SOCIOLOGICAL VISIONS

SOCIOLOGICAL VISIONS

edited by
KAI ERIKSON

ROWMAN & LITTLEFIELD PUBLISHERS, INC.
Lanham • New York • Boulder • Oxford

ROWMAN & LITTLEFIELD PUBLISHERS, INC.

Published in the United States of America
by Rowman & Littlefield Publishers, Inc.
4720 Boston Way, Lanham, Maryland 20706

12 Hid's Copse Road
Cummor Hill, Oxford OX2 9JJ, England

British Library Cataloguing in Publication Information Available

Library of Congress Cataloging-in-Publication Data
Sociological visions / edited by Kai Erickson.
    p. cm.
    Chiefly papers presented at a conference held at Yale University
in April 1992.
    Includes bibliographical references.
    ISBN 0-8476-8508-X (cloth : alk. paper). — ISBN 0-8476-8509-8
(pbk. : alk. paper)
    1. Sociology—Congresses.   2. Social sciences—Congresses.
I. Erickson, Kai, 1931– .
HM13.S573   1997
301—dc21   97-9429
                                                    CIP

ISBN 0–8476–8508–X (cloth : alk. paper)
ISBN 0–8476–8509–8 (pbk. : alk. paper)

Printed in the United States of America

⊗ ™ The paper used in this publication meets the minimum requirements of
American National Standard for Information Sciences—Permanence of Paper for
Printed Library Materials, ANSI Z39.48–1984.

Contents

PART II

Preface

It became evident early in the fall of 1991 that people at the center of the Yale administration were giving serious thought to what most members of the Yale faculty regarded as unthinkable—either to eliminate the university's already small department of sociology entirely or to cut it virtually in half. The first of those measures, of course, would have been a form of death by execution. The second would have been an amputation so drastic as to produce the same effect. The announced purpose, in either case, was to reduce costs.

The period that followed was long and painful, but it ended well for those who view sociology as one of the most important of the liberal arts. The administrative architects of the proposal were unable to persuade the rest of the faculty that their plan had any merit, and by the time that season of argument came to an exhausted close every one of them had resigned their positions. It was a conclusive defeat by any measure.

There were lessons to be learned, though. When university officials are asked to survey the academic landscape in search of programs to eliminate, they are being invited to participate in something very akin to a projective test—a process by which subjective leanings and partialities are coaxed to the surface in the name of making policy. Sociology does not always fare well at moments like these. We may never know what reservations about our field worked their way into the debate; indeed, many of the people most actively involved may not themselves know. But those reservations, whatever their form, still circulate through Yale (and other universities) like hidden underground flows. So there are good reasons for being wary. In the end, however, the commotion ended without having changed anything. Sociology at Yale is probably more secure now than it was before, and one can sense a general agreement throughout the campus that no modern university can claim distinction or even a minimal level of intellectual coverage without making a firm commitment to the discipline. The same general agreement now seems to prevail at most—alas, not all—of those other once-troubled campuses.

For sociologists at Yale, the main tasks of that season were to impress on university authorities how reckless their proposal was and to impress on other people in the community how important sociology is to the life of a major university.

One of the most conspicuous of our arguments was a five-day conference, the proceedings of which are presented here. We called it "Sociological Visions," and the announcements we posted throughout the university noted (with an edge everyone on campus understood at once):

> The teaching of sociology in the United States began at Yale one hundred and fifteen years ago. It is particularly appropriate, then, that Yale serve as host for a major gathering of sociologists and a few intellectual neighbors to celebrate the place of the discipline in the world of ideas and in the world of affairs.

Our plan was that major papers would be offered by scholars who are generally identified as sociologists, and that the papers would be followed by commentaries—themselves major statements—by scholars from related disciplines. The papers were offered by Daniel Bell, Robert K. Merton, Daniel Patrick Moynihan, Neil J. Smelser, Charles Tilly, William Julius Wilson, Alan Wolfe, and Viviana A. Zelizer, and the commentaries by Denis Donoghue, Jean Bethke Elshtain, Gerald Holton, Michael Katz, Ira Katznelson, and Margaret Weir. (Senator Moynihan may wonder about our including him in the guild of sociologists, but his hosts are certainly prepared to confer the title on him if he is prepared to accept it.)

The conference—and all the other events of that period—seemed to make Yale sociologists uncommonly reflective about the nature of their calling. So in one sense, at least, the prologue with which Part I of the volume opens and the epilogue with which it closes are both products of that experience. I was chair of the Yale Department of Sociology at the time of the conference and thus played an active role in bringing it about, and Paul DiMaggio, now professor of sociology at Princeton, was then professor of sociology at Yale and an important presence in the department.

All the authors whose work is gathered here reflect what might be called "the sociological sensibility," but no one in American sociology does so as surely or as prominently as Robert K. Merton. He presented the final paper at the Yale conference. It was different in form from the others as well as substantially longer, so it stood out, and it occurred to us as we wondered how to make a printed volume of what Merton has often called "oral publications" that the final section of the book might focus on him. He has probably done more than anyone in American sociology to formulate and give substance to the special vision that lies at the intellectual core of the discipline, and that is reason enough. But when we learned that he was scheduled to present the annual Charles Homer Haskins Lecture on the seventy-fifth anniversary of the American Council of Learned Societies—a series in which noted scholars are invited each year to speak on their "Life of Learning"—the idea took on new life. The Haskins Lecture is reprinted here with Merton's permission (as well as that of the ACLS), and it constitutes the only portion of the volume, aside from my prologue and Paul DiMaggio's epilogue, that did not originate in the Yale conference.

I have used the word "we" rather casually throughout these comments. By we I mean members of the Yale Department of Sociology and a number of other people who turned out to be particular friends. The conference was the work of many people, but they all would want to join me in a special word of thanks to Steven Brint, Paul DiMaggio, and Charles Perrow; David Fithian, Stephanie Hartwell, and Dan Ryan; Pamela Colesworthy and Ann Fitzpatrick; and in a place all his own, Joseph LaPalombara. Funds were provided by the Institution for Social and Policy Studies, Yale University, and by the John Castle Fund.

Acknowledgments

The editor and publisher wish to thank those listed below for permission to reprint these previously published chapters.

"Sociology as Science, Humanism, and Art" by Neil Smelser, 5–18; "The Two Faces of Social Science" by Alan Wolfe, 19–46; "Commentary on Sociology as Art As Science" by Jean Bethke Elshtain, 47–56; and "History and Sociological Imagining" by Charles Tilly, 57–74 all first appeared as articles in *The Toqueville Review*, vol. xv, no. 1, 1994.

"Social Science: An Imperfect Art" by Daniel Bell first appeared as an article in *The Toqueville Review*, vol. xvi, no. 1, 1995.

"A Life of Learning" by Robert K. Merton was first published as "A Life of Learning," American Council of Learned Societies Occasional Paper no. 25, © 1994 ACLS. Reprinted by permission of the author.

Part I

Prologue: Sociology as a Perspective

Kai Erikson

I

Every sociologist knows that awkward moment at the beginning of an introductory course or in the middle of a social gathering when someone asks, "What is sociology, anyway?" Most of us try to maneuver through that moment by muttering something about "the study of human society" or "the study of social life" or something equally indirect. We know we are not adding much precision to the way our craft is being defined when we speak thus, but we are not sure how the question could be answered more crisply. Colleagues in philosophy and history, chemistry and astronomy, psychology and economics—even in such neighboring fields as anthropology and political science—do not seem to share that difficulty to anything like the same degree. Why should that be so?[1]

One problem is that we sociologists tend to think of our discipline as an *approach* rather than a subject matter, as a *perspective* rather than a body of knowledge. What differentiates us from other observers of the human scene is the way we look out at the world—the way our eyes are trained, the way our intellectual reflexes are set, the way our imaginations are tuned. Sociologists scan the same landscapes as historians or poets or economists, but we select different details to attend to closely, and we sort them in different ways. So it is not *what* we see but the *way* we see that gives the field its distinction.

The prime insight of sociology has always been that there are forces out there in the world that give shape and direction to human behavior. When sociologists speak of "society," they are speaking of tides, currents,

3

forces, pulls—something in the nature of social life that induces people to behave in an orderly way at least some of the time. There are consistencies in the way people think and act, in the way they move from place to place, in the way they view the universe around them, and in the way they relate to one another. Social contexts help shape the way people conduct their lives, and those contexts have a discernable structure.

Sociologists tend to regard (and to speak of) those forces as *things*. One cannot see them or touch them, of course, but we study their properties by observing what happens to the people caught up in them—which is more or less how physicists study the properties of gravity. Human life takes place in a field of force, and we try to learn the secrets of that field in much the same way that other specialists study a galaxy, an organism, a molecular structure, or any other kind of organized matter. Few sociologists would insist that human gatherings are *like* galaxies or molecules, but we would all insist that the eye one trains on human social life is disciplined in the same way as the eye one trains on the things of the physical world.

There is pattern in the way people grow up, become adults, choose occupations, form families, and raise children. There is pattern in the way they become ill, commit crimes, compose music, or think thoughts. There is pattern in the way they make common cause with some of their fellow humans, and pattern in the way they exploit and abuse and even slaughter others of their fellow human beings as if they were not even of the same root species. Sociologists are as aware as their colleagues in the arts and the humanities that societies are made up of individuals who carve their own separate paths through life and are moved by their own private visions. Everyone who lives is a unique personality, a rare and special being. But there are commonalities in the midst of all that singularity that give social life its distinctive design. Every individual biography is at the same time part of a larger historical sweep and is to some extent caught up in it. There are no inconsistencies in that.

The social forces of which sociologists speak operate in such a way as to affect the likelihood that aggregates of people will behave in a certain way: We are dealing here with drifts, tendencies, probabilities, not with how particular individuals will act. To offer a deliberately trivial example: if you will give me a few scraps of information that can easily be contained in a paragraph half the size of this one, I will predict within a fairly small margin of error how many people will attend next year's football game between Princeton and Yale. But I will have no idea whether you (or even I) will be among them. More to the point: if another researcher were to interview everyone who belongs to the population of those who *might* attend and ask them what their intentions are in that regard, my prediction (based on such things as past attendance records, weather forecasts, and team performances) is more likely to be accurate than that survey, no matter how well done. Now any experienced director of athletics could make those calculations faster and better than I could, which is what makes this a trivial case in point. But the same logic holds in more complex social scenes. The "you's" and "I's" who make up the social fabric have our own reasons for acting as we do, but the larger aggregates to which we belong are patterned in ways that are not only observable but sometimes even predictable. This is the case for many kinds of physical matter as well. The behavior of a mass is on the whole orderly, but the behavior of its constituent particles, when traced individually, appears to be random. Worlds in motion have structure that is not reflected in grains of sand.

One of the major insights of sociology, then, is that human life is patterned, but another is that those patterns are often imposed on the powerless by the powerful. Clearly, patterning can come from old customs and usages that work their way into the grain of everyday life in ways people are only partly aware of. And, just as clearly, patterning can come from a general sense of goodness or fitness shared by the generality of those who belong to a larger gathering of people. But a good deal of patterning is simply imposed by one group of people on another. It is easy to conclude from this—and many sociologists come close to such a position—that society is best seen as a violent terrain on which class struggles and other contests for power are fought out and that sociology is at its best when it focuses on conflict. That makes good sense up to a point. At the same time, however, there is another important sociological insight to bring to bear on this matter, drawn in part from the observations of Karl Marx—that the outlooks of the powerful are often impressed upon the powerless with such force that they are simply absorbed into the moral reflexes of both on at least some level of consciousness. Thus we are dealing not just with *coercion* but with something akin to *invasion* or what animal ethologists call *imprinting*. So, Marx wants us to note, history offers the astonishing spectacle of peasants marching willingly to war to secure the interests of landlords because they have come to believe that some religious principle is involved. Or workers marching willingly to war to secure the interests of capitalists because they have come to see it a patriotic duty. A violent terrain, maybe, but a patterned one for all that.

Even at its most contentious, moreover, life in society is never a war of all against all. It is always a war of some against some. When the social terrain one has in one's sights is dominated by contests between classes or ethnic groupings or national states or any of the other divisions into which human beings manage to sort themselves, it seems logical to focus on conflict. But when one readjusts the lens and trains it on a particular class or ethnic group or nation within that larger terrain, it seems logical to focus on the sources of cohesion and solidarity that hold that collectivity together. One observer may be impressed by the sheer ferocity with which Croat and Serb neighbors slaughter one another. Another may be impressed by the ability of either of those ethnic groups to sustain a sense of communality in the face of all the troubles to which they are now exposed. And a third observer, wiser than either of the other two, may be impressed by the degree to which the ferocity and the cohesiveness reinforce each other. It is hard to imagine more chaotic human settings than the most contested parts of Croatia and Bosnia or ones more torn by conflict. But a sociologist would look for (and find) pattern even in the midst of such disorder.

Sociology often has the look of a field devoted to the study of the perfectly obvious. Sir Ernest Gowers, editor of Fowler's *A Dictionary of Modern English Usage,* and, thus, wary trustee of our language, thought he knew why that is so:

> Sociology is a new science concerning itself not with esoteric matters outside the comprehension of the layman, as the older sciences do, but with the ordinary affairs of ordinary people. This seems to engender in those who write about it a feeling that the lack of any abstruseness in their subject demands a compensatory abstruseness in their language . . . [resulting in] . . . a jargon which one is almost tempted to believe is deliberately employed for the purpose of making what is simple appear complicated.[2]

And Murray Kempton, one of the most thoughtful journalists of our time, once described a group of papers he heard at a sociology convention as "the remorseless pursuit of what everyone knew all along."

Well, something can be said for that observation. Compared to archaeologists who dig below the visible surfaces of the earth, to psychologists who try to peer into the hidden recesses of the mind, to biologists who look through instruments at tissues the naked eye cannot make out, to historians who explore a remote past—compared to them, sociologists do indeed tend to focus on those aspects of social life that seem largely familiar. In that sense, we can justly be described as specialists in the ordinary.

The fact is, though, that people in general are not really very well informed about the commonplaces of their own lives, and observers like Sir

Ernest Gowers or Murray Kempton who think they already know enough about the lay of their land or the habits of their fellow creatures have simply missed the point. Many of the things people think they know about the society in which they live really *do* belong to the realm of certified fact (although it did not become fact until specialists in the familiar studied it carefully). But other things turn out to belong to the realm of common lore, and one of the tasks of the sociologist is to try to locate the line between them.

It stands to reason, does it not, that the most tyrannical and hated regimes will provoke the most vigorous protest? In fact, things do *not* seem to work that way most of the time. It is when regimes become more moderate and begin the slow process of change that they provoke the sharpest opposition, because the promise of a better future has created expectations and nourished hopes that far exceed the new opportunities made available. By the same token, the people most likely to riot during uprisings of one kind or another are not the deeply disadvantaged, who tend to be too numbed and dispirited by the circumstances in which they live to do much of anything, but those who have been moving toward new horizons and are frustrated by the slowness of the process.

It stands to reason, does it not, that since the number of single teenage mothers seems to be growing, the number of teenage pregnancies must be going up as well? Apparently not. Recent data indicate that the number of young women who become pregnant has not increased in any significant way over the years, but that the number of pregnant women who subsequently marry has dropped appreciably. And why? One reason may well be that unemployment among the fathers is so high that fewer of them can contribute meaningfully to child support.

It stands to reason, does it not, that the best schools are the most effective in preparing persons for professional success? In fact, the reverse appears to be true. This is not because the best schools do a poorer job of teaching, of course, but because they select students who come from advantaged backgrounds in the first place—those whose life trajectories have been set long before the schools they attend take a hand in shaping their fate.

Sociologists, then, can be said to have a distinctive way of looking out at the world, a distinctive intellectual sensibility. In one sense, at least, the realities we attend to are a prospect unique to those who peer through a special disciplinary lens, and I would like now to try to describe some of the features of that lens.

It might be noted, first, that sociologists are invited by the logic of their perspective to be more concerned with *general tendencies* than with *particular events.* Our assignment in the world of scholarship has always been to move up onto the plane of generality as soon as our data allow (if not a good deal sooner), studying those regularities that form the substance of everyday human experience rather than those unique persons and moments that stand out as special (and for that reason attract the interest of journalists and dramatists and historians). Dennis Wrong writes of "the intense straining" among sociologists "for universality, for a language that transcends the particular and the commonplace by breaking through its own limits."[3] And, indeed, sociologists are at their wisest when they distrust the individual case as being too idiosyncratic and unrepresentative. Journalists and other observers whose job it is to describe social landscapes often begin their accounts with profiles of particular people, asking them in effect to portray, represent, act out the lives of larger populations. This is a way of focusing attention and establishing a tone, of giving the problem at hand a kind of personality and texture, but it is a strategy that sociologists are rarely in a position to employ. Our task is to draw group profiles with a distinct accent on numbers, percentages, tendencies, underlying structural forces. W. H. Auden wrote: "Thou shalt not sit / With statisticians nor commit / A social science." Well, the committing of a social science depends on information about wholes rather than parts, on the histories of multitudes rather than the biographies of individuals, on general contours rather than particular details. And that, in turn, entails a good deal of sitting with statisticians.

It might also be noted that sociologists are invited by the logic of their perspective to think in terms of *collateral* arrangements rather than *sequential* ones. Our stock in trade has normally been the relations that obtain at any given point in time among people and events and institutions—the way income relates to voting, the way working helps shape personality, the way migration affects urban institutions, the way poverty impacts household composition, and in all such instances, vice versa. Ours is the logic of concomitance, interconnection, comparison, correspondence, nexus. The classics of sociology—Max Weber on the relationship between capitalism and Protestantism, Emile Durkheim on the relationship between suicide and group solidarity—are of just that character. Even when sociologists trace the histories of particular events like revolutions or disasters or migrations or individual lives, the purpose of the research is almost always to draw comparisons in an effort to understand the category to which the cases belong rather than to understand the cases themselves.

And it might be noted, to offer a final example, that when sociologists contemplate a conversation between two people or an interaction among several, they are invited by the logic of their perspective to attend to the pattern that ensues rather than to the contributions of the separate participants. A distinguished law professor of a generation or so ago is supposed to have said to his students: "If you can think of the relationship between two objects without thinking about the objects themselves, then maybe you have a legal mind." I am not sure what that has to do with legal thinking, but it describes the sociologist's angle of vision exactly. Our eyes are for the most part trained on the *spaces between* intersecting individuals—on the shape of their conversation, the architecture of their transaction, the way the words spoken and the gestures enacted form a pattern that is altogether independent of the personalities and intentions of the persons who contributed to it. Georg Simmel and Erving Goffman are spectacular cases in point: the worlds they describe are compositions in which the actors seem blurred and indistinct but the patterns they collaborate to form are as clear as anything could be. Simmel and Goffman were interested in choreographies, not dancers.

In general, the sociological eye is trained on the behavior of multitudes. We are interested in the processes by which they form, persist, change, dissolve. We are interested in the bonds that link them together within those larger wholes, and in the differences that separate them. We are interested in all of the maneuverings and shiftings and skirmishes that keep social life in continual motion. There are times when one can get a sense of such forces only by counting the human particles caught up in them. How else might one describe the way populations flow from place to place, the way values change from time to time, the way money or opportunity or risk is distributed within any given social order? (Sitting with statisticians again.)

Sociologists gather material for our own kinds of portrayal in a variety of ways. We ask large groups of people identical questions, the answers to which make sense only when expressed in aggregates. Or we move out into the field ourselves, listening and watching the swirl of human activity around us in an effort to get a better understanding of its structure and rhythm. Or we look into the public record for those occasions when otherwise anonymous individuals left a mark of their passing in registries of one kind or another.

For example: There was once a man named Francis Cooper. He wrote no diaries or letters, so far as I know, and he did little else to bring attention to himself. He was born in 1672, worked as a cabinetmaker, married one of his neighbors, fathered five or six children, and died, in the fullness of his years, in 1748. I happen to know of Francis Cooper because he was once fined for an offense of some unspecified kind. It is hard to get much of a sense of this man from the fragments one finds in the historical record exactly because the world registered those of his comings and goings that he shared in common with the rest of his compatriots. Those fragments do not offer a portrait of Francis Cooper, then, but added to thousands of similar details in similar records, they offer a very rich portrait of his time and his community. Having made so brief and modest an appearance in the historical record, he disappears again under a mass of figures.

A different kind of example: Were it not for the inquiries of sociologists, very little would be known about the ways of America's inner cities or the life chances of those who live in them. One can point to an occasional novel or film that depicts the inner city sensitively and accurately, but it is in the nature of ghetto life that few voices emerge from it to provide its own portrayal. And what are the materials on which the sociological portrait is based? There are demographic analyses (the work of Otis Dudley Duncan and Stanley Lieberson offers two distinguished examples) describing the flows of people into and out of the inner city and the resources they bring with them. There are studies drawing on official estimates having to do with crime, welfare, employment, education, household composition, and many other statistical compilations that offer insight into the ways of the inner city (William Julius Wilson and Christopher Jencks are masters of that art). There are accounts of the way inner-city institutions—courts and clinics, schools and churches, police departments and welfare agencies—actually work (names like Albert J. Reiss Jr. and the team of Frances Fox Piven and Richard Cloward belong prominently on that list). And, finally, there are ethnographic field studies of the urban setting itself (by such gifted observers as Elijah Anderson and Elliot Liebow). These approaches together offer an extraordinary portrait of that crucial corner of our world—the demographic and other official data offering a kind of statistical silhouette, so to speak, and the studies of particular urban institutions and particular street corners providing a closer feel for the grain and texture of urban life.

II

The essays that appear in this volume reflect a variety of approaches to the study of social life. That is why the plural noun "visions" has such a prominent place in the title. Still, the contributors all seem to share the view that sociology is a special kind of disciplinary territory. And what makes that territory so unique is exactly the fact that so many different methods and epistemological stances and ways of looking out at the world meet there.

The collection opens with Neil Smelser, who has been for a long time one of the sanest and most measured voices in American sociology. He speaks of three "orientations" that dominate the intellectual climate of the field—scientific, humanistic, and artistic. Sociology, Smelser argues, has never tried to "seal itself into a closed paradigm," as has been the experience of so many of our disciplinary neighbors in the social sciences. This has meant, on the one hand, that the field never really quite knows "what it is," and for that reason is especially vulnerable to criticism. But it has also meant, on the other hand, that the various conflicts and dilemmas that define the field give it an unusual richness. In that sense, the intellectual center of the field is defined not so much by a core of established methods or concepts but by the competing gravitional pulls that the three orientations exert on the center. The field is at once artistic, humanistic, and scientific, and the fact that these ways of viewing social life are often inconsistent only gives our enterprise a special vibrancy.

Alan Wolfe clearly belongs in the more humanistic regions of Smelser's conceptual map of sociology, but he shares with Smelser a conviction that the tensions stretching across the field—the humanistic and the scientific being the contrasting pulls that concern him most—give shape and dimension to the sociological project. Wolfe is persuaded that a sociology that ignores the remarkable variability and unpredictability of human behavior in the interests of precision and quantification would truly be an empty undertaking. But he is equally persuaded that sociologists should avoid the view—so common in many quarters of academia these days— that the life of society is but a text that is read differently by all those who come into contact with it depending on their economic circumstances or intellectual moods. Wolfe wants to assure that sociologists do not skid too far in either direction along an axis that has a kind of mindless scientism at one pole and an equally mindless kind of postmodern antinomianism at the other—what Jean Bethke Elshtain, in her compelling commentary, calls "epistemological nihilism." Wolfe, like Smelser, sees the tensions and ambivalences of sociology as its true intellectual signature. We are at our best when we look at the world through a variety of conceptual lenses, draw on a variety of research techniques, and measure the data we gather against a variety of explanatory frameworks.

Elshtain, a distinguished political philosopher, has lived a good part of her professional life among political scientists. Many of those colleagues are attracted to the same "rigorous asceticism" that Wolfe is so concerned about within the sociological ranks. She calls the search for methods that

lend themselves to quantification and precision "utopian"—"a drive for
control, for perfection, for somehow transcending or simply expunging
from view the messiness that is the human lot." Elshtain wishes that
Wolfe had employed a different term than "rhetoric" to describe the postmodern subjectivism that both of them are at such pains to disparage, but
she clearly feels that the "messiness" of human life does not call for a
compensatory messiness in the way we approach it. On the contrary: to
study the richness of human experience properly—or, for that matter, to
respect it properly—one must take its measure in as careful and as disciplined a way as possible.

Charles Tilly has spent most of his professional career in that theoretical and methodological borderland where the study of social life and the
study of history meet and overlap. He argues that many of the rigidities
of mind found in sociology can be tempered by looking through lens
ground in the historical tradition. In doing so, he says, sociologists would
be able to avoid the common intellectual sin of "monadism"—the habit
of thinking that the basic units of social life are self-contained and similar,
that the processes through which they pass "repeat themselves in essentially the same way time after time," and that the long-term object of the
social sciences is to create invariant models to describe those units and the
regularities of their behavior.

Sociologists often take it for granted, for example, that revolutions
share a common anatomy, that cities and nations and polities of any other
kind evolve according to a natural pattern of growth, that social movements have a distinctive constitution, and so on. As an empirical matter,
Tilly argues, things just do not work that way. Every human moment has
its own place in the flows of time and has to be looked at as unique. The
character of an emerging social form is always shaped by the particulars
of the prevailing cultural setting.

In drawing attention to the particulars of human experience, however,
Tilly is not urging colleagues to give up the search for regularities. He
looks for those regularities, rather, in what he calls "interactions among
social locations." Citing research of his own, he argues that revolutions
in modern Europe simply do not look like specimens of a common genus
when studied carefully. What they share in common is that they emerged
from a similar set of historical conditions. They constitute a *type,* then,
but what makes them so is the fact that they are one of several outcomes
that can emerge from a certain combination of circumstances. The event
itself is historically singular, but the conditions from which it emerges are
at least comparable. To that extent, Tilly also wants us to make use of
the countercurrents that reach across the field by combining a historian's

appreciation for the particular with a sociologist's appreciation for the general.

Viviana Zelizer's discussion of money can almost be read as an illustration of what Tilly means by a historically sensitive act of "sociological imagining." On the surface, at least, money would appear to be the most disinterested of social goods. One would think it the very essence of rationality, impersonality, calculation, and instrumentality. It is difficult to think of anything less enchanting or magical. Simmel wrote in a passage referred to by Zelizer that money has transformed the world into an "arithmetic problem." And that is how the subject is treated in most economic and sociological research. But, says Zelizer, "once you observe the actual process of how people accumulate, allocate, use, divide, save, monies, you discover that the theory of monetary rationalization is inadequate." The rest of her essay is a fascinating account of the ways in which people imbue the coldest of cash with sentiment and personality, giving it a meaning and substance that most forms of quantitative analysis would not be sensitive enough to discern.

Ira Katznelson's brief comment is a very thoughtful look at the conceptual borderlands that figure in the papers by Tilly and Zelizer, describing the costs that must be paid for living at that point of engagement where historical and sociological ways of imagining the world meet, fuse, and create a new intellectual solvent in the process.

Daniel Bell moves across much of the same theoretical terrain as other authors in this volume, but he does so with a brilliance and a display of learning that defy easy introduction. He asks how the kinds of theorizing found in the social sciences can help us understand what is going on in the contemporary political and cultural scene, and he concludes, as his title indicates clearly enough, that ours is, at best, an imperfect art. Efforts to scan social space and find orderly structures within it are sure to disappoint sooner or later because the world we contemplate is so full of surprise and uncertainty. General theories of society and of social change always prove brittle when confronting that obdurate reality. The differences between our actual experience of the social world and the theories we fashion in an effort to make better sense of it are yet another of the contrieties that both frustrate and enrich the field.

William Julius Wilson's essay moves us into a different section of the book and onto a different level of abstraction. Wilson is concerned that policy makers and researchers alike, in their understandable eagerness to find an underlying cause for inner-city poverty, focus too abruptly on one or another of the variables that are known to have an impact. Political liberals, for example, often assume that racial discrimination must play a dominant role in the way opportunity is distributed throughout the social order, while political conservatives often assume that the ways of life found among the urban poor not only contribute to their poverty but make it difficult for them to take advantage of whatever paths out of the inner city become available. Wilson wants a broader vision, a perspective on urban poverty that can encompass all those important realities in a single conceptual frame.

Wilson then considers some of the strands that constitute the "complex web of interrelated factors" that would need to be a part of this broader vision—economic shifts in the structure of the labor market, social and cultural shifts in the structure of inner city neighborhoods, and political shifts in the nature of services to the urban poor. All these factors, moreover—the economic, the social, the political—snap at each other's heels in an ever accelerating downward spiral, giving new meaning to the expression "vicious circle."

Margaret Weir's commentary, dealing with the more political dimensions of the subject, notes that even though new forms of industrial organization are creating huge inequalities of wealth and heavily concentrated pockets of poverty throughout the modern world, there is nonetheless something distinctive about poverty in the United States. The keys to that distinctiveness, Weir suggests, are, on the one hand, the racism that works its way like a stain across the whole fabric of American social life, and, on the other, the localism of American politics. In the absence of any kind of coordination at the national level, urban places find themselves competing for business investments and higher-income residents, and in the midst of all that scrimmaging and contention the needs of the poor become a low-urgency problem.

Michael Katz's commentary adds a very important historical dimension to the discussion. Weir is arguing in effect that the inner cities of the United States are an urban form quite unlike anything to be found elsewhere in the world, and Katz points out, in his turn, that the inner cities of modern times are an urban form quite unlike anything found elsewhere in our own history. There is nothing new about urban poverty in America, to be sure, but the political and economic forces that now press in on the inner city and give it its shape have resulted in the most rigid patterns of segregation known to our history. The urban poor are segregated horizontally in the sense that they live in sharply bounded territories, but they are also segregated vertically in the sense that they have almost dropped entirely out of the bottom of the labor market. The social and economic escalators that have always offered the poor a chance of climbing out of poverty in the American past have simply come to a stop in our times, and many of those confined to the inner city have become demoralized and without any real hope of better things to come.

The title that Daniel Patrick Moynihan has chosen is a broad tent under which a fine variety of intellectual creatures can be gathered, and he takes full advantage of that opportunity. His remarks are thoughtful, learned, and full of shrewd calculations. Indeed, it is hard to think of anyone in or around government who better reflects the wisdoms of our craft. During his long public career, he has made forecasts and issued warnings that drew on his social science sensibility, and he has sometimes provoked a remarkable stir in doing so. It is very understandable, then, that he would use this occasion to review some of them.

He predicted in the late 1970s, for example, that the Soviet Union was collapsing, both because it was unstable economically and because it was unsound morally. This was long before any of the rest of us could see what now appear to have been obvious signs. And, far more to the present point, he warned in the middle 1960s that the country was "approaching a new crisis in race relations" because any society that allows large numbers of its young to grow up in "broken families dominated by women" is really asking for it. The publication of what came to be known as the Moynihan Report was an important moment in the relationship of the academy and the public forum. It was then—and probably remains now—the most prominent example of social data and sociological reasoning being brought to bear on a critical national issue in a public document. He was roundly criticized for doing so, and it is easy to appreciate that there would be some scar tissue here; but who will now call him wrong?

No one is better positioned to talk about the relationship of social science and social policy than Moynihan, and he does not seem to be very much impressed. He notes that "a tradition of pragmatic social inquiry" is as old as the republic. But to what effect? Well, we "are at the point of knowing a fair amount about what we don't know," he says, which is, after all, "useful knowledge." And the data that social scientists gather are often helpful. Beyond that, however, Moynihan is not sure that the social sciences have more than a glancing role to play in public policy.

On, then, with Part I.

Notes

1. Like many others, I sometimes find myself recycling useful passages that have appeared in other contexts to serve other purposes. Several paragraphs in the first part of this prologue have been adapted from matter first published in *The*

Kai Erikson

Rhetoric of Social Research, edited by Albert Hunter. And if that is not bad enough, I have borrowed three other paragraphs from an unfinished manuscript that may yet appear in print someday.

2. H. W. Fowler, *A Dictionary of Modern English Usage,* 2nd ed. rev. Sir Ernest Gowers (Oxford: Oxford University Press, 1965), 569–70.

3. Dennis Wrong, "Professional Jargon: Is Sociology the Culprit?" *University: Academic Affairs at New York University* 2:3–7 (1983), 7.

Sociology as Science, Humanism, and Art

Neil J. Smelser

It was about one hundred fifty years ago that William Graham Sumner was born, the son of an English machinist who endowed him with a work ethic, a sense of personal integrity, and a stubborn independence from the world—qualities that were cloned on the son in such a way that they were never shaken. Later in his life Sumner developed a love for what he called the "forgotten man"—the independent citizen who worked hard, paid his debts and taxes, dutifully raised his family, perpetuated community values. One senses that, in lamenting that this man was forgotten, Sumner might have been reviving the ghost of his father.

It was about one hundred twenty years ago that Sumner, after having been trained for the Episcopalian ministry, read Herbert Spencer, and that momentous occasion began his conversion to the infant field of sociological studies. And it was at Yale, about one hundred years ago, that Sumner offered the first academic course—in the world, it is believed—with the title of "sociology" in it. This was an event whose great symbolic import we can celebrate today, but whose full significance was, no doubt, scarcely perceived by Sumner himself.

Sumner believed his sociology to be a science—at least the beginnings of a science—and certainly not an art. But a number of his formulations fit this section's theme of sociology as art and science, and I will refer to them from time to time.

17

The Main Argument: Sociology in the
Larger Picture of Human Inquiry

As many students learn in college, one clever and sometimes effective ploy in confronting a question on a final examination—especially a question whose answer does not occur to them immediately—is to redefine the question. "Before we can consider the question, it is necessary to clarify its meaning," begins the answer. If pursued creatively enough, this strategy may consume the entire time devoted to the question and throw enough dust in the eyes of the examiner to earn a decent grade.

I promise not to take up my entire remarks with clarifications. I will, however, make an initial clarification of the assigned theme of the session, and in doing so will reveal my major argument.

Here is the clarification. Instead of addressing the topic of "Sociology as Art and Science," I will maintain that over the past century the major debates and dilemmas in our field—right up to the present—can be understood in terms of sociology's proximity to *three* intellectual outlooks that simultaneously constitute part of its environment and parts of itself. These may be referred to as the *scientific* orientation, the *humanistic* orientation, and the *artistic* orientation. At the risk of anthropocentrism, I put sociology at the center of the map, and represent the three neighboring orientations as surrounding it.

First, a few definitional notes:

- *Sociology* I will not define for the moment, and by not doing that I shorten my remarks considerably.
- By the *scientific orientation* I refer to inquiry that focuses on natural laws and logically closed theoretical formulations; on causal, even deterministic analysis; on a dispassionate and objective attitude

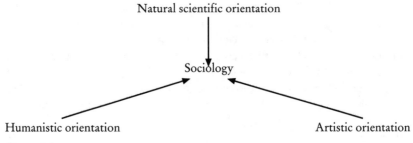

Natural scientific orientation

Sociology

Humanistic orientation   Artistic orientation

Figure 1.1

toward the subject matter under study; on empirical study; on precision and measurement; and on a method of inquiry that isolates and controls many possible causes in order to arrive at the decisive ones.

- By the *humanistic orientation* I have in mind inquiry that focuses on the human being; includes a preoccupation with the human condition (including human suffering); and deals above all with human meanings, systems of which constitute culture. What I am calling humanism overlaps in complex ways with humanitarianism, humaneness, and the disciplines in the humanities, but I will forgo trying to explicate this complex conceptual geography.
- In the *artistic orientation* I include two rather different connotations—first, an aesthetic orientation toward subject matter, or an emphasis on pattern; and, second, an emphasis on the application of knowledge, as in the "art of medical practice" or the "art of the possible."

My basic thesis is the following: sociology, having differentiated in complex ways out of *all three* of these orientations, still maintains connections with all of them. Indeed, all three orientations not only constitute the significant moral/intellectual *environments* of sociology but also are simultaneously *parts* of the sociological enterprise itself. Because of sociology's separateness from and interpretation with these several orientations, we can note immediately two kinds of intellectual phenomena that sociology as a discipline experiences:

- From *outside* the field come critical assessments that originate from standards deriving from the viewpoints of these other orientations. Natural scientists frequently take on bemused or hostile postures because sociology—or the social sciences in general—are not really as scientific as their own enterprises, i.e., they are "soft." Humanists or those in the humanities may either find sociology territorially offensive, i.e., intruding on their traditional turf, or find it arid and inhumane. Those who are artistically oriented may find sociology ugly or useless, according to which of the two connotations of the artistic orientation is invoked.
- From *inside* the field, its complex composition—deriving from its neighboring and penetrating orientations—leads sociologists to raise doubts about the field's mission, unity, and identity, and to foster debates and conflicts within the field. These debates and conflicts express the tensions and antagonisms that arise from the differences among the three orientations. The net result is that sociology has

never been able to make up its mind quite what it is. This internal dynamic has both a cost and a benefit. The cost is recurring crises of identity and self-doubts, and the benefit is living in a field that refuses to seal itself into a closed paradigm that threatens to exhaust itself, but, rather, retains the qualities of intellectual openness and imagination.

In the remainder of my remarks I will illustrate this basic argument by interpreting some central dilemmas and conflicts in sociology by locating them in the context of the map I have constructed. Among these are value-free versus value-relevant orientation; basic versus applied; knowledge-for-its-own-sake versus active intervention; positivistic versus phenomenological emphasis; quantitative versus qualitative emphasis; causal versus configurational analysis; and finally, "mainstream" versus "marginal" in the field.

A General Comparison: European and American Sociological Traditions

It is possible to gain some general insights about the different emphases of European and American sociology—ignoring many variations in each, of course—by contrasting the intellectual traditions in which the two originated. In the late nineteenth century, European sociology oriented itself above all to the intellectual traditions of European thought as represented in the study of history, philosophy, law, and the classics and in the critical intellectual traditions focusing on the state, social classes, and the economy. The current preoccupation of European sociology with macroscopic and critical issues—phenomenology excepted—and the critical treatment of each bears witness to the power of these traditions.

American sociology, by contrast, grew up in two different intellectual and social contexts. First, it made its appearance in the public institutions of higher education in this country several decades after the passage of the Morell Act of 1862, which solidly established the scientific impulse in American higher education. Second, in the 1890s the reform theme was in the air and sociology picked up that theme from both the social gospel and the progressivist movements. It is not surprising that sociology, struggling to establish its legitimacy in those days, elaborated ideas of scientific respectability and social reform as its motifs to broadcast to the academy and to the larger society. Those themes persist to the present day. They fit comfortably into the American cultural emphases on pragmatism, reform, and optimism. Also, American sociology appears to have had an odd and persisting preoccupation with how scientific it is or is not, and upon what model of the scientific method it is built.

Reading these observations in the context of my intellectual map, American sociology began with a closer identification with the scientific orientation, European with the humanistic. Insofar as both carried a humanistic impulse—that is, a preoccupation with the human condition—the European tradition was more critical and potentially revolutionary, whereas the American tradition was tamer and more ameliorative. During the twentieth century that picture has become more complex, as American sociological thought has become infused with European theoretical influences, and European sociology has developed, partly under American influence, empiricist and moderate strands. The two traditions, coming from different origins, have tended to converge to some degree.

Evolutionary Naturalism versus Progressive Evolutionism

The evolutionary perspective, propagated mainly through the influence of Charles Darwin and Herbert Spencer, was dominant in American sociology in the late nineteenth century. Within this context a debate developed between advocates of two variants of evolutionary thought: evolutionary naturalism and progressive evolutionism. To put the matter simply, the debate was between Sumner on the one side and most of the early other founding sociologists on the other. All were committed in varying ways to sociology *as a science*, as might be expected from my earlier observations. The issue, rather, was one of humanism.

On the one side stood Sumner, the evolutionary naturalist who believed in the immutable natural laws of evolution—including the survival of the fittest—that were beyond human intervention, even though he did envision the possibility of incremental improvement of the human condition through technological and material advance. Consistent with this deterministic position, Sumner took a hostile stance toward reformists and socialists alike, regarding them as unrealistic dreamers and defiers of the laws of evolution. He also took what we would now regard as a heartless, unhumanistic position with respect to social problems, social welfare, and social reform. In a dramatic moment, Sumner penned the following words about vice in society:

> Vice is its own curse. If we let nature alone, she cures vice by the most frightful penalties. . . . A drunkard in the gutter is just where he ought to be.

Nature is working away at him to get out of the way, just as she sets up her processes of dissolution to remove whatever is a failure in its line. Gambling and less mentionable vices all cure themselves by the ruin and dissolution of their victims. Nine-tenths of our measures for preventing vice are really protective towards it, because they ward off the penalty.[1]

At the theoretical level, the progressive evolutionists criticized both the materialism and the determinism of Sumner's position, and held, to the contrary, that human evolution had reached such as stage as to have liberated humanity from the dictates of nature, and that at the contemporary stage of civilization mankind had achieved a degree of freedom that permitted improvement, by deliberate and purposive efforts, of the lot of civilization and humanity.

The debate between the naturalists and the progressivists—which the progressivists clearly seemed at the time to win—was not, I suggest, a debate about science. Both sides advertised themselves as scientific. It was a debate about humanism (i.e., sensitivity to the human condition) and about art (i.e., the improvement of that condition through purposive application of knowledge). Sumner tended to reject the humanistic impulse, whereas the progressivists, in their optimism, found a way to combine the scientific and humanistic impulses in a way that nestled more comfortably into the moral and political context of the times.

The Intractable Dilemma: Scientific Dispassion versus Interventionism

Perhaps the most repetitive dilemma in the history of sociology—right up to the present day—is the tension between watching and recording the natural laws of science and intervening in the social world in the name of alleviating suffering, solving social problems, or reforging society. This dilemma, of course, is between the scientific orientation on the one hand and a kind of amalgam of the humanistic and artistic orientations on the other, i.e., to care about the world and to ameliorate or eradicate its ills through the application of knowledge.

Again Sumner provides a good lead on this issue. Given his stark Darwinian insistence on laws, his sympathy with human suffering appeared to be minimal. By the same token, the naturalistic-scientific orientation he took also predisposed him to argue against purposive human intervention, including state intervention, in things. Some have characterized Sumner as a somewhat crude apologist for laissez-faire and a sociological champion of the business interests of American high capitalism, and find many passages in his work to support this view. Others challenge this interpretation as simplistic and find other passages of their own. Be that as it may, one can see the coherent connection between Sumner's naturalism and his stress on passivity with respect to intervention.

On this score Sumner was in the minority. Most American sociologists during the first half-century of the field were ameliorationists and reformers, *while at the same time arguing that their fledgling discipline was or ought to be a science.* The moral/ameliorative strain in early American sociology has been noted often, and traced both to the religious origins of the founders and to the progressivist spirit of the era. Interpreters of a Marxist persuasion would also interpret their tame ameliorationism as an apology for capitalism as well—that is to say, focusing on the victims of the system rather than the system itself. There may be some merit in this, but I think it is perhaps more valuable to invoke Max Weber's perspective on the matter. Most of the early sociologists—including the early Chicago schools—were consciously aware and wrote critically about the social problems and evils of industrial-urban society, and often attributed them directly to industrial capitalism. Their writings also reveal a continuing romance with a vision of sturdy and virtuous rural life. But it should also be underscored that the early sociologists were something of an aspiring priestly class, seeking to establish some legitimate territory for themselves. Moreover, there were other claimants for that territory— progressive era reformers, the socialists of the late nineteenth century, and more remote exponents of revolutionary Marxism. It has frequently been noted that early American sociology was hostile to socialism and Marxism.

My point is this: The amalgam of positions taken by early American sociology can be understood when it is appreciated that the founders were a new priestly class striving for legitimacy in *two* distinct arenas. The first arena was the university system, in which science had been given great legitimacy in which economics and psychology already had a head start as human sciences. The sociologists' claim for scientific legitimacy derives above all from this context. At the same time there were good historical reasons for these sociologists to have moral and humanistic concerns, and they were striving for legitimacy as moral and reformist entrepreneurs as well. When we acknowledge this, the special formula of *amelioration through the application of sound scientific knowledge* makes sense. That formula was an amalgam of the scientific, humanistic, and artistic orientations, and constituted a complex appeal for legitimacy in both the academic and public arenas.

An interesting variant of the dilemma between dispassion and intervention appeared in the Chicago school, personified in the tension between Robert Park and William Fielding Ogburn. Park himself was committed to the scientific enterprise, was an empiricist, and was impatient with what he called "do-gooders," but at the same time he retained the preoccupation of the early Chicago school with the social problems of those who suffered in the urban laboratory. Ogburn, the quintessential antitheoretical, empirical statistician, criticized the ethnographically inclined Chicago school with not being scientific *enough,* and simultaneously launched his campaign for empirical precision, measurement, and quantification. Yet Ogburn was an ameliorationist of sorts himself. If one reads his texts in *Recent Social Trends* (1933), one observes a strict, nonpartisan remove and neutrality with respect to the great political issues of the day (especially the Great Depression), yet at the same time he argued that the accumulation of knowledge on a scientific basis would lead to social improvements and solutions through his own variant of social engineering. Again, the priestly advantages are apparent in Ogburn's position: one protects oneself from partisan criticism by standing away but promises in a general way the means to ease or solve the problems and ills around which partisanship swirls. The two catches in this formula, of course, are (1) that the farther away from the world one stands in the posture of dispassion, the more nonspecific and difficult to apply one's promised knowledge—that is, the artistic component—is likely to be; and (2) that if one holds out promises of amelioration through the application of sound knowledge, these promises, if not kept, are likely to result in disappointment in and discreditation of the field.

The 1930s witnessed a sharpening of the tension between scientific dispassion and interventionism in the dialogue between George Lundberg and Robert Lynd. Lundberg, with the friendly company of Percy Bridgeman in physics and A. J. Ayer in philosophy, was the pure positivist and operationalist, going much further than Ogburn in his scientism, yet at the same time holding on to a remote ameliorationism, as the title of his main book—*Can Science Save Us?*—reveals. Lynd, radicalized by the economic contradictions and suffering he observed in Middletown in the Depression, launched an attack on the aridity of scientism, and called for an attitude of concerned humanistic criticism and political activism. His answer to his book title—*Knowledge For What?*—was certainly not knowledge for itself but knowledge for a troubled society.

Among those sociologists who champion the interventionist or humanistic-artistic wing of sociology, one can identify three variants:

- The criticism of society that arises in identifying with the unprivileged or suffering subjects one is studying—a special sociological variant of "going native." Many of the early sociologists in the Chicago school manifested this in their studies of the prostitute, the hobo, and what was then called the jack-roller. The same impulse is found in the "labeling" approach to deviance, which portrays the "deviant" as the victim of a kind of conceptual manipulation on the part of those with authority or in power. This kind of identification is not very radical, as Alvin Gouldner once complained, because it doesn't really focus as much on the system as it does on the system's victims.

- The criticism implied by the ameliorationist approach itself. Most moderate reformists *do* start with some kind of identifiable social problem or human suffering, and much of the reformist impulse does call for some modest alteration of the system—a new regulatory agency, a new law, etc. This ameliorationist impulse is probably the most common one in American sociology, shared by the founders, the Chicago school, many positivists, and the small army of sociologists engaged in "applied sociology" and "policy-relevant" research.

- The criticism implied by the special American variant of radical sociology. In this group I include the closely related messages of Thorstein Veblen, Lynd, C. Wright Mills, and the radical sociologies that emerged in the 1960s and have persisted in radical feminism, radical theories of race, and other subfields of sociology. Most often this has not been a Marxist radicalism—Mills himself was a critic of Marx— but a more generalized critical attitude that includes a preoccupation with oppression, injustices, alienation, and contradictions. The approach also merits the term "radical" because the inequities and other societal ills at hand are characterized as faults of the system, with the implication that change must be systemic in character. Specific utopias beyond the goals of greater democracy and greater injustice are not often found in American radical sociology, however.

Except for the ameliorationist posture, most of these critical-humanist stances tend to assume a posture that, while not frankly antiscientific, is nonetheless hostile to the presumed disembodiment, coldheartedness, or political conservatism of the advocates and practitioners of positive science. As such, therefore, the critical or radical positions in sociology are reflective of the tendencies between the scientific orientation on the one side, and the humanistic-artistic orientations on the other.

Theoretical and Methodological Versions of the Dilemma

I have just mentioned the tension between positive science and concerned intervention as a special case of the tension between the several orientations that border on and are part of the sociological enterprise. I now turn to a number of repetitive dilemmas of a theoretical-methodological character. These overlap with one another and with the dispassion-intervention dilemma in various ways, furthermore, and the overlaps can be traced to the basis thesis I am advancing. The following are the variations of the conflicts I have in mind:

(1) *Positivism versus phenomenology.* Ever since the advent of Comtean positivism, one of the connotations of that term is a focus on facts, positive facts. A close corollary, espoused vigorously by Emile Durkheim in *The Rules of the Sociological Method*, is a corresponding hostility toward "inner states" such as human motivation and human meaning, largely because they are not factual—i.e., are elusive, intangible, and unmeasurable. The phenomenological alternative to positivism, in its various forms, resurrects human meaning, *as experienced by the subject under study.* The phenomenological approach lets the subjects speak in their own words, as Kai Erikson put it in his ethnographic study of the Buffalo Creek disaster. Considered as such, the phenomenological impulse is one that frequently ennobles the subject, i.e., does not reduce him or her to "behaviors" that are thought to be "determined" by external biological or social forces. Such is the Blumerian view of the actor, who is master of things insofar as they are not real and external but endowed with his or her own meanings. Such also are Harold Garfinkel's ethnomethodological actors, who negotiate culture reality rather than being subjected to it like so many "cultural dopes." Such also are Peter Berger and Thomas Luckmann's social constructors of reality, who interact to produce and reproduce the social environment they inhabit. The examples reveal the humanistic and frequently antiscientific posture of the phenomenological approach.

(2) *Quantitative versus qualitative analysis.* I have never been able to find a consistent meaning for this distinction; for example, words like "more" or "less" or "the majority" often appear in analyses that are otherwise considered qualitative. Nevertheless, the distinction continues to be a part of our discourse, and the merits of one are often compared with the demerits of the other. One meaning of the contrast that is relevant to my theme is that quantitative measures and statistical representations standardize facts about individuals and thus pull those facts from the contextual richness of individual meaning in which they are embedded and which can only be appreciated through rich or thick qualitative descrip-

tion. This is the brunt of Herbert Blumer's classic attack on the standardized survey questionnaire, which he regarded as fundamentally distorting of psychic and interactional reality. In this dialogue the tension between the scientific and humanistic orientations seems clear. There appears to be a kind of artistic complaint, too, when it is held that quantification of facts is essentially unaesthetic because it destroys a psychic reality which can be "grasped" and "appreciated" only through *verstehen* or some other kind of act of sympathetic understanding.

(3) *Formal statistical analysis of social data versus ethnographically based analysis.* This overlaps with the contrast between quantitative and qualitative analysis, but the tenor of debates often differs. Most discussions stress the more representative nature of statistical analysis and the limited generalizability of the case study, or the abstracted quality of statistical analysis and the richness and depth of the case study. At the same time, an ethnography is more likely to represent the social world as the subjects represent it, and ethnographic reports have an affinity with literary or aesthetic representations of interactional and cultural patterns; that is to say, they approximate the novel, the drama, and the biography more than the scientific report does.

(4) *Aggregative-causal versus pattern or clinical analysis.* Both experimental and social psychology are often variable-centered, taking one psychological variable (for example, tolerance of ambiguity), measuring that variable in a larger number of subjects, and determining how strongly this variable correlates with some presumed effect (for example, level of racial prejudice). An alternative mode of explanation, often referred to as clinical inference, refers to interpreting a vast range of personal material about a single individual, and arriving at a complex and coherent statement of why it is that the individual harbors such strong feelings of prejudice. The same contrast appears in political science and sociology; for example, many cross-national analyses deal with quantitative associations (e.g., between economic development and political democracy) in a large sample of nations; case studies of the political process in a single nation focus on the interplay of a multiplicity of forces that generate a democratic or undemocratic polity. Edmund Leach once went so far as to contrast sociology, with its statistical-aggregative approach, with anthropology, with its ethnographic-pattern approach. This line of contrast, which is known generically as the nomothetic mode versus the ideographic mode, is simultaneously, I would suspect, a methodological and aesthetic one, with advocates of the respective modes occupying different places on my map of sociology and its contexts.

Final Illustration: Mainstream versus Nonmainstream Sociology

One of the terms that occurs repeatedly in sociologists' discourse about their field and about one another is the term "mainstream"—implying that there is a big river in which some of us float, and smaller rivulets for the rest of us. The term also implies some kind of core and some kind of periphery. Finally, the term connotes a certain advantage or privileged place for the mainstream, a certain deficit in these regards for those on the margin.

In a field that has grown so complex—if not fragmented—as ours, it is difficult nowadays to find a consistent meaning of "mainstream." Gerald Marwell, editor of the *American Sociological Review*, reported to me that among those who submit articles for consideration, almost *everyone* claims to be and perhaps apologizes for being marginal in the field—even those who submit path-analysis models of status-attainment bolstered by a large, quantitative database. Marwell exaggerates, perhaps, but the point is made; any "core" of sociology is problematic, fuzzy, and frayed around the edges.

Notwithstanding this difficulty of consistent definition, I believe it is possible to locate two general dimensions for which "mainstream" is a kind of convenient, if unreflective, shorthand:

- By and large, the term "mainstream" in the American sociological tradition refers to that complex of orientations that lie toward the "scientific" edge of sociology on my map—that is to say, reliance on systematically gathered and representative data sets that are empirically observable and hopefully quantifiable; a search for regularities if not laws; and a posture of scientific neutrality, with an ameliorationist orientation at most. "Nonmainstream" is not a single entity, but is constituted of *all* those variants I have identified that lie on the humanistic and artistic sides of the sociological universe. I would venture to say that, if interviewed, most "nonmainstream" sociologists would define themselves as possessing one or more of those humanistic or artistic orientations. This general statement is subject to many qualifications, of course, given the vagueness of discourse on the matter.
- There is a second sense in which the term "mainstream" implies "establishment." Funding agencies, led by the National Science Foundation (its name says that it is "scientific" in orientation), tend to stress excellence of research design, hypotheses, samples, methodology,

and orderliness of design in evaluating proposals. These agencies generally send out the message that "hard science" is the thing and, correspondingly, tend to look less favorably on that which is "soft"— that is, speculative (= theoretical), qualitative, humanistic, ethnographic, and clinical. There are some exceptions, but the generalization holds. The same might be said with respect to the elite "mainstream" sociological journals, whose criteria for acceptance are primarily scientific, though one may identify some notable exceptions here as well. The resulting differential access of those in the "mainstream" to resources and recognition feeds into resentments *within* the discipline: the mainstream being regarded as "fat cats" and the nonmainstream as underprivileged and underfed outsiders (a circumstance that might provide another reason for their hostility toward scientism and their affinity with those who suffer unjustly).

Conclusion

It can be argued that sociology has some sort of intellectual core (e.g., the study of institutional life) and continuity with respect to subject matter. But with respect to intellectual orientations, it is forever struggling with conflicting images of itself, images that can be traced both to its origins and to its intellectual boundaries. Perhaps my arguments have provided you with some degree of understanding of why it is that sociologists have a running preoccupation with defining themselves and finding an intellectual home. The truth is that they have many homes, but it is difficult for them (us) to tolerate this kind of perpetual ambiguity in the context of an intellectual tradition that holds out an expectation that a science should have unity and coherence above all. It is equally certain, moreover, that any effort to define the field in certain and simple terms is likely to cause disputation, because the field itself is, in reality, so ambiguous and complex in its orientations.

Note

1. William Graham Sumner, "The Forgotten Man," in Stow Persons, ed., *Social Darwinism: Selected Essays of William Graham Sumner* (Englewood Cliffs, N.J.: Prentice-Hall, 1963), 122–23.

The Two Faces of Social Science

Alan Wolfe

From biology in the late nineteenth century to information theory in the late twentieth century, the social sciences have turned to the natural sciences for inspiration. Yet the expectations have never fully been satisfied. After more than one hundred years of effort, the ability of social scientists to say anything with certainty about human behavior is not very impressive. We remain close to where we started, developing theories, trying to test them against data, arguing about methodology, and disputing conclusions. The social sciences have neither the public legitimacy nor the self-confidence that comes from the practice of "real" science.

There are numerous explanations for the failure of the social sciences to develop along the lines of the natural sciences, but surely among them ought to be included the special subject of the social sciences: human beings. The aim of a science is to describe and predict the behavior of the subjects it studies. Human subjects, because they can interpret the world around them, create sacred worlds of meaning out of their profane everyday affairs. A science of the human species that ignored one of the most significant aspects of what humans do would be like physics without the atom. It is anything but science to borrow the insights of those who study mindless subjects and apply them to those who possess mind. Nor does it satisfy the first criterion of science to understand those whose complex affairs are governed by the search for meaning on the basis of self-regulating systems that function without any special realm for meaning whatsoever. The social sciences, unlike the natural sciences, must incorporate the study of great humanistic texts in order to be a science. Because the opposition between the sciences and the humanities is as a false opposi-

31

tion, those who would study human affairs by using one rather than the other are doomed to discover very little.

Emboldened by the failure of a scientific model based on the natural sciences to predict much more than the obvious, and impressed by the fact that the social sciences remain more divided than ever in how they pursue their affairs, some people, reflecting a postmodern inability to define the world with precision, have claimed that science itself is suspect. In those accounts, usually referred to as the "strong program" in the sociology of science, science is understood as little more than rhetoric; the acceptance of a truth by scientists is not the result of a clever experiment or the marshaling of convincing data, but the end product of an inexhaustible rhetoric campaign in which the winners use every available strategy to browbeat the losers.[1] If "we must eventually come to call scientific the rhetoric able to mobilize on one spot more resources than older ones," the tables are reversed.[2] Rather than sociology turning to the natural sciences intent on envious borrowing, now sociologists claim to have the only method capable of understanding "science in action." The imperialism of the natural sciences over the social sciences is reversed if "adequate *social* studies of the sciences turn out to be the necessary foundations upon which more comprehensive and less distorted descriptions and explanations of nature can be built."[3]

If the sciences, including the hardest of them, are in reality rhetoric, then rhetorical tools can be used to understand everything, including society. What is coming to be called "the rhetorical turn" uses the techniques of rhetoric to understand social phenomena just as a previous generation of sociologists used the techniques of science.[4] Rhetorical tools have been applied to many disciplines, but because sociologists study social interaction, they are viewed as particularly suited to an emphasis on rhetorical tools. "As sociologists," Albert Hunter has written, "we cannot but see truth claims as examples of social interaction, and their refutation or acceptance is an inherently social process."[5] Once that insight has been accepted, the ways ideas are presented become at least as important as the ideas themselves. And the tools of literary analysis come to the fore; society is understood as a "text" to be read by sociologists sensitive to postmodernist techniques.[6]

The rhetoric turn in the social sciences adds a much needed element of skepticism to the belief that a rigorous, almost algorithmic, understanding of human behavior is possible. But it would be a loss if the social sciences, in liberating themselves from the natural sciences, were to fall heads over heels into the arms of rhetoric. If they did, those who claimed that the laws of the social science should be reduced to those of biology or biochemistry would be replaced by those who claim that their laws can be reduced to tropes and language games. And even more important, with respect to one key issue—the question of whether human beings have any special and unique characteristics—both the positivists and many rhetoricians, for all their differences, agree: they do not.

Positivists who would turn to the natural sciences for a model of how to do social science of necessity see no sharp break between natural and social phenomena. To argue that biology or physics provides a fruitful approach for humans is to make a case that the subjects of the one—other animal species or atoms—exist along the same continuum with the subjects of the other—people. Arguing that "the scientific analysis of social phenomena follows exactly the same general principles whether the objects of that analysis are human or nonhuman organisms," Walter Wallace believes that "sociology is, in its actual practice as well as its abstract design, one of the natural sciences—that is, much more akin to biology, chemistry, and physics than to philosophy, poetry, and religion. . . ."[7] From such a perspective, Wilhelm Dilthey's distinction between the cultural and the natural sciences would make no sense.[8] At some point, if not already now, sociology as a human science would make no sense. Either the study of people will become the study of the physical parts out of which people are made, or the study of all living organisms that exist together in groups will be viewed as fundamentally similar whether those organisms have human properties or not.

Approaches that deny the possibility of a firm and unshakable grounding for knowledge share with positivism an unwillingness to make a distinction between the subjects of inquiry. In much feminist and postmodern thought, any sharp break between nature and culture is suspect. It therefore follows that any effort to distinguish between a science of nature and a science of culture is also problematic. From Sandra Harding's perspective, "we must be skeptical about being able to make any clear distinctions between the physical and the nonphysical."[9] Harding, consequently, explicitly accepts the notion of a "unity of science" associated with the prime representatives of twentieth-century positivism, the Vienna Circle, even if she would reverse the hierarchy and place the moral sciences over the physical ones. Richard Rorty comes to a similar conclusion. His argument that we have no "sky hook" we can use to hitch ourselves to reality applies to both physics and the social sciences. Rorty instead urges that "we avoid using Dilthey's suggestion that we set up distinct parallel metavocabularies, one for the *Geistes-* and one for the *Naturwissenschaften.*"[10] The only difference between the social and the natural sciences, from such a perspective, lies in the way those who claim such titles do their work: "If we say that sociology or literary criticism is not a science, we shall mean merely that the amount of agreement among sociologists or literary critics on what counts as significant work, work which needs following up, is less than among, say, microbiologists."[11] In Rorty's ideal world, disciplinary designations ought to refer to communities of scholars "whose boundaries were as fluid as the interests of their members."[12] There would be no reason to divide disciplines by their claims over "chunks" of the world that interfaced with other chunks.

If reality for the positivists is seamless in its intelligibility, for Rorty, Harding, and many postmodernists reality is seamless in its opacity. They may differ sharply with positivists on epistemological ground, but they have no essential difference with those who would model social science on the natural sciences, for in both cases the world is equally unchunkable. Just as for positivists the social world has only a transitory autonomy—sitting there waiting to be colonized by the tools of the natural sciences—so for the postmodernists the social world is an arbitrary convention, an illusory attempt by people to believe they can control and organize chaotic forces that are really out of control. The distaste toward the self and the society found in so many postmodern writers is merely a continuation of a similar distaste that once came from biologists and physicists, or those who would emulate them.

To be faithful to human beings and their capacity to create meaning out of the things around them, the social sciences can turn neither to the hard sciences on the one hand nor to postmodern rhetorical or literary theory on the other. Sociology has long sought a third way between the market, the subject of economics, and the state, the subject of political science. But as a social science, it joins with those disciplines in seeking a third way between science as usually understood and the humanities as currently understood. Unlike the natural sciences, it must account for the interpretative capacities of those it studies. Unlike rhetorical and postmodern understandings, it must recognize the reality of human subjects. The social sciences must combine elements of both science and literature into a synthesis that fully resembles neither.

The best social theory has, in fact, always been in between the sciences and the humanities."[13] "While many of its roots are in the novel . . . ," Bruce Mazlish has written, "sociology still aspires, and should, to be a form of science."[14] Committed to a philosophical anthropology that understood humans as a unique species, the classic social theorists of the late nineteenth and early twentieth centuries hoped to fashion a social science that would be faithful simultaneously to science and to the human subject. Emile Durkheim turned to biology as his guide in his earlier work, but concluded his studies with a humanistic emphasis on meaning, only then to try and classify, like a taxonomist, everything there was to know about human beings.[15] Georg Simmel could be formalistic like a scientist but could also be characterized as "impressionistic" like an artist.[16] Florian Znaniecki called for a "humanistic sociology" but also argued that it should meet "the highest standard of logical exactness compatible with the nature of social data."[17] And Max Weber may have been the most ambivalent of all, appreciated because of his stress on "value-free" research, while seeming to embody a Nietschean heroic resistance against rationalization.[18]

In more recent years, this ambivalent position between science and the humanities has continued, even though, in postwar America, a positivistic model of the social sciences reached its pinnacle. Under the inspiration of Talcott Parsons and especially Robert Merton, European grand theory was transformed into "middle-range theorizing" that would generate hypotheses suitable for testing by models borrowed from the natural sciences. The idea was that knowledge would accumulate slowly but systematically, to the point at which sociologists could speak with authority about human behavior. Yet the victory for a social science based on a normal science of data collection and hypothesis testing was always more apparent than real, for the most interesting work in the field tended to remain ambiguous toward both science and the humanities.[19] Merton himself illustrates the point. Although a consistent advocate for middle-range theorizing, Merton was nonetheless rather ambivalent toward the natural science model; indeed ambivalence was one of his favorite concepts.[20] Recognizing that sociology "oscillates" between the humanities and the sciences, he noted that "only a few sociologists adapt to these pressures by acting wholly the scientific role . . . or the humanistic one."[21] Although he is well known for his work in the sociology of science, Merton's stylistic brilliance, copious references to literary sources, and love of irony and paradox make him a first-rate humanitarian. If we consider the subtext—the way Merton presented himself—over the text—his arguments for sociology as a science—the influence of the literary model is undeniable: Merton's references are to very old sources such as Francis Bacon; his footnotes are in literary, not scientific, form; and he published his books with leading New York houses. In postwar America, the best of scientific sociology was also humanistic at heart.

Because it falls into neither the sciences nor the humanities, sociology cannot present its findings in ways similar to those other ways of knowing. Merton has shown how, in the sciences, the gradual accumulation of knowledge develops in such a way that what were mind-boggling problems to mathematicians or logicians in an earlier period become the subject matter of introductory exercises in contemporary textbooks. Hence only very recent work tends to be cited in scholarly production, which makes the journal article—premised upon relatively quick publication followed by relatively quick obsolescence—the most appropriate. In the humanities, by contrast, older works are not only cited frequently, but often held to embody a wisdom beyond the reach of contemporary scholars. Given the longer expected life of the ideas involved, books—which are designed to be not only more permanent, but also more easily obtainable from shelves (as opposed to being stored on microfilm)—become the obvious mode of publication.[22] A thoroughly scientized sociology would, like the natural sciences, develop an almost exclusively article culture, yet the fact is that sociology, even to this day, has a book culture as well.[23]

Sociology's two cultures are as different from one another as they can be, each claiming more in common with neighborly disciplines than with others in the same disciplines. They all too often have little to do with each other, clustering themselves in different kinds of universities and promoting careers in different kinds of ways. Yet the very fact that each culture is associated with a particular kind of university in a particular location suggests a certain arbitrariness in the way sociology is practiced. Sociology's fate, as Kai Erikson has written, is to have no permanent home:

> . . . sociologists occupy a kind of border territory, positioned between the holdings of historians and literary critics, say, who often use language to reach out to larger audiences, and the holdings of economists and statisticians who circulate material to one another written (if that is the right word) in a species of code. To the first set of neighbors we look inelegant; to the second we look inexact.[24]

Given the subject that sociology studies—human beings who live simultaneously in the worlds of nature, culture, and mind—such bifurcated ways of doing and presenting research, however awkward, are also somewhat understandable.

It would be a mistake for the social sciences to lose their ambivalent status between the sciences and the humanities. The task for the social sciences is to develop a way of knowing that on the one hand grounds knowledge in something more than rhetorical argument while on the other hand recognizes that the truths so obtained have about them a tentative and even transitory nature. The something on which knowledge can be ground is the human subject, for human beings exist in the real world, have capacities that define what is special about them, and can be understood once those capacities are recognized and appreciated. But the truths obtained must be tentative because what is special and unique about human beings is their capacity to interpret, and thereby change, the rules that govern what they do. Because the subjects we investigate "talk back" to us, their behavior requires what Anthony Giddens calls a "double hermeneutic," since the subjects of study already exist in a "pre-interpreted" world.[25] The techniques, methodologies, and epistemologies of the social sciences must be as distinctive as the subjects they study.

How, then, ought we to do social science if we are to remain faithful to the interpretative capacities of the subjects we study? The question cannot be ignored, but neither can it be answered too literally, as if there were one way, and one way only, to do social science. Recognizing the particular capacities of human subjects leads to at least three general injunctions. (1) We ought to develop multiple methodologies because the people we study have multiple characteristics. (2) We ought to be committed to a form of sociological realism, because once one dismisses other animal species or machines as analogous to humans, real humans are all one has left. (3) We ought to understand and take seriously our calling as social scientists because we, like the people we study, are ultimately responsible for what we do.

Methodological Pluralism

In the ever present struggle to represent reality, academic disciplines traditionally begin by putting methodology first and the real world second. Those who would use the tools of the natural sciences to describe human social behavior already know, even before looking at the behavior they plan to observe, how it should best be studied. There are certain tools that have been perfected by the natural sciences. These tools—the experimental method, the verification of hypotheses, the accumulation of data, the interlinking of confirmed propositions into a theory about the world—are what defines science, not the world that the science would seek to understand. The facts of the social world are there waiting to be discovered, but it is more the search than the find that stimulates the intellectual juices. Indeed, once found, the facts often turn out to be trivial or boring. To practice social science based on the assumptions of the study of nature is to spend far more time learning method than learning content.

In a similar way, the application of rhetorical technique to the social sciences also puts method in the foreground and examines real world behavior as an afterthought. Rhetorical analysis is primarily concerned with the techniques used to persuade an audience. Actual discoveries of fact—what social scientists usually believe themselves to be doing as they study the real world—may or may not be very important in the application of such techniques. From a rhetorical perspective real world facts are not so much trivial as they are slippery. In some accounts they have no real existence at all but are instead the construction of the investigator who, knowingly or unknowingly, is engaged in a struggle for power with his or her audience. To practice social science from a rhetorical perspective is to spend far more time examining how the world is presented rather than how it actually is.

There is a long-standing debate in the social sciences, one that parallels the division between science and the humanities, dividing those who claim that human behavior is so constant that it can be predicted and those who argue that because humans are so unpredictable, their affairs can never achieve the regularity needed by science. Both positions miss the point. Humans live in both nature and culture. They possess qualities of mind but do not always use those qualities. The first task of any social science investigation is to gain a sense of the degree to which the individuals one is studying have accepted their world as given by nature or culture or have made the world around them through mind. The social sciences need a methodology for determining which methodology is appropriate.[26] There can be no fixed methodology for the social sciences because there can be no fixed assumptions about human nature.

Nonetheless a certain methodological imperialism runs rampant in the social sciences, and from all sides. On the one hand, those who argue from positivistic premises usually share a commitment to a certain kind of methodology, even if they are pluralistic with respect to theory. Wallace, for example, has attempted to provide an eclectic theoretical overview of all contemporary schools of sociology in the belief that a latent consensus exists among them. Wallace's reach is broad, as he finds common ground not only between Marxists, Parsonians, symbolic interactionists, and neofunctionalists, but also among sociobiologists and ethologists. But if his theoretical range is inclusive, his methodological focus is exclusive. When he turns to methodological questions, consequently, Wallace looks only at techniques borrowed from the natural sciences. None of the objections to the appropriateness of such techniques for the study of human behavior strike him as convincing.[27]

Yet the case is not especially different on the part of those who dissent from the positivistic consensus. Herbert Blumer, whose conception of sociology as embodying "symbolic interactionism" is probably closest to the emphasis I have been making on human beings as interpreting creatures, has little positive to say about methods borrowed from positivistic conceptions of science. The use of concepts and methods from the natural sciences imposes a kind of "captivity" on the researcher from which he ought to be "released." Only a close "inspection" of the real situations in which people find themselves, Blumer argues, constitutes an empirical science. Scientific approaches are a "travesty on methodology," generating techniques that "are grossly inadequate on the simple ground that they deal with only a limited aspect of the full act of scientific inquiry. . . ." It is possible that techniques borrowed from the natural sciences might supplement Blumer's emphasis on symbolic interactionism, but he never specifies how. What begins as an effort toward methodological pluralism winds up polarizing "rather sharply the opposition between naturalistic inquiry, in the form of exploration and inspection, and the formalized type of inquiry so vigorously espoused in current methodology."[28]

All forms of methodological monism reduce human beings to one of their capacities or another. Either they are organisms essentially similar to all other living organisms, as they are in Wallace's view, or what characterizes them is always and everywhere their irreducible need to make sense out of the situations they are in, as in Blumer's account. Yet whether human beings act as predictably as honeybees or are so idiosyncratic that no science can chart their affairs is not an a priori but an empirical question. Even sociobiology does not argue that all living organisms act in similar ways; some species can symbolize and others cannot, and among those fifteen or so species believed to be capable of imitation and learning, the relative abilities between them is never the same.[29] Nor does it follow that the capacity to use mind to shape both culture and nature is a given, as if the development of modernity automatically produces autonomous individuals capable of mindful action. While there clearly is a historical relationship between the kind of subject one studies and the way one studies it—modern people, in general, are in positions to use their minds more than traditional people (and perhaps more the postmodern selves who reputedly will come after them)—there are occasions on which very modern people will act instinctively and unthinkingly. To argue that mind is always and invariably present is to negate what it is about mind that makes it important.

Human behavior is never the product only of nature, of culture, or of mind. In the interaction between them, three general parameters of human action can be discovered. To the degree that human beings struggle for mere existence in a way similar to the natural world, their behavior, like that of other animal species, will be more or less amenable to a natural science such as biology. (Or, to consider the world of machines, to the degree that people adapt their behaviors to the computers around them, they would be better subjects for the sciences that explain those computers.) To the degree that human beings exist closer to the cultural world, by contrast, their behavior will be best charted by a combination of physical and cultural science, in the fashion, for example, of Durkheimian sociology or fin de siècle anthropology. And to the degree that human beings liberate themselves from the constraints of both nature and culture—in the process using their minds to alter the rules that govern what they do—an understanding of their behavior requires more of an interpretative science.

Some combination of methodologies will in most cases be necessary to understand human behavior in all its forms. There is no reason to denounce methodologies borrowed from the natural sciences on the grounds that people are never predictable. Sometimes their behavior is very predictable. They do tend to vote in ways that one can anticipate. Reduce their income, and they will most likely be less generous toward strangers. Put them in crowded jail cells with little hope for release, and they may act like rats in a cage. Remove socialization, and biology may well become more important. Understood as one methodology among many—appropriate for particular circumstances if not for others—the traditional techniques of science have an important role to play in the social sciences. Unfortunately for those who would model social science on the natural sciences, that role is not only limited, it becomes more irrelevant the more modern the society, if modernity is understood as the ability of people to understand the world around them. The flaw in positivist conceptions of social science is the belief that the more societies rely on natural science, the more its tools can be borrowed by the human sciences. The relationship is actually the other way around.

In a similar way, there is little or no reason for adherents of a positivistic conception of social science to rule hermeneutical approaches outside their purview. Even when people's behavior is in general predictable, not everyone's is, and it ought to be just as much a goal of science to understand those who deviate from the statistical norm as it is those who do not. There is no example of an insight gained by applying the methodological tools of the natural sciences to a social phenomenon that could not be deepened and improved by an accompanying "thick description" of particular cases.[30] What kind of science can possibly result when the assumptions that govern its view of its subject are simplistic, the tools use to gather evidence are partial, and the theoretical perspective into which the findings are to be incorporated ignores the special features of the subject under investigation? Self-referential sciences are only partially appropriate to subjects that possess culture. Cultural sciences, especially those committed to strong versions of structuralism that attribute little importance to human agency, are only partially appropriate to subjects that possess mind. When both nature and culture loosen their grip, hermeneutical methods provide the straightest road to a human science; that the road will contain detours only reflects that both the drivers and the destination do as well.[31]

A commitment to methodological pluralism makes one demand: that doing social science not be formulaic. It makes little sense to study phenomena in the real world by developing a tight research design that, to achieve presumed scientific validity, takes all the imagination out of doing social research. The predictability of much "scientific" social science is generally matched, however, by the formulaic quality of much "rhetorical" social science, which also applies its own pre-experiential methods to the study of social reality. If the social sciences are to be neither science nor rhetoric, their methodology has to be open-ended and multiple. There is nothing wrong, and a good deal right, with studying the same thing from many methodological standpoints. To the scientists, the results will be untrustworthy because they are unreplicatible. To the rhetoricians, some of the methodology will smack of positivism. But because neither alone can grasp the complexity of real human beings in all their biological, cultural, and mindful complexity, both together will have to suffice.

Avoiding furious battles for the soul of the social sciences, methodological pluralism picks and chooses from all contending parties depending on circumstance and situation. Driven by subject rather than method, such choices will tell us something about the world we want to understand. If methods borrowed from the natural sciences dominate, that will be because people are not using the powers of mind that modernity makes available. If hermeneutic methods dominate, that will be because people's interpretative capacities will be at their fullest. In this way, the social sciences as disciplines will be intimately linked with society as a subject, the one telling us what the other requires, and vice versa.

Sociological Realism

Methodological pluralism is rooted in the idea that the social scientist must begin with real world facts and then develop the appropriate methodology for understanding them. But are there real world facts? Anyone who argues from a "realist" position tends to be on the defensive in a postmodern epistemological atmosphere marked by skepticism toward such grandiose claims.[32] But my argument for realism is a minimalist one, based on the distinction between the human and other species, both natural and artificial. In the real world, I have been arguing, there are some chunks of reality that possess interpretative capabilities and others that do not. It then follows that one should try to get some sense of which kind of subject one wants to study, and how that subject is acting and thinking, before deciding which methodology is appropriate to understanding it. Rather than methodology first and reality second, this way of proceeding would put a slice of reality first and tailor its methodology afterwards.

Realism has not only a philosophical meaning, but it is also used as well in a political sense—as the opposite of idealism. A "realist" is one who takes the world as given in deciding between strategic alternatives. Statesmen are realists to the degree that they accept human nature as what they believe it is. They ask what is in their own and their opponents' interest, not what is right or ethical according to some impartial standard of justice. While there need not necessarily be any relationship between these two meanings of the term, some thinkers embody them both. Max Weber is one, Raymond Aron another.

To be an appropriate science for the humans it would study, a social science has to be realistic in both senses of the term. But if the belief in philosophical realism can be weak, premised only on the assumption that some chunks of reality possess mind while others do not, the belief in a political form of realism ought to be strong. Once one drops the assumption that human behavior can be modeled on the study of rats, pigeons, or computers, there are no appropriate subjects left for a human science except humans. Social scientists have to understand people as they really are because people as they really are are the only things social scientists can study.

The best social science, therefore, is inevitably marked by a commitment to realism that is similar to the realpolitik of a great statesman. Such realism has usually been associated with the ethnographic tradition in the social sciences—a tradition especially under attack from postmodernism's suspicion of authorial omnipotence. Ethnography prides itself on understanding people as they really are, not as we would like them to be. Such realism is closely aligned with a "debunking" tendency in modern sociology, a tendency to look behind official rationales, platitudes, and spaces to the "realities" that lay hidden behind them. For this reason, the sociology of the professions has long had a realistic dimension, since professionals are usually defined by their formal commitments to codes that are often violated in practice.[33] The same is true of what used to be called "deviant behavior," for merely by calling attention to problems that society generally prefers to ignore, the social scientist plays a realistic role. Studies of crime, for example, are grist for the realist's mill, rarely better exemplified than in Jack Katz's indictment of criminologists for not understanding why crime is pleasurable to the criminal.[34] Even the perception of crime so drastically changes the way in which people live that only an observer sensitive to the silent codes of dress, deportment, and language can obtain a realistic picture of urban life at the present time.[35]

Few sociological careers have better illustrated this commitment to realism than that of Herbert Gans.[36] At a time when white ethnic cultures were barely understood, Gans painted a vivid picture of Italian life in Boston.[37] A few years later, when it was common among intellectuals to denounce as tacky and inhuman the newly built suburbs that sprouted in the years after World War II, it took Gans to discover that inside those little houses were not conforming dupes spawned by an abstraction called "mass society" but real people struggling with the dilemmas of real life.[38] Finally, in his account of "middle American individualism," Gans continues to bring real people face to face with the prejudices that intellectuals and academics often have against them.[39] In his methodological reflections on *The Urban Villagers,* Gans concluded that he did not carry out a "scientific study" in Merton's sense of the term. His goal, rather, was to to get as "close to the realities of social life" as he could.[40] The juxtaposition is what is most interesting here, assuming, as it does, that what is realistic is not necessarily scientific and vice versa, as if a science of human behavior could be based on something other than the real world.

Given this juxtaposition, it is perhaps not surprising that realism actually has quite a number of opponents in contemporary social science. The reasons advanced are generally of two kinds: theoretical and political.

C. Wright Mills made his reputation through his criticisms of theory and method that were divorced from reality.[41] Much of what he says about abstracted empiricism and grand theory is still relevant, even if the matters to which it need be applied have changed. Rational choice theory, which has its origins in biology as well as economics, is one theory-driven approach to the social sciences that is primarily concerned with modeling behavior according to certain assumptions and only occasionally with testing those assumptions against real world behavior. In James Coleman's view, for example, there are two significant kinds of actors: natural actors, or people, and corporate actors, or organizations. The assumption that both will act to maximize utility ignores many "deviations from rationality" such as, in Coleman's terms, "weakness of will, precommitment, preference reversals with changes in proximity, failure to meet the criterion of independence from irrelevant alternatives, and others." This failure to account for the reality of the self in the empirical world represents a "central weakness of a theory based on rational action."[42] But Coleman is convinved that the problem is not as important as critics have made it out to be. On the one hand, "the theoretical predictions made here will be substantially the same whether the actors act precisely according to rationality as commonly conceived or deviate in the ways that have been observed."[43] On the other hand, it is possible to imagine the internal structure of actors by generalizing back from corporate actors to natural people in ways that will enable us to develop a more complete view of the self. Coleman's understanding of the self actually resembles more a self-recurring computer than a flesh-and-blood person: "The receptor, linkage, and actuator constitute a kind of control system, and the perfect purposive actor could also be described as an optimal control system."[44] Determined to solve the problem of deviations from the model of rationality as a thought experiment, the one thing Coleman never considers is an ethnographic account of real people living in conditions of real life.

If theoretical interests were not enough of an obstacle to understanding real world people in all their complexity, there are also political ones. While social theory and politics always overlap, there are differences between them, and the most important of those differences involves the question of realism. To be true to social science, one must suspend judgment about how people ought to be and first consider how they are. But to be a political activist, one necessarily wants to overcome people as they really are and make them into people as one wants them to be. Just as methodologists put an approach first and consider reality secondarily, political activists have a theory of human nature to which reality has to be adjusted. Conservatives think of people as inherently limited, whereas radicals tend to view them as essentially good. But both know what they want to know about people without consideration for how they actually are. That is why social scientists can be political, but can never let their politics substitute for their commitment to social science.

A commitment to realism cuts across the existing right–left dimension that characterizes political attitudes. Conservatism, for example, was once almost synonymous with realism, but no longer. Contemporary conservatives long for a world that no longer exists, lamenting, in the process, the fact that real world people have not only made their compromises with modernity, but sometimes find it appealing and would have it no other way. Even if families could afford it, women are unlikely to leave the workplace, stop having abortions, and devote full-time to their families, no matter how vigorously conservatives urge them to do so. To be a realist is to accept that gender relations have changed precisely because people have minds as well as bodies and that, once changed, they are never again likely to be the same. Conservatives who demand legislation requiring parental approval for abortions, in appealing to an imagined family structure, are no different from postmodernists who call for androgenous social arrangements; the one is as unreal as the other. If liberals often have a hard time accepting that people can be racist or inegalitarian, conservatives refuse to accept that homosexuals will not go away, secularism is here to stay, most people have minds of their own, and modernity survives because most people find it rather beneficial. It is precisely because conservatives have lost touch with realism that their proposals often seem so radical.

But radicals and leftists also have difficulty accepting realism. At first glance this is somewhat surprising, since being able to accept the real world, even in all its unpleasantness, is a prelude for changing it, which is perhaps why Karl Marx and Friedrich Engels understood themselves as realists (and why they liked novelists such as Honoré de Balzac). Yet many on the left seem unwilling even to acknowledge unwanted realities for fear that to admit their existence is to accept their inevitability. This is a particular person for many sociologists, who generally tend to lean toward the left in their personal politics. To the degree that sociologists understand themselves as critics and dissenters from society as it is, realism seems just another term for reaction. A book like Jonathan Rieder's *Canarsie*, which allows its subjects the room to express a point of view that most sociologists would find racist and repugnant, exemplifies sociological realism at its best, but it remains, for many sociologists, an uncomfortable book. It becomes easy to confuse the messenger with the message, to criticize Rieder for not confronting his subjects with their politically incorrect attitudes, as if the task of sociology were to create a world other than the one that exists, rather than understanding the world we have. Even as sophisticated a realist as Gans was disturbed by Rieder's book, wishing the author to be "less the dutiful ethnographer" and more the "systematic" analyzer of the causes of what he found.[45]

For those who see sociology as a way of taking the side of the underdog, realism is treacherous, a dangerous, lurking presence that will, if we are not careful, seduce us into a false complacency. In developing what she calls "a feminist sociology," Dorothy Smith argues that the everyday world is "problematic": "we cannot understand how it is organized or comes about by remaining within it." Instead we have to shift our attention from the world of everyday practices to the world of discourse, understanding the latter as constituting in large part the former. Ethnography can never stop with the real world but can only begin there. "The ethnographic process of inquiry is one of exploring further into those social, political, and economic processes that organize and determine the actual bases of experience of those whose side we have taken." And if realism is dangerous, so is sociology, for it too is, in Smith's phrase, "part of the ruling apparatus."[46] Realism in general, and sociological realism in particular, are epiphenomenal. What really counts are structures of power, and we need to work through the real world to find them. In imagining how her subjects ought to be in the world, the sociologist deprives them of their own imaginative capacities, should the subject choose to imagine herself in roles—such as loving mother, wife, or homemaker—that the sociologist believes inauthentic because inscribed in power. By contrast, realistic feminist ethnographers should, as one of them put it, "learn to respect and understand some of the social appeals of widespread nostalgia for eroding family forms" characteristic of the political movements they otherwise oppose.[47]

The denial of reality is strongest among those influenced by postmodernism. If reality is little more than the arguments one makes about reality, one can always look elsewhere, beyond the text of everyday life, endlessly deconstructing what appears to be until finally one is satisfied that the imperfections have been removed. Pauline Rosenau has shown why postmodernist assumptions, so attractive in the humanities, are of more limited appeal to social scientists.[48] The reason surely is that taken to its logical conclusion, postmodernism leaves no real social facts to be discovered or analyzed. Any particular social fact could illustrate the point, but the one that is most salient, because it lies at the postmodern disenchantment with reality, is the fact of difference. For the sociologist, borders, boundaries, and divisions are the heart of the matter; people are organized, or organize themselves, by time, space, ethnicity, race, age, gender, taste, status, and any one of a number of relevant sociological categories.[49] For the postmodernist, difference is suspect. Distinctions and boundaries are artificial. Socially constructed, they can be deconstructed. A product of power, they can be abolished by power. The task becomes one of imagining worlds, or at least trying to develop public policies, where difference is no longer invidious.[50] Sociology tends toward exclusion, since groups usually develop their identity by keeping others out. Postmodern thought tends toward inclusion, the incorporation of the other as no longer foreign and strange. An imagined world without distinctions may be fairer and more just, but from a sociological standpoint, it is also likely to be less interesting and less richly textured. With postmodernism, we reach the pole that is diametrically opposite to sociology's long fascination with the real world.[51]

Despite pressures that derive either from theoretical or from political premises, sociology must be a realistic science. When we prejudge people's actions and beliefs—by coming to them with a predetermined methodology or a predetermined set of political attitudes—we fail to give them the benefit of what makes them human: the capacity to interpret the world in ways different from the ways we, who are observing them, interpret the world. The only check we have on the tendency for either our theories or our politics to run wild is an obligation to turn to the real world from time to time to see where we are. The people we find in the real world are unlikely to give full support for any theoretical or political position advanced in their name. Their motives are likely to be mixed, conforming neither to the dictates of rational self-interest nor to an automatic recognition of the claims of the other. And their politics will rarely be as decisive as the politics of those studying them, making any effort to substitute our politics for theirs not only bad social science, but also, in the long run, bad politics. To be a sociological realist is to accept that people are neither perfect nor imperfect, neither biologically determined nor socially created, neither embedded in structures nor free of constraint, neither predictable nor idiosyncratic. What makes them real is precisely that they resist monistic assumptions—whether methodological, theoretical, or political—of who and what they are.

Social Science as a Vocation

Neither the scientific nor the rhetorical approach to social science has an adequate understanding of the obligations of those doing social research. Just as the subjects one studies are not very interesting if one knows in advance which methodologies or political attitudes are appropriate to them, the person who studies them is not very interesting if that person follows formulaic conventions without much regard for his or her own interpretative qualities. Being true to the human subject requires not only taking seriously the people one studies, but also how one goes about studying them.

The scientific model that became so attractive for sociologists in the years after World War II never did generate the patient accumulation of fact upon which complex theories could be built. Surely part of the reason, as I have argued throughout this essay, is that, in borrowing models from the study of other than human species, much of scientific social science failed to understand its own subject. But whatever the reason for its failure, the scientific model did possess one significant advantage, which may explain why it continued to live. Under the scientific model, the rules of how social scientists were expected to comport themselves in their professional work were fairly clear. Unlike earlier thinkers—in America sociology developed as an explicitly moralistic substitute for Protestant theology—scientific sociologists would be circumspect about injecting their own values into their scholarship.[52] Instead of writing books for general audiences that any good journalist could do as well, they would subject themselves to the hard discipline of peer review, submitting articles to publication in journals that would be read— anonymously—by impersonal judges concerned only with fidelity to agreed upon standards.[53] Decisions about hiring, promotion, and tenure would be based, not on what Parsons dismissed as affective and subjective criteria associated with premodern *Gemeinschaft* communities, but on the universalistic judgments of the "invisible college" and its standards. (The Parsonian scheme—stressing affective neutrality over affectivity, universalism over particularism, achievement over ascription, specificity over diffuseness, and collectivity-orientation over self-orientation—may or may not have been an adequate description of how sociologists understood the world, but it was undoubtedly a very accurate description of how professional sociologists wanted the world to understand them.)

The scientific model may not, finally, have taught all that much about social reality, but it did deal extremely well with the reality of who social scientists were and what they aspired to be. Its set of rules for professional behavior enabled its practitioners to resolve some exceptionally awkward questions about what social scientists, as opposed to social science, ought to do. Social scientists could attempt to be objective, even if social science could not. Social scientists could follow well-known rules, even if reality did not. Methodological debates involved the behavior of practitioners, not the nature of the social world. A model of science as a profession was far more appealing to American social scientists than a model of science as an epistemology.

Nonetheless, the inability of the scientific model to generate significant new increments in social knowledge created a void in which at least some are tempted toward a postmodern response. But if it is the case that epistemological assumptions not only structure how we try to comprehend reality, but also how we establish standards of professional comportment, what would be the consequences of a postmodern understanding of professional obligations? If one no longer believes that no one reality exists outside the efforts of observers to describe it, what consequences follow for how one understands one's professional obligations? Is it possible to retain one's belief in the neutrality of knowledge and the relatively dispassionate, value-free professional code upon which it was based, if knowledge itself is understood to be so slippery as to be almost beyond grasp? If we can no longer be sure which practices are "deviant" and which "straight," if norms are contingent and contextual rather than universal, if the self is little else than a series of presentations, then an entire structure of professional obligations based on the assumption that what validates academic inquiry is an adequate description of social reality becomes difficult to maintain.

There may well be dangers in practicing the postmodernism one might be tempted to preach.[54] If there is no real social world whose laws can be understood, there is no way to judge whether any social scientist has a better understanding of the world than any other. The academic enterprise is one that is essentially concerned with making distinctions, yet distinctions themselves are suspect from postmodern assumptions. Unable to make judgments and distinctions based on merit, since merit would likely be dismissed as a construction through which some try to obtain domination over others, other criteria would almost have to become the basis for making judgments with respect to appointments, publication, and tenure. Such criteria would include politics, on the grounds that all knowledge is tainted by politics in any case. The criteria might also include the background of the scholar, if one believes that those who have been excluded from dominant ways of knowing "can provide the grounds for a less distorted understanding of the world around us."[55] A vocation organized by postmodern assumptions would not be a vocation that could recognize social science as an autonomous way of knowing. Sociology would be another form of politics, just as for the positivists sociology was another form of science.

Both those who would model sociology on the natural sciences and those who would turn toward postmodern epistemologies have an insufficient understanding of what the vocation of a scholar demands. When sociology modeled its professional standards on the practices of physical scientists, its practitioners believed, even if incorrectly, that they could count on reality to help them out: ideas would be proven by hypothesis testing or they would not. Because it was reality that was believed to hold the secrets, the observer of reality played an essentially passive role. The multiple authorship and jargon-laden language of scientific sociology— represented in that side of sociology that sought publication in journal articles—symbolized the impersonal and antibiographical nature of the quest for truth. Good writing was unimportant, since nature wrote and the scientist merely transcribed what she had in mind. No strong theory of vocational conduct was necessary because it finally did not matter what the sociologist did or did not do; reality itself would determine what happened in the world.

Although practitioners of the new postmodern epistemologies believe themselves highly critical of positivistic science, their understanding of the vocation of the scholar is essentially the same. Since reality can never help us out, since the whole quest to discover laws of the real world can only uncover the rhetorical strategies by which its investigators frame their arguments, attention shifts from the world to the observer of the world. But such a point of view attaches no particular importance to the observer, since texts take on their own dynamics irrespective of the intentions or desires of their authors. The death of the author means the death of the sociologist as author. There need not be any conception of the right way to carry out one's vocational duties if one has no autonomy, no selfhood, no authorship. It ought not to be surprising, consequently, that although postmodernists tend to publish in books rather than in journals, one finds the same jargon-filled prose and "authorless" quality found in scientific articles. In both cases, research writes itself, making irrelevant any notion that observers of the world have any particular responsibility when carrying out their observations.

Sociological realists and methodological pluralists, who can neither ground their claims in the study of other species nor be satisfied that all claims to truth are rhetorical, cannot find satisfactory rules of conduct in either. Instead they have to resurrect the notion of an authorial responsibility that is missing in both scientific and rhetorical approaches. Because the sociologist cannot allow the nature of the world to solve problems of conduct for her, she, as author, has to solve them herself. The more skeptical her epistemological assumptions, the more ordered must be her professional standards. The more she understands social reality to be colored by politics, the less she can allow her search to understand the reality to be colored by politics. The greater her appreciation of interpretation and meaning, the less she can rely on self-reflexive models that attach more importance to information than to meaning. Postmodernism, for those who like it, comes with a price: to the degree that we allow the content of what we do to be influenced by it, we must resist allowing the form by which we do it to be similarly influenced. Indeed, the case can be put even more strongly. Precisely because we can no longer be convinced that there is a relatively uncomplicated social reality out there to be measured and described, we need even more to have deeply entrenched professional standards by which we go about conducting our business.

Because social scientists, in trying to understand the world, are also trying to understand themselves as part of the world, the subject and object of social investigation are difficult to distinguish. If humans have no special capacities of interpretation, then social scientists—who are also human—lack them as well. Thinkers like Niklas Luhmann, who imagine the world in completely self-referential terms, allow little room for autonomous social scientists because there is little room for autonomous selves of any sort. But if the concern of the social sciences is with chunks of reality that possess mind, then included within that chunk of reality are social scientists themselves. An adequate theory of the human subject can never be developed if it stops short of including those who study and write about other humans.

Is Sociology Necessary?

Although they once believed themselves the queen of the sciences, sociologists are no longer certain they have anything to offer the world. Surely the tendency to borrow from elsewhere—to turn to the sciences and then to the humanities, to borrow from economics and then political science— reflects an intellectual insecurity quite at odds with the assertive, often imperial, tone of Auguste Comte and Emile Durkheim. The longer sociology has been in existence, the less it seems to know what it wants to do, a state of affairs that confirms those who believe that sociology is little more than jargon in the first place.

Compared to the 1960s, when sociology was a booming business, there is reason to question whether sociology is any longer necessary. It was, after all, a field that established itself not only late, but also with some difficulty, as conservative elites in both Germany and France viewed sociology as little different from socialism.[56] With the dramatic turn against socialism that started in the 1980s, a turn against sociology would also become inevitable.[57] And to the degree that any anthropocentric assumptions have been challenged by the emerging worldviews described in this essay, the case for a distinct science for the human species seems even more problematic. An intellectual milieu that distrusts utopianism and is simultaneously attracted to antihumanism is not one in which sociology is going to flourish.

One response to this state of affairs would be to proclaim the death of sociology, to view its classic objectives as overtaken by developments in neighboring fields. This is essentially what both the scientific and the rhetorical turns imply, the one absorbing sociology into biology and physics, the other into argumentation and textual analysis. But it is also possible to view sociology's ambivalence as a sign of strength—an indication of the need for a mature science to stand on its own feet, accept its own subject matter, and develop its own methodology, irrespective of whether what it does conforms to the epistemological and ontological views of others. In that sense, the challenge to sociology that emerges from events in the real world, as well as from developments in the realm of thought, forces sociology back to its origins in order to be able to stand on its own disciplinary feet.

Both science and rhetoric tend not to lead back to origins such as classic texts, founding documents, or significant statements. It is a hallmark of science to ignore works written long ago, no matter how important for their time, on the grounds that new knowledge is always the most relevant knowledge. It is a hallmark of contemporary literary criticism to treat classic texts iconoclastically, as if their appearance were a matter of contingency and luck. Because sociology is concerned—some would say obsessed—with its founding classics, it is, once more, different from both science and rhetoric.[58] In their location between the sciences and the humanities, in their attempt to discover a science of the human between the world of God and the world of nature, in their effort to find a place between the sacred and the profane, the classic thinkers in the sociological tradition broke new ground. Whatever has changed since, the ground is firm enough to provide the footing necessary for a distinct science for a distinct subject to walk forward.

But it has to be a walk, not a run. To practice a social science that recognizes its subjects as interpretive creatures in the real world means learning to live with ambiguity. The social scientist, as Thomas Scheff has argued, will practice "being a jack-of-all-trades, as well as an expert in a particular field."[59] Such a social science will present itself in many ways. It will publish its findings in both book and article form. Its methodology will be inherently pluralistic, borrowing from the biological and cultural sciences while stressing social science as a distinct way of knowing. It will accept the existence of a real world, but not in a strong sense and never in the sense that what is found in the real world settles all epistemological and moral issues. It will develop a calling rooted in understanding the social scientist on the same terms as those he or she studies. This is not a formula for certainty, as if social science provides the key that unlocks the secrets of human beings. But it is a formula for a more realistic social science, one that, in rejecting both science and rhetoric as its proper model, meets the human beings it presumes to understand more than halfway.

Notes

1. Barry Barnes and David Bloor, "Relativism, Rationalism and the Sociology of Knowlege," in Martin Hollis and Steven Lukes, eds., *Rationality and Relativism* (Cambridge: MIT Press, 1982), 21–47.

2. Bruno Latour, *Science in Action: How to Follow Scientists and Engineers through Society* (Cambridge: Harvard University Press, 1987), 61.

3. Sandra Harding, *Whose Science? Whose Knowledge? Thinking from Women's Lives* (Ithaca: Cornell University Press, 1991), 15.

4. Herbert W. Simons, ed., *The Rhetorical Turn: Invention and Persuasion in the Conduct of Inquiry* (Chicago: University of Chicago Press, 1990); Donald McCloskey, *The Rhetoric of Economics* (Madison: University of Wisconsin Press, 1985); John S. Nelson, Allan Megill, and Donald McCloskey, eds., *The Rhetoric of the Human Sciences: Language and Argument in Scholarship and Public Affairs* (Madison: University of Wisconsin Press, 1987).

5. Albert Hunter, "Introduction: Rhetoric in Research, Networks of Knowledge," in Albert Hunter, ed., *The Rhetoric of Social Research, Understood and Believed* (New Brunswick: Rutgers University Press, 1990), 3.

6. Richard Harvey Brown, *Society as Text: Essays on Rhetoric, Reason, and Reality* (Chicago: University of Chicago Press, 1987).

7. Walter L. Wallace, *Principles of Scientific Sociology* (New York: Aldine, 1983), 4, 5.

8. Wilhelm Dilthey, *Introduction to the Human Sciences*, vol. I of *Selected Works*, edited, with an Introduction, by Rudolf A. Makkreel and Frithjof Rodi (Princeton: Princeton University Press, 1989), 55–72.

9. Sandra Harding, *The Science Question in Feminism* (Ithaca: Cornell University Press, 1986), 23, 246.

10. Richard Rorty, *Objectivity, Relativism, and Truth,* vol. I of *Philosophical Papers* (New York: Cambridge University Press, 1991), 79.

11. Ibid., 40.

12. Ibid., 45.

13. Wolf Lepenies, *Between Literature and Science: The Rise of Sociology,* trans. R. J. Hollingdale (Cambridge: Cambridge University Press, 1988).

14. Bruce Mazlish, *A New Science: The Breakdown of Connections and the Birth of Sociology* (New York: Oxford University Press, 1989), 24.

15. See Emile Durkheim and Marcel Mauss, *Primitive Classification,* trans. Rodney Needham (Chicago: University of Chicago Press, 1963).

16. David Frisby, *Sociological Impressionism* (London: Heinemann, 1981). See also Donald N. Levine, "Simmel as a Resource for Sociological Metatheory," *Sociological Theory* 2 (Fall 1989), 161–73.

17. Robert Bierstedt, "Introduction," in Florian Znaniecki, *On Humanistic Sociology: Selected Papers* (Chicago: University of Chicago Press, 1969), 16.

18. The first effort to insist that the "value-free" Weber was the incorrect one is Wolfgang J. Mommsen, *Max Weber and German Politics 1890–1920*, trans. Michael Steinberg (Chicago: University of Chicago Press, 1984). Many recent books bring out Weber's relationship to literary themes, especially Harvey Goldman, *Max Weber and Thomas Mann: Calling and the Shaping of the Self* (Berkeley: University of California Press, 1988); Lawrence A. Scaff, *Fleeing the Iron Cage: Culture, Politics, and Modernity in the Thought of Max Weber* (Berkeley: University of California Press, 1989); and Alan Sica, *Weber, Irrationality, and Social Order* (Berkeley: University of California Press, 1988).

19. This point is made forcefully by Donald N. Levine, *The Flight from Ambiguity: Essays in Social and Cultural Theory* (Chicago: University of Chicago Press, 1985).

20. Robert K. Merton, *Sociological Ambivalence* (New York: Free Press, 1976).

21. Robert K. Merton, *On Theoretical Sociology: Five Essays, Old and New* (New York: Free Press, 1967), 28.

22. Ibid., 1–37.

23. I have explored these differences at much greater length in Alan Wolfe, "Books Versus Articles: Two Ways of Publishing Sociology," *Sociological Forum* 5 (September 1990), 477–89.

24. Kai Erikson, "On Sociological Prose," in Albert Hunter, ed., *The Rhetoric of Social Research*, 26.

25. Anthony Giddens, *New Rules of Sociological Method* (New York: Basic Books, 1976), 158. Rorty disagrees; see *Objectivity, Relativism, and Truth*, 97.

26. On this point, see Donald W. Fiske and Richard Shweder, eds., *Metatheory in Social Science: Pluralisms and Subjectivities* (Chicago: University of Chicago Press, 1986).

27. Wallace, 477–93.

28. Herbert Blumer, *Symbolic Interactionism: Perspective and Method* (Berkeley: University of California Press, 1969), 24, 26,47.

29. The argument that fifteen or so species have an advanced form of protoculture comes from Charles J. Lumsden and Edward O. Wilson, *Genes, Mind, and Culture: The Coevolutionary Process* (Cambridge: Harvard University Press, 1981), 2–5.

30. The reference is to Clifford Geertz, "Thick Description: Toward an Interpretative Theory of Culture," in *The Interpretation of Cultures* (New York: Basic Books, 1973), 3–30.

31. On the role of interpretation in social science see Paul Rabinow and William M. Sullivan, eds., *Interpretive Social Science: A Second Look* (Berkeley and Los Angeles: University of California Press, 1987).

32. One exception is the school generally labeled "new social realist," whose assumptions are close to, but not the same as, my own. See Roy Bashkar, *A Realist Theory of Science* (Sussex: Harvester Press, 1978); Rom Harre and Paul Secord,

The Explanation of Human Behavior (Totowa, N.J.: Rowman and Littlefield, 1972); and Giddens, *New Rules of Sociological Method.*

33. Howard S. Becker, et al., *Boys in White: Student Culture in Medical School* (Chicago: University of Chicago Press, 1961).

34. Jack Katz, *Seductions of Crime: Moral and Sensual Attractions of Doing Evil* (New York: Basic Books, 1988).

35. Elijah Anderson, *Streetwise: Race, Class, and Change in an Urban Community* (Chicago: University of Chicago Press, 1990).

36. Gans describes his own career in Herbert J. Gans, "Relativism, Equality, and Popular Culture," in Bennett M. Berger, ed., *Authors of Their Own Lives: Intellectual Autobiographies by Twenty American Sociologists* (Berkeley and Los Angeles: University of California Press, 1990), 432–51.

37. Herbert Gans, *The Urban Villagers: Group and Class in the Life of Italian-Americans* (New York: Free Press, 1962).

38. Herbert Gans, *The Levittowners: Ways of Life and Politics in a New Suburban Community* (New York: Pantheon Books, 1967).

39. Herbert J. Gans, *Middle American Individualism: Political Participation and Liberal Democracy* (New York: Oxford University Press, 1991).

40. Gans, *The Urban Villagers,* 349–50.

41. C. Wright Mills, *The Sociological Imagination* (New York: Grove Press, 1959).

42. James S. Coleman, *Foundations of Social Theory* (Cambridge: Belknap Press of Harvard University Press, 1990), 932–46.

43. Ibid., 506.

44. Ibid., 504.

45. Herbert J. Gans, "They Drew the Line," *New York Times Book Review* (March 31, 1985), 26.

46. Dorothy E. Smith, *The Everyday World as Problematic: A Feminist Sociology* (Boston: Northeastern University Press, 1987), 109, 119, 177.

47. Judith Stacey, *Brave New Families: Stories of Domestic Upheaval in Late Twentieth Century America* (New York: Basic Books, 1990), 5.

48. Pauline Marie Rosenau, *Post-Modernism and the Social Sciences: Insights, Inroads, and Intrusions* (Princeton: Princeton University Press, 1991), 42.

49. For some recent treatments, which themselves demonstrate the tension between sociology and postmodernism, see Eviatar Zerubavel, *The Fine Line: Boundaries and Distinctions in Everyday Life* (New York: Free Press, 1991); Judith Gerson and Kathy Peiss, "Boundaries, Negotiations and Consciousness: Reconceptualizing Gender Relations," *Social Problems* 32 (April 1985), 317–31; Michele Lamont and Marcel Fournier, eds., *Cultivating Differences: Symbolic Boundaries and the Making of Inequality* (Chicago: University of Chicago Press, 1992).

50. An interesting effort along these lines is Martha Minow, *Making All the Difference: Inclusion, Exclusion, and American Law* (Ithaca: Cornell University Press, 1990).

51. I have elaborated the themes of this paragraph at greater length elsewhere.

52. Arthur Vidich and Stanford Lyman, *American Sociology: Worldly Rejection of Religion and Their Directions* (New Haven: Yale University Press, 1985).

53. For an argument to the effect that such methods of publication constitute "quality control" standards for the profession, and that such standards are breaking down, see Hubert M. Blalock, "The Real and Unrealized Contributions of Quantitative Sociology," *American Sociological Review* 54 (June 1989), 447–60.

54. I have written about these dangers at greater length in "Sociology as a Vocation," *American Sociologist* 21 (Summer 1990), 136–48.

55. Harding, *Science Question in Feminism*, 191.

56. For interesting accounts of the hostile reception of sociology on the part of German and French officials, see Karl-Siegbert Rehberg, " 'Anti-Sociology:' A Conservative View on Social Sciences," *The History of Sociology* 5 (Spring 1985), 45–60, and Steven Lukes, *Emile Durkheim: His Life and Work: A Critical Study* (London: Penguin Books, 1973), 100–108.

57. On the relationship between sociology and socialism, see Tom Bottomore, *Sociology and Socialism* (New York: St. Martin's Press, 1984).

58. An effort to reexamine the founding texts of sociology for future purposes is Buford Rhea, ed., *The Future of the Sociological Classics* (Boston: Allen Unwin, 1981).

59. Thomas J. Scheff, *Microsociology: Discourse, Emotion, and Social Structure* (Chicago: University of Chicago Press, 1990), 151.

Disciplined Artfulness and
the Human Sciences

Jean Bethke Elshtain

When I first read the essays by Neil Smelser and Alan Wolfe, I was somewhat bereft: I found myself in rough-and-ready agreement and much in the debt of the authors for their forthrightness and illuminating commentary. I had nothing substantive to detract and I was unsure of my poor powers to add. Then it hit me. I thought of one good, self-interested reason for why sociology of the interpretive, humanistic sort must not only survive but flourish—we political philosophers need all the help we can get. We too are often somewhat forlorn laborers in the vineyard of an enterprise—political science—that numbers among its practitioners, perhaps the majority, those devoted to the rigorous asceticism of a method that eschews or finesses questions of meaning. By meaning, I refer to the meaning to and for complex human subjects with their rich and often raucous lives.

It follows that the political scientist frequently wishes that the political philosophy enterprise had not only begun but ended with Plato and Aristotle and the Greek polis. I will not indulge this line of commentary, save to indicate that the study of politics features its own versions of the three intellectual outlooks discussed by Smelser, as well as its particular variations on the sin of opting out of reality to which Wolfe devoted the bulk of his commentary. I shall call these the seduction of dissociated method, on the one hand, and the lure of hypertextuality abstracted from concrete social context, on the other. My own discipline, then, is not immune from the desire to transcend what Hannah Arendt calls the human condition

57

and what the great political philosopher Isaiah Berlin sometimes refers to as the human predicament.

The founding fathers of Western political thought were torn between visions of the good, perhaps even the best, life: was it the *vita activa*, the *vita contemplativa*, or some salutary combination of the two worked out in ordered harmony through the prudent use of one's faculties? To achieve the good in the best way the "Sublime Plato," as many of his disciples through the centuries sighingly refered to him, proffered a determinedly utopian vision of the ideal city. Because the absolutism of method—whether scientific or discursive—is also a manifestation of the utopian impulse, I will begin with a few thoughts on the often dangerous fantasies of political theorists and textmakers.

Consider Plato's *Republic*.[1] For some present-day theorists, this is a story congenial to their own ends and purposes. Why, Plato even lofts a few good women upward (the spatial metaphor is unavoidable) to become members of his Guardian-Warrior-Philosopher elite! Plato describes this world that never was as a "city in speech," and he makes quite clear what is required of the utopian as a ruler. You must take "the dispositions of human beings; as though they were a tablet . . . which, in the first place, they would wipe clean, and that's hardly easy."[2]

Hardly! All those stubborn, already formed human beings stand in the way. Plato devises various methods: pack off all children over ten years of age (too old, we now know, to be altogether unformed); censor and forbid speeches about the gods; get rid of those dangerous poets who inflame the lower human impulses; create for the Guardian class a system of "women and children in common," with a eugenic breeding regimen to guarantee reproduction of the best and to preclude any woman from getting attached to her own, or any other, particular child; and so on.

Plato is explicit about why all this wrenching. The city must be as one. There can be neither discord nor disunion. Private homes and sexual attachments, devotion to friends, dedication to many aims and purposes militate against single-minded devotion to the ideal city, he cries. Have we any greater evil for a city than what splits it and makes it *many instead of one?* Or greater good than what binds it together and makes it one?[3] Scattered throughout the *Republic* are words that evoke a sense of chaos and disintegration: asunder . . . destroyed . . . dissolved . . . overwhelmed . . . split. . . . Other terms are designated as potent enough to prevent anarchy: dominate . . . censor . . . expunge . . . conform . . . bind . . . make one. For Plato every conflict is a potential cataclysm; every difference, a threat portending disintegration; every debate, an embryonic struggle unto death; every distinction, a possible blemish on the canvas of harmonious and unsullied order, the purity of an aesthetically constructed ideal city. Plato's *Republic* offers peace at a very high price.

So it is with all utopians past and present, including twentieth-century systematic ideologizers riding the train of history to an often murderous end of the track. Well, just in case you hadn't sniffed this out, I have a long-standing animus against philosophers and political model-builders who disdain our ordinary humanity and who, in their quest for a comprehensive, airtight universal standpoint, wind up, in Martha Nussbaum's words, making "the humanly possible work look boring and cheap."[4] To this one must add: the humanly responsible work of explaining and interpreting the humanly possible work.

The quest for a utopianism of method, making the discourse as one, is, like the quest for a utopian polity, a drive for control, for perfection, for somehow transcending or simply expunging from view the messiness that is the human lot. A scholar of the human sciences, faced with that messiness, might be tempted to throw in the towel in a second way: to begin and to end with what philosophers call the "incorrigibility of first person statements." Meaning whatever anyone says is what *is*, and one can merely report that fact. That, of course, would leave scholars with nothing to do save reportage.

I take my colleagues Smelser and Wolfe to be urging something else upon us: a scholarly vocation that begins with the complex and various social realities in which complex and various human beings find themselves, but does not end there. Rather, the scholar must go on to account for variations and differences and to discern whether there are patterns and similarities. To be avoided is a headlong rush into the arms of a universal standpoint and an equally headstrong plunge into the opacity of incommensurable particularism. This enterprise demands an artful science, a scientific, disciplined artfulness. Smelser calls for a combination of dispassion and intervention.

In a book I wrote in 1981, *Public Man, Private Woman*, I talked rather grandly—or so it seems to me from my present vantage point—of the need to "proffer coherent proposals for reordering public and private worlds." At the same time, I recognized that "life is too various, diversity too dear, to give it over to a single definition or purpose."[5] The second recognition, however, is more important than ever, and happily, it is the place Smelser and Wolfe wind up—with a call, not for mushy tolerance of alternative perspectives, but for robust debate and a plurality of approaches in the human sciences and recognition of the plurality of the human condition.

Building on Wolfe's engagement with the social and political contests,

I will now offer a few comments on the theme of what it means to be a civic philosopher in and for our time. It means, I believe, the need to embrace a necessary pessimism about our ability to control events and to shape and reshape our lives as well as the lives of our polity. Pessimism *not* cynicism, not hopelessness, but a recognition of the unavoidability of conflict. Wolfe saves some of his most intense fire for those he sees immersed in a *rhetorical* project that is, at best, incoherent. His reading of this situation is that those who have taken the rhetorical turn have followed the road off the edge of a cliff and into the abyss. It is the case that it would be impossible to do serious study in the human sciences if one pushed something called the "subject position" far enough. This holds that I can understand the world only from my own standpoint, whether I am white, black, male, female, and so on. It follows that genuine dialogue and genuine understanding are, quite simply, impossible. But I'm not sure that this move toward incommensurability and epistemological nihilism is best captured by the notion of rhetoric.

A modest version of the rhetorical turn is, in fact, wholly compatible with Wolfe's call for a methodological pluralism within which it remains both possible and necessary to assess the power of alternative explanatory frameworks. This takes me back, once again, to the Greeks. Here briefly is the story. Modern American culture is of at least two minds on the question of political rhetoric. Either (a) it's mere rhetoric and doesn't matter anyhow because nobody really believes what those guys (and, increasingly, gals) are saying, or (b) we're all being manipulated by smooth-talking politicians—or academicians—who are capable of getting just the results they want from us by pulling the right rhetorical strings. In scenario (a) we are knowing listeners who take everything with a grain of salt; in scenario (b) we are a passive mass seduced by the wily few, whose eloquence is a trap for the vast unwary many.

The "mere rhetoric" school of denigration, interestingly, finds its most eloquent champion in Plato and subsequent interpreters who accept his sharp divide between rhetoric and dialectic, between opinion and knowledge. Greek oratory was preeminently forensic in nature and intent— speeches delivered in courts of law and aimed at securing the acquittal or condemnation of the accused. We would call such an actor a lawyer. What lowered rhetoric irredeemably in Socrates' eyes was its instrumentalism. Rhetoric had a functional purpose: to persuade in the interest of winning or losing a case. The high-minded search for truth should not look anything like that, he insisted; hence the emergence of a dialectic of knowledge in opposition to a rhetoric of persuasion.

Some of the Sophists, those who formed schools and proposed a *techne* or rhetorical handbook larded with tricks of the trade, played directly into Socrates' hands. They, he claimed, pandered while he opened a quest for the truth. If the Sophists were spellbinders, Socrates was a truth-teller or discoverer. Between the spellbinders and truth-discoverers lay a great incommensurable divide. Socrates proves his point by stretching poor Gorgias to the end of his rhetorical tether in the Platonic dialogue that bears the name of Socrates' hapless interlocutor.[6] Socrates maneuvers Gorgias into declaiming that oratory is not concerned with "helping the sick learn how to live in order to become more 'well.' " It is not, in other words, concerned with *the* good but with making men "good at" speaking.

Gorgias rebuts "that the art of oratory is the art of speech *par excellence*" and that this involves not only "freedom" for "oneself" but "the power of ruling" one's countrymen by convincing them to concur with one's argument "in a court of justice . . . and any other gathering of citizens whatever it may be." With this definition, Gorgias plays into Socrates' hands and the master administers the coup de grâce with mock innocence: "If I understand you aright, you are saying that oratory is productive of conviction and that this is the be-all and end-all of its whole activity." Gorgias repeats that this is indeed the case. Socrates has all he needs to put Gorgias away by noting that Gorgias, by his own admission, has shown that oratory does not teach "about right and wrong." Instead the orator "merely persuades," making of oratory a subdivision "of pandering . . . a spurious counterfeit of a branch of the art of government."[7]

"Mere rhetoric merely persuades": The Platonic view decocts to this locution. Something of that temperament is at work in Wolfe's brief against rhetoric. But it may, in fact, be that it is possible to recoup and retrieve a view of rhetoric that is not only compatible with Wolfe's commitment to methodological pluralism and democratic politics, but constitutive of it. For ancient suspicion of mere rhetoric went hand-in-hand with the disparagement of the messiness of politics. A contemporary comedian gets laughs when he proclaims, "Comedy isn't pretty!" Neither is politics, especially democratic politics, and democratic politics without rhetoric, without attempts to persuade, is impossible.

Plato's contrast between rhetoric, which he attacked, and dialectic, which he defends, is, in James Boyd White's view, a way of highlighting the difference between ways of speaking and being and "of establishing community with others."[8] But White errs in going with the flow of Socrates' representations in his brief against rhetoric, accepting the stipulation that the power to persuade others is synonymous with reducing them to one's will.[9] This reduction of the other follows only if one endorses the

Socratic insistence that dialectic, or the quest for true knowledge, and persuasion are opposites, the former treating people as "ends in themselves," the latter constituting them as means to one's ends.

The comeback of the rhetoricians would be that the end of rhetoric is neither monological nor definitive. Rhetorical persuasion is on this occasion, to these people, for this possible end. But its master is not an object of knowledge (say the Platonic forms) but a complex dialogical situation in which any sharp line between the performative uses of language and other sorts of deeds disappears. By incorporating the performative dimension of language, rhetoric elides the distance between words, speeches, and actions.[10]

Wolfe refuses to sign on with an approach that collapses altogether the distance between truth and rhetoric, between knowledge and persuasion. I am with him on this, but I want to suggest that rhetoric, or attempts to persuade within a particular language community, are part and parcel of any coherent attempt to arrive at the truth. For the truth in a social world must involve entering a world of meanings shared, but not shared perfectly; a world that simultaneously constrains and imposes limits to rhetoric, persuasion, and mutual understanding even as it makes possible all three. Those with whom Wolfe most strongly disagrees are *not* at all committed to rhetoric, for they have given up on any notion of dialogue or persuasion. Instead the approach of so-called "subjection-position postmodernism" is to stake out one's single position, to proclaim that no one else has entrée to it unless that person shares one's subject position, and to claim further that politics is about nothing but who has power to bully, coerce, or silence whom. This is not rhetoric. This is, in fact, a vulgar form of essentialism and a retreat from democratic politics.

When I was in graduate school, in the late 1960s, it was in vogue to mock the warnings of Sir Isaiah Berlin about the dangers inherent in many visions of positive "liberty," turning as they did on naive views of a perfectible human nature and sentimental views on the perfectibility of politics. Berlin was accused of being a liberal sellout, a fainthearted compromiser. But compromise, not as a mediocre way to do politics, but as the only way to do democratic politics, flows from a recognition that no one group is in possession of the whole truth. Democratic moderation lacks the panache of revolutionary violence. Compromise does not stir the blood in the way a nonnegotiable demand does. But it presages a livable future, for in any democratic politics there are choices to be made that involve both gains and losses. Here we are reminded of words from the great George Eliot: "Reformers, martyrs, revolutionists are never fighting against evil only. They are also placing themselves in opposition to a good—to a valid principle which cannot be infringed upon without harm."

Conflicts about moral claims are about what it means to be human. We laborers in the vineyard of the human sciences must lift up this recognition as central if we are to recapture an appreciation of the ambiguities and cross-purposes of our individualities as well as our lives in common. For political life is a permanent *agon* between incompatible goods. This both Smelser and Wolfe recognize in their explicit endorsement of approaches to the human sciences respectful of that messy reality that is our lot.

Let me conclude by suggesting that we live in an era in which we are not well served by the old political categories. We are witnessing, to our astonishment, the realities of a half-century crumple and give way. The drama of democracy, of conflict and compromise, turns on our capacity for making distinctions and offering up regimens. It turns on our recognition that the roles and values that flow out of private relationships— loyalty, intimacy, fidelity—are not altogether transferable to public relationships where different criteria, including the capacity for provisional alliances, are required. We need ever more to teach ourselves and our children what it means to be held accountable to the diverse and various rules of public life and private relationships if we are to avoid a disastrous overfamilializing of politics. To engage in politics is to be called out, to go beyond, to enter the unfamiliar.

Ours is a complex moral universe, a world of justice and mercy, autonomy and caring, particular ties and universal aspirations. In such a universe the self is very much a modern identity at once committed yet aware of the irony and limits to all commitments, prepared to sacrifice but wary of all calls to sacrifice.[11]

The generosity of outlook and method suggested to us by Smelser and Wolfe also suggest that we are often best instructed in our own understanding of democratic politics and practices by turning to those who are struggling to learn how to create a democratic polity. One of the thinkers I have found most helpful to my own work is Václav Havel, Czech dissident and president of the Czech Republic. It is with reflections on Havel's overturning of old political categories in the service of even older truths and recognitions now made fresh again that I will conclude.

What Havel brings to our consideration of the human sciences as the century draws to close is this: He reminds us that to continue to think in inherited categories of right, left, progressive, regressive is, in his words, to give one a "sense of emerging from the depth of the last century." He writes: "It seems to me that these thoroughly ideological and many times mystified categories have long since been beside the point."[12] Such sure and certain political labels fail to capture the complexity of social life and cannot come close to the content of our actual beliefs and actions. In language that makes contact with contemporary awareness of and emphasis on difference and plurality, yet never abandons the hope for commonalities, Havel insists that between the aims of what he calls "the post-totalitarian system" and life in all its "plurality, diversity, independent self-constitution, and self-organization there lies a yawning abyss." The post-totalitarian system, whatever its political self-definition, pushes to "bind everything in a single order": again we see the monistic impulse and the drive toward absolute control at work. Havel's word for a world in which this distorted imperative reigns supreme is that of the "social auto-totality," a system that "depends on demoralization and cannot survive without it."[13]

What the fragile new democratic movements and theories of civil society share in common with some strands of contemporary American political and social discourse is the attempt to eschew worn-out categories, to insist on the centrality of self-reflection and critical interpretation, and to remain committed to debate and dialogue with those with whom one disagrees. Recognition of the stubborn reality of the other before me yields a scholarly vision capable of acknowledging a world of political conflict and debate without end. This is a way of thinking and working respectful of, and attuned to, our perils and our possibilities, our creatureliness and our creativity, our irreducible plurality and our search for truths we can cling to and act on, however provisionally, in solidarity with others.

Notes

1. Of course, there are those who argue that Plato's ideal city and speech are to be taken wholly ironically. Both Plato's detractors and defenders have, through the years, denied this claim. Whether Plato meant it or not, it is the case that the drive to monism on display in the *Republic* is an impulse shared by all utopians, whether revolutionaries or political theorists.

2. Plato, *Republic*, Book VI, 500c–501b.

3. Plato, *Republic*, Book V, 461e–462d. I draw upon portions of my discussion of Plato from my book, *Public Man, Private Woman: Women in Social and Political Thought* (Princeton: Princeton University Press, 1981), 20–21.

4. Martha Nussbaum, *The Fragility of Goodness. Luck and Ethics in Greek Tragedy and Philosophy* (Cambridge: Cambridge University Press, 1986), 258.

5. Elshtain, *Public Man, Private Woman*, 351.

6. Plato, *Gorgias*, trans. Walter Hamilton (New York: Penguin Books, 1971).

7. Ibid., 23, 28, 30, 32, 44.

8. James Boyd White, *When Words Lose Their Meaning* (Chicago: University of Chicago Press, 1984), 93–94.

9. Ibid., 109.

10. Ibid., 59.

11. See Jean Bethke Elshtain, "Sovereignty, Identity, Sacrifice," *Social Research* 58, 3 (Fall 1991), 545–64, and Charles Taylor, *Sources of the Self: The Making of Modern Identity* (Cambridge: Harvard University Press, 1989).

12. Václav Havel et al., *The Power of the Powerless: Citizens Against the State in Central Eastern Europe* (Armonk, N.Y.: Sharpe, 1985), 59.

13. Ibid., 72. Portions of these reflections are drawn from my essay, "The Power and Powerlessness of Women" in Jean Bethke Elshtain, *Power Trips and Other Journeys. Essays in Feminism as Civic Discourse* (Madison: University of Wisconsin Press, 1990), 145–46.

History and Sociological Imagining

Charles Tilly

Sociology without history resembles a Hollywood set: great scenes, sometimes brilliantly painted, with nothing and nobody behind them. Seen only as the science of the present or—worse yet—of the timeless, sociology misses its vocation to fix causation in time. It thereby vitiates its vital influence on historical thinking, its influence as the study of social mechanisms operating continuously in specific times and places. Although after years of living in the borderland of the two disciplines little lectures on the complementarity of sociology and history burst from me as easily as bubbles escape from champagne, that pleasant cohabitation will not be my subject here. Instead, I want to advocate theoretically informed historical inquiry as a solution to a major difficulty that social scientists, especially sociologists, frequently create for themselves.

What difficulty? Let us call it monadism. Monadism involves the adoption of three closely related assumptions. First, that the elementary units of social life are self-contained, self-directing monads, especially human individuals but also aggregates of individuals up to the level of something vaguely called a "society." Second, that regularities in the social world consist of structures, sequences, and directional processes of those monads that repeat themselves in essentially the same way time after time. Third, that the central task of social science is therefore to create invariant models, one per structure, sequence, or directional process, match them to as many relevant cases as possible, then perfect each model in accordance with observed discrepancies from careful observation of the relevant cases.

Thus sociologists create models of social mobility in which characteristics of fathers cause characteristics of sons, with coefficients varying from one setting to another, all within the same basic structure of causation by human capital. In the same mode, urban sociologists formulate invariant models of urban growth and decay within presumably self-contained cities based on the average experience of older capitalist cities, then cope with vastly contrary patterns in Third World cities by postulating a second urban species to which a quite separate model is supposed to apply. Likewise, we find specifications of the necessary and sufficient conditions for democracy, with little allowance for variation in time and space.

Following the same design, sociologists of revolution create unitary models of true revolutions as incidents in the lives of "societies," line up multiple cases of revolution, tug and haul to make those models fit each and every relevant case . . . and then, not incidentally, spend much of their polemical time demonstrating that theorist X's model doesn't apply properly to revolution beta or gamma, an exercise that leads instantly to minor revisions of X's model. Similar models purport to explain crime, war, divorce, secularization, employment discrimination, racial conflict, suicide, homelessness, and dozens of other lugubrious phenomena sociologists have cheerily made their own. The models vary enormously in structure and scope, but have in common the presumption that at bottom the subject concerns a unitary phenomenon having a relatively invariant structure, sequence, or process, a phenomenon happening to some self-contained social unit or aggregate of them.

By no means all models in the social sciences conform to the invariant plan. Some explicitly undertake to account for variation, as in Arthur Stinchcombe's brilliant discussion of the influence on policing of property's spatial distribution (1963). Others represent recurrent and coherent causal mechanisms having wildly variant outcomes, as in Harrison White's extraordinary account of identity-formation (1992). Still others, and many of them, create representations of a single nonrecurrent social structure or process, as in Immanuel Wallerstein's portrayal of the capitalist world-system. My polemic concerns only one manner of modeling in the social sciences, but a common one: postulating an essentially invariant structure or process in a self-contained social unit. I aim to make you wary of that common procedure, wary because in actual social life invariant structures and processes are rare or nonexistent. By no means, as you will see, am I advocating historical particularism or epistemological nihilism. Nor am I arguing that social life has no coherent recurrences or that it is fundamentally unknowable. I am advocating clearer reflection about ontology, about the character of the phenomena we purport to describe and explain.

History is not immune to monadism. Such reasoning appears as often in history as elsewhere in the social sciences, if only because invariant models of structures, sequences, and processes infest the folk sociology on which historians so regularly draw without being self-conscious about their reasoning. Throughout the labyrinthine historical literature on political conflict in which I spend much of my own time wandering, for example, a limited number of competing models, each invariant, recur in explanations of mass collective action. In caricature, we might call them misery models, madness models, and mobilization models. I confess to having contributed one or two of the latter to the literature myself; my most general representation of mobilizing actors postulates precisely that every person or group that acts collectively is responding in a similar way to an array of interests and opportunities (e.g., Tilly 1978: chapters 3 and 4). The maker of such a model characteristically presumes that every time large numbers of ordinary people band together and challenge authorities the same basic process of mobilization, collective action, and demobilization unfolds. Historical knowledge does not automatically eliminate that presumption.

Nevertheless, history provides its own antidotes to overdoses of singularity. For real history, carefully observed, does not fall into neat, recurrent chunks; it winds and snarls like a proliferating vine. What is more, in real history time and place make a difference to the way that ostensibly universal processes such as industrialization and secularization unfold; just as the flows of rivers, for all their common properties, depend intimately on the terrain through which they pass, and those terrains result in important part from previous flows of the selfsame rivers, the power of history means that social processes follow strong regularities yet do not repeat themselves; the regularities lie in causal mechanisms, not in recurrent structures or sequences.

Among analysts who are self-conscious about such matters, invariant-model reasoning has its own distinctive method, codified by Charles Ragin as the Comparative Method. Ragin reports that he developed the method out of his dissatisfaction with the application of multivariate statistical techniques to a number of problems that interested him (1987: vii). As a distinctive procedure, he says, comparative analysis in general uses combinatorial logic to explain the characteristics of whole cases. The cases are most often "societies." In Ragin's variant, Boolean logic applied rigorously over a number of cases singles out those differences that can actually make a difference. The argument rests ultimately on John Stuart Mill's paired procedures: the method of agreement, the method of differences (1892: 221–34). (Mill actually distinguished four experimental methods—

agreement, difference, residues, and concomitant variation, but somehow his provocative treatments of the latter two have disappeared from social scientific discussions of comparison.)

There is, alas, a catch. Mill himself pointed it out: For the pair of methods to be foolproof, the analyst must be able to specify, observe, and even manipulate all possible causes, a circumstance that lies beyond the reach of nonexperimental social sciences. Hoping nevertheless to identify all the obvious candidates for causes of a given outcome, however, adepts of invariant-model arguments commonly forge ahead with comparisons of cases that display the outcome with others that do not, searching for those other conditions that occur uniquely with the outcome. They habitually practice closest-case comparison. Their procedure follows the example of epidemiology in searching for the necessary conditions of a distinctive disease. Thus they conduct comparisons of whole countries to discern the special conditions that distinguish those experiencing major declines in fertility or great gains in per capita income from all others.

What's wrong with this standard modus operandi? Nothing much would be wrong with it if the social world did, indeed, consist of self-contained units, if it did, indeed, fall nicely into recurrent structures, sequences, and directional processes. Mill, as a matter of fact, thought it did. He ended his discussion of Historical Method with this bright promise:

> If the endeavours now making in all the more cultivated nations, and beginning to be made even in England (generally the last to adopt whatever does not originate with herself) for the construction of a Philosophy of History, shall be directed and controlled by those views of the nature of sociological evidence which I have (very briefly and imperfectly) attempted to characterize; they cannot fail to give birth to a sociological system widely removed from the vague and conjectural character of all former attempts, and worthy to take its place, at last, among established sciences. When this time shall come, no important branch of human affairs will be any longer abandoned to empiricism and unscientific surmise: the circle of human knowledge will be complete, and it can only thereafter receive further enlargement by perpetual expansion from within. (Mill 1892: 565)

Francophiles and sociological chauvinists will be happy to know that Mill's chief example of Historical Method's proper application was Auguste Comte, coiner of the word "sociology." If we should have learned anything from the fifteen decades of systematic social science that separates us from Mill, however, it is that social life doesn't work that way: Boundaries of social units are porous, structures keep changing, sequences never quite repeat themselves, ostensibly directional processes stop, reverse, or split, what has happened before affects the character of the next structure, sequence, or process.

Taken as entire events, neither wars, occupational careers, spurts of urban growth, racial conflicts, nor any of the other social phenomena to which sociologists have commonly applied the suspect modus operandi display enough invariance to make such models useful. The repetitions within them, furthermore, are superficial, at the level of the proximate causes that (given extensive separation of home from work, employment in large workplaces under time-discipline, and reliance on mechanical transportation) produce rush-hour transport peaks twice a day (but not on Sundays or holidays); the knowledge involved is not trivial, especially for transportation planners and traffic cops, but it is superficial and highly vulnerable to changes in boundary conditions. Try applying standard American models of daily traffic flow to today's Sarajevo or Mogadishu!

In such circumstances, the search for necessary and sufficient conditions becomes a wild goose chase. Discovering these difficulties, optimists who persist in holding to invariant models conclude that the models need more refinement; pessimists conclude that the world is too complicated for the location of regularities; skeptics that social life is unknowable in any reliable, systematic sense; pragmatists that for the time being we need more than one model, yet far fewer than one model per observation.

We have, however, a more hopeful alternative. We could begin to see that the elementary units of social life are neither individuals nor "societies" nor groups but interactions among social locations. We could recognize that great social regularities do not occur at the level of whole structures, full sequences, or total processes but in the detailed social mechanisms that generate structures, sequences, and processes. Whole networks do not resemble each other in lawful ways, but the principles by which networks form and change do. Wars do not follow standard sequences or burst out in only one set of circumstances, but they conform to very strong principles of logistics, organization, and strategy. We could, in short, rediscover history, rediscover the interplay among causal mechanisms, idiosyncratic events, and powerful contingencies. In this sense, we could become historicists.

To rediscover history, however, is not to fit invariant models, huge or modest, to great slabs of time and space. Stinchcombe ends his *Theoretical Methods in Social History* with a ringing declaration that regrettably, often rings the wrong bells in readers' minds: that "it is the details that theories in history have to grasp if they are to be any good" (1978: 124). Contrary to a superficial reading, Stinchcombe is not recommending barefoot empiricism, but examination by analogy with other historical situations or the actual mechanisms that generate social structures, sequences, and processes. Properly conducted, historical research has the great virtue of requiring the investigator to locate social actions in time and space, to specify their interrelations, to search for their causes in concrete circumstances. It also leads, as we shall see, to recognizing the tight interdependence and instant mutual modification of culture (conceived as shared understandings and their objectifications) and social structure (conceived of as durable relations among people).

Three recent inquiries of my own made me aware of the difficulty, which had bothered me for years without my being able to articulate it well. The topics differed greatly: European revolutions from 1492 to the present, American immigration during the nineteenth and twentieth centuries, British popular politics between the 1750s and the 1830s.

The first inquiry was a book on European revolutions from 1492 to 1992. On agreeing to write the book, I had implicitly assumed that it would be easy, almost a potboiler, an exercise in locating the best model of revolution around—perhaps Theda Skocpol's, Michael Kimmel's, or Jack Goldstone's—polishing it up a bit for my own purposes, then fitting it to a number of European revolutions: the old game of Improving Karl Marx that self-appointed theorists among us all play so confidently. (These days the thinker improved is more likely to be Max Weber, Anthony Giddens, Jürgen Habermas, or heaven help us, even Talcott Parsons rather than Karl Marx, but the rules remain the same: Explicate the mode; single out one or two elements for criticism; correct those elements; glue the updated model back together; congratulate yourself; publish the result.) But I wanted to connect the analysis of revolution to those of state formation and collective action in which I had been dabbling for some years.

At length I realized that I was yoking a lion and a hippopotamus together for plowing; I was starting mayhem rather than the neat cultivation of a field. Why? Because my favored models of state formation and collective action concerned continuous variation rather than recurrent invariant phenomena. Although I had perpetrated invariant models of both earlier in my career—we remain creatures of our educations so long!—through protracted struggles with historical material I had first rejected one-track models, then began to formulate accounts of variable trajectories by searching for deep causal mechanisms. Meanwhile, the available models of revolution, at least in their most general forms, all purported to specify the necessary and sufficient conditions for revolution, conceived of as a relatively invariant bundle of structures and processes. The misfit soon became obvious.

Attention: I don't claim to have found the Deep Causes of all changes in the character of states or of all variations in collective action. I only claim to have recognized that the regularities lie in the generating mechanisms rather than in the recurrence of whole structures, the repetition of whole sequences, the reappearance of the same unilinear processes. Such a recognition does not preclude typologizing states or collective actions, mapping sequences of conflict, or even tracking long processes of transformation, but it does entail recognizing that those operations do not yield explanations. They simply specify what is to be explained.

In the case of revolution, then, I found that I had to rethink the phenomenon as one zone in a much larger field of variation including many political interactions no one would label revolutionary, then search for clues as to why some peoples, places, and eras spent a lot of their time in that zone while others barely approached it. My first crude device for doing so consisted of analytically separating the conditions for revolutionary situations from those for revolutionary outcomes—revolutionary situations consisting of open splits within polities, revolutionary outcomes consisting of substantial transfers of power over states. I argue that the two sets of conditions vary and change in partial independence of each other.

My second crude device was to treat each of those conditions as a continuum, for example from no split whatsoever in a polity to a split putting every political actor on one side or another. My third was to treat major changes in the organization of states, state systems, and armed forces as determinants of the position of different states and polities on those continua. My answers surely contain defects, but they illustrate another way of thinking about revolution than as a one-track phenomenon. They represent a historicizing of the problem.

Any vendor of standard models of revolution, for example, will have trouble selling them to specialists in early modern European history who go beyond fitting their appliances to the English revolution of 1640–60, the Fronde, and the revolt of Catalonia to asking why so many more forcible attempts to seize state power—revolutionary situations, roughly speaking—occurred, and why so many of them actually succeeded. Close study of the circumstances of those centuries' revolutionary situations does not produce a new General Model of Early Modern Revolutions. It does, however, reveal the grounding of revolutionary situations in prevailing conditions of indirect rule, military expansion, and dynastic competition.

Take the factor of dynastic competition: In Muscovy, then in the Russian empire that grew with Muscovy as its kernel, for there centuries after

1492 every time a czar died without an adult, militarily competent son or
brother to succeed him a serious struggle for the throne ensued, often
with wide popular support for one faction or another. During the seventeenth and eighteenth centuries the serious claimants at different times
even included thirty or forty men pretending to be czars or heirs whom
everyone else had believed dead—often murdered at the behest of the
late ruler. Cossack Emilian Pugachev, who led the great peasant-Cossack
rebellion of 1773–75, proclaimed himself Czar Peter III. A number of the
claimants actually made it to the throne: Boris Godunov, his successor
the False Dmitry, Ivan V, his brother Peter the Great himself—all became
czar irregularly, outside the standard inheritance rules, through the use of
force. Russia was no more extreme in this regard than Poland, Hungary,
and a good many other early modern states. Yet by the nineteenth century
militarily contested successions had become rare in European mon-
archies.

The whole story of that transition would take too long to tell, and
would require too many allowances for variations among, say, Iberia, the
Balkans, and the British Isles. But one cluster of factors nicely illustrates
my general point: the tight interdependence in early modern European
states among the organization of great families, the existence of huge
patron-client chains attaching officials, servitors, and tenants to those
great families, the embedding of military force in those patron-client
chains, and the adoption by great families of outmarriage strategies ac-
complishing three purposes: first, giving their heirs claims on aristocratic
and royal successions elsewhere; second, providing local members of the
family (including emperors or kings) with some call on military assistance
from grandees or rulers outside their own countries; and third, arranging
another place to survive comfortably if life became too dangerous at
home.

Together, these circumstances meant that almost every royal succession
constituted an opportunity, or at least a hope, for some rival to the most
obvious heir, often a foreigner in whom another royal family also had an
interest. Where the inheritance was unclear or the heir incompetent, the
opportunity became a strong incentive to employ autonomous military
force, and enlist aggrieved popular support, for a dynastic coup. When
Protestant lords invited fellow-Protestant William of Orange to England
in 1688 to displace Catholic King James II, they did not simply call on
an experienced statesman from a distinguished family; they called on a
grandson of Charles I and son-in-law of James himself. An explanation of
the Glorious Revolution requires much more than knowledge of William's family background. Nevertheless, no one will understand it and

other revolutions of the time without exploring the mechanisms by which great families attached themselves to each other and to regimes. Such an exploration is deeply historicist. In it, structure and culture interact.

Let me underline what this means and what it does not mean. Considered as wholes, neither lineages nor revolutions had recurrent structures besides those they shared by definition. Invariant models of lineages and revolutions would serve us badly. On the contrary, the regularities lie in the ways that kinship ties affected the formation of alliances, the probability of war, and the claims to succession to supreme positions in dynastic states, which in turn affected the probability and character of revolution. These are not invariant structures or processes, but wide-ranging causal mechanisms whose combinations produced the actual unique histories we observe.

The second inquiry concerns inequality and American immigration in the nineteenth and twentieth centuries. As Ewa Morawska (1990) has well documented, recent work on immigration has challenged the two dominant models of earlier generations: human capital and assimilation. Human capital models escape my strictures somewhat by deliberately accounting for differential success as a function of variable resources, broadly defined; they deserve suspicion, nevertheless, for their reliance on an invariant model of market-mediated success. Assimilation models clearly qualify as invariant insofar as they posit only one standard path into American life, the chief variation being the speed at which different groups travel that path. As Morawska says, an anti-invariant historicist view helps make sense of the connections between migration and durable forms of inequality, including those forms people organize as ethnicity—as structured differences according to imputed national or racial origin. In thinking about American immigration as a whole, and about my current collaborative studies of nineteenth-century French silk workers in Paterson, New Jersey, and of twentieth-century Italian peasants in Mamaroneck, New York, I find it useful to ask how the social organization of migration constrained the subsequent opportunities of different groups of migrants and their descendants.

In the case of Paterson, Florence Baptiste and I are trying to find out how textile workers from Lyons and its vicinity entered the expanding silk industry of Paterson after 1860, as well as what impact those circumstances had on their experience, and that of their children, in the American labor force. As for Mamaroneck, Philippe Videlier and I are attempting to compare post-1900 migrations from a few villages in the Frosinone, near Rome, to the Lyons metropolitan area, to Mamaroneck and nearby towns, and perhaps eventually to Buenos Aires, São Paulo, and Toronto as well, in order to see how differently the survivors of those migrations turned out at their various destinations.

How well immigrants do in a new country, and whether they return to the old, depends mainly on five factors: the extent to which they integrate on arrival into networks that embrace a wide range of employment opportunities; the opportunities for individual income with which their networks give them contact, especially at the start; the opportunities for collective capital accumulation at the destination; the degree of obligation to support people and enterprises in the place of origin; and the relative opportunities for reinvestment of accumulated capital at the origin and the destination. On the whole, the more the migrant group or its subdivisions serve as an accumulator of capital, the greater the incentive to pass jobs through kin and paesani. Thus durable inequality among immigrant groups and their descendants depends on the initial organization of migration and its capacity for accumulation of collectively available capital. While it sounds strange to put warm matters so coldly, immigrants and their descendants actually know these principles well; their stories of connections, favors, and ethnic differences reek of them.

Networks transformed or created by migration create and maintain inequality. Members of immigrant groups often exploited each other as they would not have dared to exploit the native-born. Every act of inclusion, furthermore, also excludes. North American immigration produced a remarkable specialization of work by origin, although the precise specializations varied from one locality and migrant stream to another. The characteristic story of Mamaroneck is the present domination of landscape gardening and related fields by Italian immigrants and their heirs, that of Paterson French, British, German, and Italian workers from well-defined industrial locations entering specific branches of Paterson's industry.

Any student of migration can tell similar tales of occupational specialization by regional or national origin. The actual tales refute grand stage schemes of immigration, illustrate the combination of bounded contingency with constraint in social life, and show us powerful causes working consistently as links among events. Generalized, that observation makes my case against monadic ontologies and invariant models, for historicism concentrating on the discovery of mechanisms that generate social structures, sequences, and processes. Again, culture and structure interact.

A third area of research that made me think about these topics concerns changes in the forms of collective contention—for example, why and how sit-ins and similar deliberate occupations of contested spaces rise and fall. For the shared delusions of collective behavior theorists, sociologists of the 1960s and 1970s generally substituted models of collective rational action: public choice, resource mobilization, political process, and so on. In so doing, however, they (perhaps I should say "we") stuck unwittingly to monadism, assuming that the main problems were (a) to explain the behavior of one coherent actor (individual or collective) at a time, and (b) to identify a single model of collective action that, with no more than nudges of a parameter or two, accounted in principle for all instances. In the study of social movements, for example, this reformulation rejected earlier portrayals of prohibitionism or feminism as irrational reactions to the stress of social change, but retained the assumption that the social movement was a kind of self-contained group whose behavior could be explained by the group's social situation. Similar, Mancur Olson's (1965) injection of collective-goods models into the analysis of what sociologists previously called collective behavior sent sociologists scurrying for alternative invariant models that would accommodate identity, loyalty, and self-satisfaction (see Cohen 1985, Gamson 1990).

Let me spare you a detailed critique of standard models for social movements and collective action. Suffice it to say that monadic analyses of contention ignored the strategic interaction among challengers, competitors, and sometime allies that pervades real episodes of contention. (As participants and benevolent observers of social movements, many formulators of monadic models had ample practical awareness of strategic interaction, but failed to draw the appropriate theoretical conclusions from their own experiences.) A combination of influences tipped the balance toward interaction: the infiltration of game-theoretic reasoning from economics and political science; the creation of large catalogs of events as alternatives to the treatment of one group, movement, or action at a time; above all, the historicization of polemology (as francophones call the systematic study of conflict).

In this setting, historicization meant installing time and place as major determinants of contention's character rather than as proxies for other more elusive variables such as modernization or level of grievance. To historicize the study of contention meant recognizing that collective claim-making entails the simultaneous use and recasting of relations, including shared understandings, among local actors. It meant seeing that each locality and each interacting set of claimants, both challengers and authorities, accumulates its own particular experience, memory, understanding, practices, and accumulation that strongly constrain current contention. My own formulation of these insights adopts the theatrical language of repertoires; contentious actors perform in dramas in which they already know their approximate parts, during which they nevertheless improvise constantly, and of which the exact outcomes remain uncertain.

In this formulation, potential actors choose strategically among available performances, engage other actors, including objects of their claims, in those performances, and improvise their way to some conclusion. The conception is at once deeply interactive—that is, structural—and deeply cultural. It reeks of culture, as Stinchcombe has pointed out, in insisting that shared understanding and their objectifications constrain social interactions (1987).

My current research on the subject uses catalogs of British "contentious gatherings" between 1758 and 1834 to examine how claim-making changed during a period that brought Great Britain the demise of Rough Music, collective machine-breaking, invasions of enclosed fields, and many related forms of interaction, as well as the rise of public meetings, demonstrations, petition drives, popular associations, firm-by-firm strikes, and more now-familiar forms of struggle.

A contentious gathering, for the purposes of this study, is an occasion on which ten or more people gathered in a publicly accessible place and visibly made claims that, if realized, would bear on the interests of at least one person outside their number. The main machine-readable catalog provides detailed descriptions of 8,088 contentious gatherings that occurred in southeastern England during thirteen scattered years from 1758 to 1820 or anywhere in Great Britain during the seven years from 1828 through 1834. Among other things, my group is analyzing the events in that catalog and complementary evidence to determine whether a strong version of the repertoire model actually holds up to close scrutiny. We are unquestionably seeing profound changes in the texture of British contention, as seizures of grain, invasions of fields, mocking ceremonies, and related forms give way to processions, demonstrations, petition drives, and their kin. The changes pivot on the years of war with revolutionary and Napoleonic France, and bear plausible relationships to the transformations of the state and economy during the war years. That much verifies at least a weak version of the metaphor.

For stronger versions, we must look at innovation and variation within and among contentious gatherings. We think we are finding evidence, for example, of Parliament's increased salience as an object of contentious claims and of the role played by public meetings, local assemblies, and popular associations in that shift. We think we can trace the influence of innovators such as John Wilkes, Lord George Gordon, Francis Place, and Daniel O'Connell on cumulative shifts in contentious repertoires. We have some grounds for claiming that collective actors constantly innovate in small ways, and do so at a faster pace when political opportunities are changing rapidly, but that innovations in the forms of contention only stick when associated with visible success for one actor or another. But many questions remain open.

I won't bore you with other results, technical details, and historical problems. I am trying here to illustrate how historical thinking, properly conducted, combats monadism and helps reveal the tight interdependence of culture and social structure. For in the analysis of British contentious repertoires, as in the study of revolutions and of immigrant itineraries, we find the cumulative intersection of history, social ties, and shared understandings.

What, then, are these elusive causal mechanisms I have identified as the true locus of regularities in social life? In the case of revolutions, they consist of rapid and visible diminutions of state power, splits in control over the major means of coercion, formation of antiregime coalitions, and other political shifts that singly neither guarantee revolution nor constitute parts of its definition. In the case of immigration, the crucial causal mechanisms consist of the transmission of information about opportunities within existing ties of kinship or neighborhood, the pooling of capital or credit, the hoarding of access to remunerative work, housing, and social life, the remittance of money and other resources to the place of origin, and other collective actions that shape the structure of opportunities, rights, and obligations; all of these operate outside of immigration, indeed quite outside of residential mobility of any kind. In the case of changes in contentious repertoires, we must look for causes in the transformation of political opportunities by innovations associated with successful claim-making, in alterations—incremental or sudden—of various political institutions' capacity to deliver rewards or punishments, in the creation or rupture of links among potential collective actors, and in similar mutations of shared incentives and organizational resources. If revolutions, immigration, and changing repertoires defy invariant models, that is not because they know no regularities. It is because their regularities do not lie in recurrent structures or sequences but in powerful causal mechanisms that in different combinations produce both those phenomena and a host of others.

Note

A few passages in this paper come from "Cities and Immigration in North America," Working Paper 88, Center for Studies of Social Change, New School for Social Research, September 1989, which contains much more extensive discussions both of historicism and of migration.

References

Cohen, Jean. 1985. "Strategy or Identity: New Theoretical Paradigms and Contemporary Social Movements," *Social Research* 52: 663–716.

Gamson, William A. 1990. *The Strategy of Social Protest*, 2nd ed. Belmont, Calif.: Wadsworth.

Goldstone, Jack A. 1986. "Introduction: The Comparative and Historical Study of Revolutions," in Jack A. Goldstone, ed., *Revolutions: Theoretical, Comparative, and Historical Studies*. San Diego: Harcourt Brace Jovanovich.

————. 1991. *Revolution and Rebellion in the Early Modern World*. Berkeley: University of California Press.

Kimmel, Michael S. 1988. *Absolutism and Its Discontents: State and Society in Seventeenth-Century France and England*. New Brunswick, N.J.: Transaction.

————. 1990. *Revolution: A Sociological Interpretation*. Philadelphia: Temple University Press.

Mill, John Stuart. 1892. *A System of Logic, Ratiocinative and Inductive, Being a Connected View of the Principles of Evidence and the Methods of Scientific Investigation*. London: Routledge. First published in 1843.

Morawska, Ewa. 1985. *For Bread with Butter: Life-Worlds of East Central Europeans in Johnstown, Pennsylvania, 1890–1940*. Cambridge: Cambridge University Press.

————. 1990. "The Sociology and Historiography of Immigration," in Virginia Yans-McLaughlin, ed., *Immigration Reconsidered: History, Sociology, Politics*. New York: Oxford University Press.

Olson, Mancur. 1965. *The Logic of Collective Action*. Cambridge: Harvard University Press.

Ragin, Charles C. 1987. *The Comparative Method: Moving Beyond Qualitative and Quantitative Strategies*. Berkeley: University of California Press.

Skocpol, Theda. 1973. "A Critical Review of Barrington Moore's Social Origins of Dictatorship and Democracy," *Politics and Society* 4: 1–34.

————. 1979. *States and Social Revolutions. A Comparative Analysis of France, Russia, and China*. Cambridge: Cambridge University Press.

Stinchcombe, Arthur L. 1959. "Bureaucratic and Craft Administration of Production," *Administrative Science Quarterly* 4: 168–87.

————. 1963. "Institutions of Privacy in the Determination of Police Administrative Practice," *American Journal of Sociology* 69: 150–60.

————. 1975. "Merton's Theory of Social Structure" in Lewis Coser, ed., *The Idea of Social Structure*. New York: Harcourt Brace Jovanovich.

————. 1978. *Theoretical Methods in Social History*. New York: Academic Press.

————. 1986. "Milieu and Structure Updated," *Theory and Society* 15: 901–13.

————. 1987. Review of Charles Tilly, *The Contentious French, American Journal of Sociology* 92: 1248–49.

————. 1990. "Work Institutions and the Sociology of Everyday Life," in Kai Erikson and Steven Peter Vallas, eds., *The Nature of Work: Sociological Perspectives*. New Haven: Yale University Press.

Tilly, Charles. 1978. *From Mobilization to Revolution*. Reading, Mass.: Random House.

———. 1993. *European Revolutions, 1492–1992*. Oxford: Blackwell.

———. 1995. *Popular Contention in Great Britain, 1758–1834*. Cambridge: Harvard University Press.

White, Harrison C. 1970. *Chains of Opportunity: System Models of Mobility in Organizations*. Cambridge: Harvard University Press.

———. 1988. "Varieties of Markets" in Barry Wellman and S. D. Berkowitz, eds., *Social Structures: A Network Approach*. (New York: Cambridge University Press).

———. 1992. *Identity and Control: A Structural Theory of Social Action*. Princeton: Princeton University Press.

The Many Enchantments of Money

Viviana A. Zelizer

When it comes to gift-giving, matters of pricing are usually delicate, sometimes perplexing, and often troublesome affairs. Just think of the embarrassment when we neglect to remove the price tag from a wedding gift or a birthday present—even when the price is high. Or consider the efforts we make to distinguish cash gifts from other transfers. The same uncertainty reappears in many other spheres: deciding whom to tip and whom not to tip, reckoning whether a gift certificate will offend its recipient, knowing what favors require payment, and which forbid it. First we fret over when it is appropriate to give a gift of money, then we worry about the proper sum, and finally we must decide how to present the money properly. Economists insist that cash is the most efficient gift but overlook the work it takes to give cash: selecting crisp bills, designating the cash for a particular use, disguising the quantity involved.

People care deeply about the finely tuned economics of gift exchanges. The wrong gift means more than incompetence, it can offend, anger, confuse, or hurt the recipient. Today's etiquette books spend pages on monetary gifts; *Emily Post's Etiquette*, for instance, offers advice ranging from when and how to give money gifts, to special formulas for acknowledging money gifts, and even techniques for the tasteful display of wedding-gift checks. "It is quite proper," we are reassured, "to display checks with the amounts concealed. This is done by laying them out on a flat surface one above the other so that the signatures alone are disclosed. The amount of the one at the top is covered with a strip of opaque paper, and then a sheet of glass laid over them all, to prevent curious guests from taking a peek."[1]

By no means is this a recent concern. Consider the following 1920s vaudeville routine: an anxious mother about to send her married daughter a fifty-dollar bill as a Christmas gift first tries hard to erase the price mark because she didn't want her daughter to know how much the gift cost. The mother was broken-hearted when she later heard that her daughter had used the money simply to pay her grocery bill—worse still her son-in-law's.

What sort of money is this, that should carry no price tag and be restricted only to special purchases? In the 1920s gift money was not just vaudevillism coinage; in real life, people were also working hard to invent a special currency for gift-giving; women's magazines of the early 1900s describe the many time-consuming and often elaborate strategies for converting an ordinary dollar into a gift; gold coins hidden in cookies or concealed by Christmas seals; dollar bills decorating a belt buckle or encased within a picture frame. American Express began advertising money orders as "the acceptable Christmas gift," Hallmark marketed specially designed cards to send holiday or birthday money to friends and relatives, while department stores invented gift certificates. Etiquette manuals introduced advice on money gifts for weddings, anniversaries, and christenings.

Gift money seems a peculiar, puzzling currency. If money is the perfect medium for rational market exchange, how can it also serve to express the care and affection of personal ties? Let me try to show how historical "imagining," as Charles Tilly puts it, that is, the use of comparative historical materials to challenge old theories and construct new ones, can help us not only solve the specific puzzle of gift money but also break the larger spell of common but erroneous ideas about money and its impact on social life. For despite the widespread assumption that modern money rationalizes and homogenizes inexorably, we will see that people constantly create new monies, invent different uses for old currencies, and designate special uses for particular transactions.

We often see money through filters imposed by classical theories of modernization. Such theories treat the rational and impersonal market as a relentless invader of social spaces. And a dangerous one, necessarily replacing personal bonds with calculative instrumental ties, corrupting cultural meanings with materialist concerns. Classical theorists assumed that money, as the "most abstract and 'impersonal' element that exists in human life," as Max Weber put it, spearheaded the process of rationalization. It was the perverse magical wand that disenchanted modern life. Money, Georg Simmel observed, transformed the world into an "arithmetic problem." The revolutionary power of money presumably came from its complete indifference to values. Free from subjective restrictions, indifferent to personal relations, money's liquidity and divisibility were infinite, making it the perfect medium of market exchange. It allowed, Karl Marx claimed, the "equation of the incompatible."[2]

Sociologists, reputedly the specialists in direct observation of contemporary social life, have remained half-blind to people's actual monetary practices. Contemporary sociology still clings to the utilitarian model of money as a single currency, absolutely fungible, qualitatively neutral, entirely homogeneous. Consider for instance Jürgen Habermas's argument that money is the medium by which the economic system "colonizes" the world of routine social life, irrepressibly and systematically undermining "domains of action dependent upon social integration."[3]

Social scientists have thus accepted with a remarkable lack of skepticism an intellectual inheritance that endows money with a quasi-magical power to objectify, depersonalize, and homogenize all social life. Money's "colorlessness," as Simmel saw it, repainted the modern world into an "evenly flat and gray tone." All meaningful nuances were squeezed out by the new quantitative logic that asked only "how much" but not "what and how." Or, as Gertrude Stein put it more succinctly a few decades later: "Whether you like it or whether you do not money is money and that is all there is about it."[4]

Starting in the nineteenth century, the American state worked vigorously to create the Simmelian "colorless" currency; a standardized national money. How did it do so? It taxed thousands of state-issued paper currencies out of existence, suppressed the private issue of tokens, paper notes, or coins by stores, businesses, churches, and other organizations, and stamped out the personalization of money by individuals. The government, for instance, even forbade the common late nineteenth-century practice of inscribing coins with sentimental messages, calling that practice "mutilation." After 1909, a law forbidding the mutilation of coins turned the popular "love token" gifts into an illegal currency. As the supreme court of Indiana declared in November 1889, the government "has a right to provide a currency for the whole nation, and to drive out all other circulating mediums by taxation or otherwise."[5]

It was a losing battle. Although the American state did achieve a significant degree of standardization in legal tender, people continually disrupted monetary uniformity, actively creating all sorts of monetary distinctions. As Simmel's *Philosophy of Money* went to press in 1900, the real world of money in the United States belied his observations. For as the consumer society was being established, distinction among the meanings and uses of monies multiplied and became more complex than ever. Con-

sider for instance the domestic economy. Listen first to Mrs. M's letter to
Woman's Home Companion in the early 1920s about her financial strategy
to keep the family's multiple monies apart: "I collected eight little cans,
all the same size, and pasted on them the following words, in big letters:
groceries, carfare, gas, laundry, rent, tithe, savings, miscellaneous . . . we
speak of those cans now, as the grocery can, carfare can etc."[6] Other
families used jars, china pitchers, envelopes, or boxes to physically distinguish their monies; often segregating different types of income for particular expenses. In a parallel way, immigrants religiously marked a portion
of their hard-earned wages for transmission to relatives back in their
home villages.

Sometimes families set particular monies, such as "Christmas money"
or "summer vacation money," apart by handing them over to an institution, such as the popular Christmas clubs or vacation clubs, which usually
paid no interest, but simply served as collective "piggy banks." A bit
earlier than Christmas clubs and the like, poor people had already been
putting their monies into penny provident banks, which charity organization societies invented and the poor used as a way to set aside small sums
for designated expenses.

Increasingly, too, a wife's money became differentiated from her child's
or her husband's. Home economists as well as families debated: What
should be the proper money for the modern housewife and her child?
Was the allowance a "good" income for wives or was it demeaning?
Should children be given an allowance, or was it their duty to earn it
through household chores? Should husbands hand over all their salaries
to their wives, or how much could they keep for themselves? What made
"personal money" seem more legitimate for men than for their wives? A
Japanese visitor to the United States in the 1910s was shocked to hear
from "men and women of all classes, from newspapers, novels, lecturers,
and once even from the pulpit . . . allusions to amusing stories of women
secreting money in odd places, coaxing it from their husbands . . . or
saving it secretly for some private purpose."[7] Even when women earned,
their wages were treated differently from their husband's. For instance, a
wife's income was considered pin money regardless of its quantity, defined as a less fundamental kind of money than her husband's income,
and used only for designated family expenses, such as a child's education,
a vacation, or a household appliance.

Monies multiplied outside the household as well. Charities, for instance, invented a new kind of cash relief for their clients, distinct from
the nineteenth-century dole and clearly set apart from a wage. Coined
by social workers and home economists, the new charitable cash was an

instructional currency, providing not just purchasing power but lessons in consumerism, showing the dependent how to divide their monies properly. The poor, on the other hand, made their own distinctions among monies; to charity workers' dismay, for instance, "burial money" was a budgetary priority even for families on relief. For the poor, a pauper's burial was a more degrading form of poverty than a meager diet.

Prisons also debated the right kind of money for inmates, while orphan asylums and foster care supervisors created a separate currency for dependent children. Some industrial firms paid their employees with scrip or trade checks redeemable only at the local company store. Legislatures debated whether tips were an acceptable kind of money or a punishable misdemeanor, while businesses defended in court the legitimacy of coupons, trading stamps, and premiums to promote their products.

Even Congress resisted when the government's efforts to homogenize currency went too far. Consider for instance the intense debate provoked in 1908 by the proposal to restore the inscription "In God We Trust" on U.S. gold coins, which had been removed by a presidential order. While a few congressmen applauded President Theodore Roosevelt's sensible decision, insisting that "our coin . . . is a medium of secular, and not sacred, transactions," their more successful opponents argued eloquently in favor of the ritual marker, insisting that while "the removal of [the motto] did not depreciate [money's] monetary value . . . it depreciated its sentimental value." America, warned the representative of Georgia, should not coin an "infidel money."[8]

Is this Weber's disenchanted currency? Or Habermas's colonizing money? Once we take history seriously, when we examine actual social practices, when, more specifically, we recognize that people routinely assign different meanings and separate uses to particular monies, the standard historical account of a rationalized modern world quickly breaks down. Invariant theoretical models, as Tilly so persuasively demonstrates, only work by ignoring history. If you took only one snapshot of legal tender, you might think classic theorists were right, but once you observe the actual process of how people accumulate, allocate, use, divide, and save monies, you discover that the theory of monetary rationalization is inadequate.

This realization made me look at materials as exotic as court cases, etiquette books, instructions for charity workers, annual reports of charitable organizations, immigrants' manuals and memoirs, household budget studies, contemporary novels, plays and vaudevilles, general periodicals, newspapers, womens' magazines—including feature articles, fiction, letters to the editor, and advice columns—consumer economics and home economics textbooks, popular household manuals, and advertisements. Exploring people's changing understandings and uses of money as they manage their multiple, variable, and contested social relations makes us also listen carefully to the pronouncements of social arbiters such as etiquette and magazine writers, social workers, or legal authorities. Down here in historical detail reenchantment occurs.

Thus, when it came to money, classical social theorists had their magical script wrong. Money did not cast a blanket rationalizing spell over social life, but instead social life cast multifarious, constantly changing spells over money. How, then, should we interpret this manifold enchantment? Let me propose an alternative differentiated model of money as continually shaped and reshaped by diverse networks of social relations and varying systems of meanings. Money is neither culturally neutral nor socially anonymous. It may well "corrupt" values and social ties into numbers, but values and social relations reciprocally transform money by investing it with meaning and social patterns.

In general, an attentive examination of monetary practices reveals five striking features. First, as government agencies strive to standardize and regulate legal tender, ordinary people, organizations, and even some branches of government continue to introduce new distinctions and to create specialized currencies to match them. Second, the parties involved in this differentiation of currencies employ an array of earmarking techniques: physical transformation of legal tender, conversion of other objects into currencies, invention of new objects such as tokens and tickets, physical segregation of different currencies, and strict separation by use. Third, the distinctions involved do the work of creating and maintaining significantly different sets of social relations; they correspond to distinct social ties and their meanings. Fourth, this differentiation involves extensive symbolic work, ranging from the invention of categorical systems to the creation of rituals; it adapts old cultural forms and creates new ones. Finally, people care enough about these distinctions that they struggle when other people attempt to impose different systems of earmarking upon them.

Despite its transferability, people make every effort to embed money in particular times, places, and social relations. Thus, there is no single, uniform, generalized money, but multiple monies: people earmark different currencies for many or perhaps all types of social interactions, much as they create distinctive languages for different social contexts. And people will in fact respond with anger, shock, or ridicule to the "misuse" of monies for the wrong set of social relations, such as offering a $100 bill to pay for a newspaper. Money used for rational instrumental exchanges is not "free" from social constraints but is another type of socially created currency, subject to particular networks of social relations and its own set of values and norms.

How does this process of social earmarking work? After all, the physical homogeneity of modern currency is indisputable. How, then, do people distinguish between monies that can so easily remain indistinct? Anthropologists provide some intriguing insights into the differentiation of monies, but only with regard to primitive money. For instance, ethnographic studies show that in certain primitive communities, money attains special qualities and distinct values independent of quantity. How much money is less important than *which* money. Multiple currencies, or "special-purpose" money, using Karl Polanyi's term, have sometimes co-existed in one and the same village, each currency having a specified, restricted use (for purchasing only certain goods or services), special modes of allocation and forms of exchange, and sometimes, designated users.

For instance, in Rossel Island, a small traditional community in the southwestern Pacific, separate, lower-value coins were reserved exclusively for women. And in Yap, one of the Caroline Islands in the western Pacific, mussel shells strung on strings served as women's money, while men monopolized the more desirable large stones.

These special monies, which Mary Douglas has perceptively identified as a sort of primitive coupon system, control exchange by rationing and restricting the use and allocation of currency.[9] In the process, money sometimes performs economic functions serving as a medium of exchange, but it also functions as a social and sacred "marker," used to acquire or amend status, or to celebrate ritual events. The point is that primitive money is transformable, from fungible to nonfungible, from profane to sacred.

But what about modern money? Influenced by economic models, most anthropologists established a sharp dichotomy between primitive, restricted "special-purpose" money and modern "all-purpose" money, which, as a single currency, unburdened by ritual or social controls, can function effectively as a universal medium of exchange. Only recently have anthropologists begun to cast off the fallacy of a culturally neutral currency. An important collection of essays edited by J. Parry and M. Bloch demonstrates the heterogeneity of money, showing how the multiple symbolic meanings of modern money are shaped by the cultural matrix.[10] But because their cases are restricted to societies outside the centers of capitalism, they cannot fully challenge established assumptions.

A sociological model of money must show how, how much, and why, even in the heartland of capitalism, different networks of social relations and meaning systems mark modern money, introducing controls, restrictions, and distinctions that are as influential as the rationing of primitive money. Multiple monies in the modern world may not be as visibly identifiable as the shells, coins, brass rods, or stones of primitive communities, but their invisible boundaries work just as well. How else, for instance, do we distinguish a bribe from a tribute or a donation, a wage from an honorarium, or an allowance from a salary? How do we identify ransoms, bonuses, tips, damages, or premiums? True, there are quantitative differences between these various payments. But surely, the special vocabulary conveys much more than diverse amounts. Detached from its qualitative differences, the world of money becomes undecipherable.

One might argue that the earmarking of money is an individual phenomenon. Indeed, in psychology, new studies now reject the notion that money is psychologically general, maintaining that instead money involves "multiple symbolizations." An exciting literature on "mental accounting" challenges economists' assumption of fungibility by showing the ways individuals distinguish between kinds of money. For instance, they treat a windfall income much differently from a bonus or an inheritance, even when the sums involved are identical.

Modern money, however, is marked by more than individual random preferences. As Marcel Mauss observed in 1914, money is "essentially a social fact."[11] The earmarking of money is thus a social process: money is attached to varying sets of social relations, rather than individuals. And there are a number of different techniques for this social production of multiple monies: restricting the uses of money, regulating modes of allocation, modifying its presentation, attaching special meanings to particular amounts, designating proper users, earmarking appropriate sources. To be sure, this phenomenon is not restricted to the uses of state-issued money but applies as well to other objects: from tokens and commercial paper to art objects, and even including kitchen recipes or jokes—anything, in fact, that is socially exchangeable. At issue here, however, is to show that precisely where interpreters of modernity see the utmost depersonalization of life, in the circulation of state currency, people continually introduce distinctions, doubts, and directives that defy all instrumental calculation.

My most recent research has focused on fundamental transformations of this earmarking of money in the United States between the 1870s and 1930s. I have selected three general social settings to explore and explain patterns of variation in the conditions and techniques of differentiating monies: the domestic economy, gifts exchanged by relatives and friends, and charitable currencies. Why choose these three areas? Why not examine, for instance, the social construction of market money and take on economists in their own turf? Quite deliberately, I chose areas where according to the traditional dichotomy between the market and personal relations, rationalization should have succeeded best: commodifying core personal and social relations and rationalizing sentiment: family, friendship, charity, death. I show instead that it is very hard work to suppress the active creative power of supposedly vulnerable social relations.

Reenchanting money not only challenges social theorists' standard modernization scripts, it takes money away from economists' intellectual pocketbook, where it has been sleeping for too long. A historically grounded analysis of multiple monies strongly defies economic models of a single, fungible, infinitely divisible, impersonal currency. Of course, in real life, economists acknowledge the nonfungibility of monies. Take Paul Samuelson. Some years ago, after being criticized for doing a series of spot commercials for Allied Van Lines ("I am Paul Samuelson of MIT. I won the Nobel Prize for my book in economics. One thing economics teaches is the importance of controlling risks. One risk that worries me is the cost of a household move. That's why I like Allied Van Lines"), Samuelson recognized this was a "demeaning" way of earning money for a scientist. He "laundered" his embarrassing fee by donating the money to a charity.[12]

I can, of course, hear Simmel's reply: So you found a few ripples. The current is still running strongly in my direction. Just wait, and money will disenchant the world. Haven't you noticed the way that electronic transfers of money are converting all monies into a single, invisible medium? At first glance, Simmel's ghost seems to have a point. But consider the following: as of 1993, a record-breaking 26.6 million welfare recipients bought their food with government-issued food stamps. Millions of other Americans trade regularly in frequent-flier miles—a currency created about two decades ago by the airline industry. Frequent-flier monies are not restricted to the travel market: they can be earned by, among other ways, eating in certain restaurants, buying flowers, investing in particular money market funds. Furthermore, they can be spent for hotels, cruises, even pianos, or donated to a designated charity. Think also of the flourishing national barter market described by the *New York Times* (March 14, 1992), where $6 billion a year in barter trades are paid not with dollars but with scrip or trade checks created by a barter exchange network, or the vouchers devised by Berkeley, California merchants and charitable organizations to encourage "good panhandling" by making their coupon-currency redeemable only for food, bus fares, or other essentials but not for alcohol, cigarettes, or illegal drugs.[13]

Christmas clubs and special account deposits are still around. Only a few years ago, American Express issued the successful gift check as a new form of "gift money." Or take household monies: witness the recurrent findings that in some dual-career families, despite larger paychecks, women's money is still earmarked, designated for special purposes, such as child care, housekeeping services, or vacations, or to pay the rent. Reflect also on the mother in Chicago's public housing, as Alex Kotlowitz describes, who in the midst of deep poverty sets aside $80 a month for burial insurance on her children.[14]

One last item: Some time ago the *New York Times Magazine* (March 15, 1992, p. 37) described how Rabbi Menahem Mendel Schneerson—the late head of the Lubavitcher group—each Sunday offered his thousands of visitors not only a blessing but also a crisp dollar bill that was supposed to be deposited in a charity box set in a nearby wall. Instead, many visitors rushed out to the street where, reportedly, "enterprising Russian immigrants wait to laminate them, melting the Rebbe's stern, fatherly portrait over the benign face of George Washington."

Once you look past the textbooks on legal tender, and into the actual process of how people identify, classify, organize, re-create, and use money, it is clear that enchanted monies are more than an antiquarian tale of anxious mothers erasing dollar bills.

Notes

This essay, written en route to my completion of *The Social Meaning of Money* (New York: Basic Books, 1994), can now serve as an introduction to that book's themes. In modified versions, most segments of this text also appear in the book. Instead of detailed documentation, which is in the book, I have restricted my citations here to direct quotations.

    1. Elizabeth L. Post, *Emily Post's Etiquette* (New York: HarperCollins, 1992), 591.

    2. Max Weber, "Religious Rejections of the World and Their Directions," in H. H. Gerth and C. Wright Mills, eds. *From Max Weber: Essays in Sociology* (New York: Oxford University Press, [1946] 1971), 331; Georg Simmel, *The Sociology of Georg Simmel*, ed. Kurt H. Wolf (Glencoe, Ill.: Free Press, [1908] 1950), 412; Karl Marx, *Grundrisse* (New York: Vintage, [1858–59] 1973), 163.

    3. Jürgen Habermas, *The Theory of Communicative Action*, vol. 2 (Boston: Beacon Press, 1989), 327.

    4. Simmel, *The Sociology of Georg Simmel*, 414; Georg Simmel, *The Philosophy of Money*, trans. Tom Bottomore and David Frisby (London: Routledge &

Kegan Paul, [1900] 1978), 259; Gertrude Stein, "Money," *Saturday Evening Post* 208 (July 13, 1936): 88.

5. *Hancock et al. v. Yaden*, 366 Supreme Court of Indiana at 371 (1889).

6. Alice Bradley, *Fifty Family Budgets* (New York: Woman's Home Companion, 1923), 7.

7. Etsu Inagaki Sugimoto, *A Daughter of the Samurai* (Garden City, N.Y.: Doubleday, [1926] 1936), 176.

8. *Congressional Record*, 60th Cong., 1st sess., 1908, 42, 4:3387, 3389.

9. Mary Douglas, "Primitive Rationing," in Raymond Firth, ed., *Themes in Economic Anthropology*, (London: Tavistock, 1967).

10. J. Parry and M. Bloch, *Money & the Morality of Exchange* (Cambridge: Cambridge University Press, 1989).

11. Marcel Mauss, "Les origines de la notion de monnaie," *Institut Français d'Anthropologie*, Compte rendu des séances, vol. 2 (1914): 14–19.

12. *New York Times* (May 20, 1982).

13. *New York Times* (July 26, 1991, September 19, 1991).

14. Alex Kotlowitz, *There Are No Children Here* (New York: Doubleday, 1991), 17.

Sociology and History:
Terms of Endearment?

Ira Katznelson

When Charles Tilly showed his essay to Viviana Zelizer and me he noted that "we have an opportunity to make an unusually integrated presentation, even where (if anywhere) we disagree." My worry is that we will be too self-congratulatory. The landscape on which history and the social sciences currently are engaging is, at once, the most promising terrain in the social sciences, yet it also is a region fraught with pits and snares. I should like to underscore some of these by commenting about the "said" and "not said" of the two preceding essays, then I shall raise for discussion some more general questions about history and sociological imagining suggested by the essays.

Each of the two preceding papers effectively pleads the case for the constitutive engagement of social science and history both in hortatory fashion and by way of illustrations of the concrete research programs Tilly and Zelizer currently have underway on revolutions, immigration, and money; no small subjects for students of modernity, whatever their disciplinary identification.

Tilly and Zelizer tell us with great clarity about the kind of work they prefer: a theoretically informed historicism, a consideration of embedded processes and social relations, and a focus on networks, flows across boundaries, and variations in structure and meaning even in the embrace of generating mechanisms that impel toward regularities. They also identify the kinds of work they do not much like. These commit the sins of "monadism" and "societism" for Tilly, the sins of economism and a flattening of history and variation for Zelizer, and the sins of disembedded essentialism and a reification of differentiated categories and units of action for both.

These critiques and programs, it might be noted, are directed less to the issue of how sociology and history should engage each with the other than with the ways in which both sociologists and historians continue to conceptualize the world and its units of action in terms of isolated individuals and societies, abstracted and disembedded money and markets, self-contained and competing models, insensitive to variation, complexity, mutual constitution. On this, Zelizer and Tilly profoundly agree, as do I.

But the essays also speak implicitly, and critically, to interrogate each other. First, from Tilly to Zelizer: Is the market itself not an interactive social mechanism that generates "structures, sequences, and processes" that are broadly similar despite the cultural specificities of time and place? In this light, does not Zelizer's denial of the "colorlessness" of money (Georg Simmel's language) practice a reciprocal destandardization that runs the risk of obscuring the terms of engagement between the generative qualities of markets and money as the economists and modernizers have understood them and the multifarious meanings of money that are given heft and constitution by the networks, cultures, and practices within which they play out? Zelizer implies that her program to "embed money in particular times, places, and social relations" represents a stark alternative to claims about the inherent, even remorseless, logic of market and money relations. Why make this choice? Why not, rather, interrogate their mutual constitution?

From Zelizer to Tilly: How are your generative structures and mechanisms embedded in and shaped by variations in meaning and in the identities of agents? If we all would agree with Edward Thompson's formulation that history knows no regular verbs, are not the distinguishing irregularities that mark the "interactions among social locations" themselves causal? Does your case "against monadic ontologies and singular models" suggest that we replace these with more satisfactory, more complex, more interactive models without resolving whether these provide contexts for, or explanations of, human action and choice? What do you make of Trevor Roper's valedictory lecture claim that "free will, the choice of alternatives, is in the actor; the historian's function is to discern those alternatives"? Does your distinction between revolutionary situation and revolutionary outcome do the trick? What is the role of revolutionary leaders and their choices?

And to both Tilly and Zelizer I would ask, while agreeing wholeheartedly with their skeptical view of dominant tendencies in history and the social sciences, why are the alternative visions they reject so powerful, so seductive, and so influential as representations of social reality? More precisely, why do the differentiated categories of state, market, and civil society seem so compelling to so many, even at the costs they have identified? Without argument, let me claim that such is the case because the most fundamental aspect of the divide in the West between the feudal and postfeudal worlds—whatever paths we have taken to get from here to there—has been the separation of property and sovereignty, and with it a number of other separations: between state, economy, and civil society; and between states claiming sovereignty over territory and people from each other without an integrated context of values or rule. Other separations follow, such as that between the state and the person of the ruler, and between markets as processes and markets as places. Mine is not a call for a social science or history of differentiation. Rather it is a plea that our social science and history of interactions, networks, and relationships specify the distinctive institutional and normative units that interact to define the qualities and rules of their transactions.

*   *   *

I have called this comment "Sociology and History: Terms of Endearment." Which sociology? Which history? What terms of endearment?

Opening the entry on "History" in the *Encyclopedia of the Social Sciences* (1932), Henri Berr (who sought to make history the integrating science of the social sciences) and Lucien Febvre wrote:

> There is no branch of knowledge which in the course of intellectual evolution has exhibited more varied modalities and answered to more contradictory conceptions than has history. There is none which has had and continues to have more difficulty in discovering its definitive status.

Of course, they might have been writing about sociology. What kind of history and what kind of sociology should engage with each other? These are the issues Tilly and Zelizer have addressed, yet even on the terms they sketch a number of crucial questions remain to be asked, which might be condensed as questions about attenuation: how much thinning is required by sociology and by history for each to be capable of joining with the other in a powerful historical sociology or a compelling sociologically informed history? And are the gains of such a thinning worth the costs to history and sociology, each on its own terms? I would say yes, but only if we take great care with and are very self-conscious about questions of evidence, qualities of presentism, the multiplicity of perspectives, ambiguities of agency and choice, and the character of our intra-and interdisciplinary conversations.

Here are two caricatures of "thick sociology" and "thick history." A thick sociology stresses the advantages of scientifically created evidence over the utilization of the necessarily partial relics left to us from the past; its agenda is generated by the urge to understand the patterning of relationships between variables and processes—mobility, stratification, deviance, and the like—rather than events in actual places. A thick sociology crafts scientific hypotheses about the causal determinants of choice by impersonal factors, most of which operate behind people's backs. Most of its questions are driven by contemporary concerns, on the assumption that time and place do not change basic social processes very much: the way we decide to vote today is thought to be much like the way our great grandfathers decided to vote (for those of us who had great grandfathers who could vote!). A collective action problem and a transaction cost are treated as much the same irrespective of context and meaning, at least for broad swaths of time. From this view, one articulated by John Goldthorpe, history, and even historical sociology, suffer from inadequate evidence, and a kitbag of impossibly loose and ad hoc methodologies.[1]

A counterposed and equally caricatured view of "strong history" was asserted clearly by Geoffrey Elton in his 1984 inaugural lecture at Cambridge University: "A history," he wrote,

> simply is not equal to a collection or even a sequence of technically analyzed sociological states . . . we, as historians, do not write history for the use of the moment; we are the guardians and distributors of the truths of history and should at least try to make sure that when current partisans plunder history for their own purposes they have a non-partisan and real history to stand over them.

In full knowledge of the potential costs, historical sociology and sociological history must reject the claims of thick sociology and thick history. Practitioners of the engagement of history and sociological imagining *construct* evidence from relics; they do not just take them as they are. Their work recognizes, as Paul Cézanne did, that it is possible, even desirable, to paint not just a singular tree but a multiplicity of partial visions of a tree. How these are joined in a single painting depends on the relationship the observer chooses with the object of representation. As practitioners, we are suspended uneasily, as it were, between science and humanistic criticism; we utilize concepts and comparisons both to differentiate *and* to universalize the objects of our concern; and we promote provocative hypotheses that in some sense deliberately distort in order to correct empirical or analytical imbalances in our fields.

Because the relationship between history and sociology (and, more broadly, the social sciences) always hovers between mutual constitution and mutual threat, their engagement demands special caution and care. There is no use in a joining of sociology and history that naively imports arid social science concepts into history or that is unreflective about the kinds of history that social scientists utilize for case materials. Nor can such a joining be unaware of its tacit assumptions. Medieval historiography assumed the universal cogency of Christendom. What comparable assumptions have we made our own? Think for a moment of the crisis for sociologists and historians of the working class entailed not only by what Eric Hobsbawm has called "the forward march of labor halted" but by the collapse of socialist alternatives to liberal democratic capitalism. It is easier to do good work by disciplinary standards as thick sociologists or as thick historians, but the limits of both are far more severe than those imposed by the self-conscious imbrication of a less thick sociology with a less thick history. No one, however, should gainsay the difficulties in this engagement. But how much poorer would we be without the kinds of efforts Viviana Zelizer and Charles Tilly have presented to us to shatter deeply inscribed categories and interrogate complex and meaningful patterns of human action in the past so that, in part, we may learn to better understand and navigate the present.

Note

1. John H. Goldthorpe, "The Uses of History in Sociology," *British Journal of Sociology* 42 (June 1991).

Social Science: An Imperfect Art

Daniel Bell

Politics is almost always, in some measure, an argument about the future. And we cannot escape either the normative debates as to what kind of future we may want, or the empirical assessments as to the kinds of futures that may come. But how do we understand "the future"? One can assume that all outcomes are chance (or there are some magical formulas, like mantras of the rainmakers, to compel the clouds of nature). Or believe with Thucydides that the passions and vanities of men are always the same—". . . and from these passions proceeded the violence of parties once engaged in contentions"—so that when law breaks down, men take upon themselves the prosecution of revenge, a story he tells of the Corycerean revolution, and which is now repeated in Bosnia-Herzegovina. Or, there is the social determinism of a Frederick Engels, for whom the domain of History is subject to a "necessity" which, given the direction of history, manifests itself in a materialist outcome that in "the last analysis" is not in doubt.[1] Thus history is not made by "great men" or by event-making men (to use the phrase of Sidney Hook) but by men who represent the impersonal social forces of history.

Few persons today, I assume, would hold any of these positions completely. We know that men and women, by actions and wills, can seek to realize choice and intentions, yet we recognize, as well, the constraints—of habits, interests, resources, unintended or contradictory consequences, or clashing values—which limit what can be achieved.

My purpose, here, is to deal with that dialectic of intention and constraint, and lay bare the theoretical assumptions of that imperfect art. The difficulty is how to unravel that tangled web without ending up with the

Gordian knot (what sailors once called "the Turk's head") whose strands
are so cunningly concealed that no loose ends are visible and we do not
know where to begin. The assumption we make is that there are some
necessary distinctions—distinctions about the kinds of phenomena, and
distinctions about method—that may allow us to sort out the ones that
may lead us to what Auguste Comte once called *prevision.*
    We begin with theory, rather than narrative. Theory directs our atten-
tion, orders our experience, provides explanation, evaluates likely outcomes, and gives us confidence about our understandings. In that respect,
what this essay attempts to do is to follow the logic of theory in the social
sciences and to see in what ways theory can go beyond description in
helping us understand the breakup of the institutional structures that are
roiling our world today.

    In his treatise *De Divinatione*, the wise but sad Roman statesman Mar-
cus Tullio Cicero observed: "It is an ancient belief . . . that there exists
within mankind an undeniable faculty of divination. The Greeks called it
mantike, that is the capacity to foresee, to know future events, a sublime
and salutary act that raises human nature most nearly to the level of divine
power. . . . There is no nation, whether the most learned and enlightened
or the most grossly barbarous, that does not believe that the future can
be revealed and does not recognize in certain people the power of foretell-
ing it."
    In the *De Divinatione*, Cicero distinguishes two kinds of prophecy:
one due to art, the other to nature. He was, in fact, adopting Plato's distinction between *inductive* or artificial divination (*technike*) and *intuitive*
or natural divination (*adidakatos*). The first of these was based on observations, as that of the soothsayer inspecting the entrails of the animals.
(As Robert Flaceliere observes in his *Greek Oracles*, the method, though
it rests on irrational assumptions, is rational.) The second consists of a
kind of madness (*mania* in Greek, *furor* in Latin), an ecstasy of divine
possession. (In the Greek, ex-stasis means leaving one's body.) It was the
kind relied upon by seers and prophetesses, the Bakis or Sibyls, who were
regarded as being directly inspired by the gods without any perceptible
intermediation. For Plato the second kind, because it was religiously derived, was more authentic, so that only in that instance did the word *mantike* apply.
    There is, however, one obvious difficulty in defining genuine *mantike*.
A number of years ago I gave some lectures at Leningrad State University,
the theme of which was man's powers and the development of *techne*.
When I had finished, a sad and wise man arose and spoke, Professor Bell,

you have given us a wonderful lecture about the future, but as we look about us, wouldn't it have been better if it had all been left up to God? I thought the audience would hoot, but most nodded sympathetically. What does one say in that circumstance? I replied that this was a profound question, one that had been asked repeatedly over the millennia. The difficulty was that we did not know, truly, to whom God spoke. If we did, most of our problems would have been solved long ago. As it was, over the millennia individuals have killed one another for possession of the claim to that answer.[2]

Beyond the inductive and the intuitive certainties, there is a profound, third kind of answer: the prophecy by ambiguity—such as we find at the Pythian oracle at Delphi. The answers were wrapped in circumlocution and equivocation, so that the meaning would be hidden from others, while the questioner sought to unravel it. Perhaps the most famous Delphic utterance, which Socrates reported, was "Know thyself." (That was the answer; but what was the question?) The pythia spoke, as we know, from the *omphalos*, the navel in the belly, and such prophets are called belly-talkers. But that takes us back to politics and ambiguity.

So, we are left with the imperfect art.

II

If we start with nature, we have to consider whether there is order in nature, for if we can find that order we would know the sequence of events and its regularities. But there are also two further questions. If nature is not static but changing, are there some determinate patterns in the modes of change? And, perhaps the most difficult of all: are man and society part of nature; i.e., is the social order, such as the family and polis, "natural," or is there some qualitative change in a move from nature to culture; and if so, are there determinate structures, or consistent patterns of change, in culture?

Again, distinctions are in order.

The first distinction is between *contingency* and *entelechy*. Contingency is chance or random events, something unforeseen or unexpected, outside the order of things. As Hegel once said, there is no science of the particular. Yet we know that in large numbers, there are patterns which we now call probability, for beneath all the randomness, some regularities do emerge. (Many years ago, the Rand Corporation published a "book" entitled *A Million Random Numbers and a Hundred Thousand Digits*, to provide tables for statisticians and engineers who needed "chance" num-

bers for their control experiments; but even that was not wholly successful, and today high-speed computers are used to generate "random"
numbers.) And, on the "micro" level, as the 19th-century French mathematician Antoine-Augustin Cournot once remarked, chance is the encounter between two series of events that are independent of one another.
Yet if one can retrace the tracks of the two, then we can follow the logic
of the encounter.

Entelechy is the intrinsic inner design of all phenomena. Since all things
have determinate beginnings (*archai*) they move, unless impeded, to their
natural end, or *telos*. The trajectory of *archai* and *telos* is the path of
knowledge.

The terms, of course, are Aristotle's. Aristotle, born in Macedonia, but
spending time on the seashore, for him the world was one of change and
becoming. The science in which he was most at home was biology, which
combined observation and reasoning, and often his basic metaphors were
biological. His emphasis was on the functions and purposes of things, so
that all explanation was primarily functional—the relation of the part to
the whole, and the realization of "natural ends."

As he wrote in *De Partibus Animalium:* "we do not find any chance
being formed from a particular seed . . . that from which the seed comes
is the *archai* and agent out of which it comes . . . while the end (*to telos*)
is something that has to come to be (*ousia*). Acorns grow into oak trees,
not pine trees; human infants will grow into men and women, not don-
keys." There is *potentiality* and *actualization*, What has the power to become, will under appropriate conditions become.

This natural teleology becomes generalized by Aristotle for all phenomena. In art (painting and sculpture) there is *hyle*, or inchoate matter,
which, as shaped by the artist, becomes "realized form," which is its perfection. In music, random sounds become organized by a determinate
logic, into a specific form. Since man and society are also part of nature,
each also must seek to realize their nature, to achieve fulfillment. As Aristotle writes in the opening line of his *Metaphysics*, "All men, by nature,
desire to know," i.e., to achieve understanding. And for society, the natural end, its purpose, is virtue and justice.

For sociological analysis, a large theoretical claim is at stake. These
processes are *immanent*, they are logical unfoldings in the exploration by
the artist or scientist of the variety of forms. To place the issue in respect
to the sociology of knowledge, these developments are "internal," and
not a result of outside or social forces. In music, the sonata form, from
the classical period to the twentieth century, is the developing relationship
between an initial thematic modulation from the tonic to a new key, and

answered by a complementary modulation from the new key back to the tonic. The variations in the form, such as chromaticism or novel keys, which one finds in the later developments, are not responses to "external" or "social" forces, but the variations that are opened up in the exploration of the form. For later composers, the sense that the form is fully developed or "exhausted" may lead to new structural arrangements such as atonality, twelve-tone compositions, or serial music—or the aleatory devices of a John Cage, who, by reacting against received forms, may have "reflected" the temper of the time. But in the end these are all "dialogues" with a past which is part of the repertoire of every composer.

In painting, the change from romantic and mythological subjects to the mundane world of the spectacle, the studio, and the self, becomes the setting of the Impressionist and Post-Impressionist pictures, yet the modes of expressing these, from the daubs and patches of pigment on the surface (rather than smooth brushwork) to the siting of the multiplicity of views, rather than a single center, to define a picture plane, as in the marvelous Mont Sainte-Victoire series of Cézanne, or the successive foreshortening of interior depth within an illusionistic frame—which may have led to the pronouncement of Maurice Denis that "we must close the shutters," i.e., to paint on the surface itself—all of these are the *formal* developments which extend the "actuality" of painting itself.

And in the history of science, there is the famous debate initiated by B. Hessen, the Russian Marxist philosopher who in 1931 sought to establish the "social sources" of Newton's cosmology, and was answered by Alexander Koyré, who argued that the research agenda of physics from Galileo to Newton was dictated by the logical unfolding of theory, in seeking to make sense of observations and measurements of motion and gravity. The influential thesis of Thomas Kuhn (from which he backed away somewhat in the second edition of his *Structure of Scientific Revolutions*) may be seen as combining both elements, since "normal science" has a logical progression until its "program" is realized, and following an epistemological *coupure* (a term first used by the French philosopher Gaston Bachelard, 1884–1962, before Foucault,) a new paradigm becomes established.[3]

The epistemological rupture with the idea of natural *entelechy* arises with Hegel. For Aristotle, Reason lay in Nature, and the idea of natural "ends." But for Hegel, man is outside nature, living (where the process of rationality takes hold) in History.[4] Man begins (as with any animals) with consciousness, but in reflecting upon himself and the world, in the exercise of reason, he achieves self-consciousness, and the awareness of a divided self. The theme of the divided self is a central one in the history of Christian thought, for after the Fall, man lives alienated from salvation and God, and only at the end of time (in the *parousia*, the second coming in Augustine's sense) can man achieve redemption.

For Hegel, there is a *philosophy* of history; that is, a determinate structure of unfolding and meaning, juts as the religious drama was the unfolding of God's purpose on earth. For Hegel (as for Marx) the meaning becomes embodied in man's powers so that, in the end, he may achieve a Faustian vision, which is God-like knowledge. For Hegel, man is divided into nature and spirit (as the objectification of consciousness), and, in the unfolding of Reason, which is "the ultimate design of the World," there is the further movement of Spirit through History. The *telos* of reason is the "end" of History, the time when all dualities are overcome, and man achieves the "realization" of the self in overcoming all alienation.[5]

For Marx, whose thought is a palimpsest over Hegel, the cunning of history lies not in reason as the self-reflection on the plane of ideas, but in *techne*, man's powers as *homo faber*, in making things, and gaining mastery over, and reorganizing, nature, to satisfy man's needs. And where Hegel located the dualities of self in thought, Marx gave these a naturalistic location: the division between mental and physical labor, between propertied and propertyless, between town and country, between men and women. As man develops *techne*, he gains new needs and new wants and an expanded sense of his new powers. As Marx once put it, man does not have a "nature," but a history, and man is defined not by "human nature," but by his changing historical self. The end of history is the "leap," as Engels once put it, from the Kingdom of Necessity to the Kingdom of Freedom.

In this "inner design," the immanent unfolding of man's powers (either through reason or *techne*) there is thus a *direction* to history. The "end" of History is Universalism, the dissolution of all particularities. On the intellectual level, the dualities of subject and object would be eliminated, and man's actions would no longer be limited by subjectivity or constrained by objective circumstance; as in Zen, perhaps, where the individual and the act are "one," as with the dancer and the dance. On the sociological level, the division of labor and the claims of property are abolished, for economic plenty abounds. And on the political level, men would renounce their national, class, and ethnic identities and become world citizens of the world community.

Is there—could there be—an end to History? On a superficial level, we have recently witnessed the claim, given garish publicity, of Mr. Fukuyama's End of History. What Fukuyama argues is that with the collapse of Communism, there is no longer any other single, all-embracing "universal" idea, claiming validity for all society, than the idea of democracy. And since, like Hegel, he believes that the Idea foreshadows eventual Actuality, it is only a matter of time for the Idea to become fully "universal."

But all that is a foolish misreading of Hegel, or of his devious epigones such as Alexander Kojève, who at one time believed that Communism (through the cunning of reason embodied in Stalin) would become the Universal idea. For Hegel, the end of History was the beginning of *philosophy*, the reunification of thought, of myth and wonder, of the speculative and the scientific, of the changelessness of Parmenides, which has been "dirempted," or torn apart when the "totality" of spirit (of aesthetics and tragedy, of work and the polis) has lost its unity.

The end of history, like the end of time, remains a utopia. But the effort to "realize" history, like previous efforts to realize the Kingdom of God on earth, has led to the slaughter of millions of persons by the Zealots of History, from Lenin to Mao, who have proclaimed themselves generals in the long march of history.

Whether there is a "direction" to history is a questionable, if not discredited, idea. Hegel (and Marx) thought that there were "historic" nations and "backward" nations, and they justified wars against the latter as being historically "necessary." Morality was tied to the level of history, and transcendental judgments were ideologically suppressed in the interests of the higher "class" morality. (And proletarian novels, by the logic of the argument, were superior to "bourgeois" novels.) On the level of material circumstances, the premise of Communism and the end of history was the possibility of abundance, an abundance that was being withheld only by the class power of the property owners.

Yet, as we realize today, sadly, abundance is a chimera and scarcity rules. And given the overwhelming rise of demand (for goods and services, such as health care) against the limited resources, when choices have to be made as to who is entitled to what, we may be back to *triage*, the ethical questions as to who shall live and who shall die.

And in the break-up of nations and empires today, we see not the move to universalism, but the "return of history," as individuals and groups cling to primordial and particular identities, especially in defining themselves against one another, as the find themselves swamped by the tides of history.

Yet the idea of *entelechy* still has its claims. The worlds of art and of science are not arbitrary, so rules of change have meaning in the exploration of form. And in seeking to distinguish between civilization and barbarism, the idea of "natural ends" may be right. What we have to forgo are the chains of a strict determinism in the realization of form and in the design of social institutions. We live necessarily, with surprise and uncertainty.

III

To return to theory. If History does not provide the determinate trajectories for plotting the directions of social change (or, similarly, the sociological variants such as modernization theory or world-systems analysis), the logical alternatives are a unified-field theory or a general theory of society and of social action.

To be fully effective, however, both require a "closed system." In a physically closed system, the relevant parameters establish the limits of other variables (e.g., no vehicle can go faster than 16,000 miles an hour within the earth's orbit, for that is the escape velocity which pitches a vehicle into outer space). Or within a closed environment (such as Raymond Pearl's population experiments with fruit flies), growth follows a logistic or S-shaped curve where the rates of change above the line of inflection reverse the rates of the earlier exponential acceleration, until the ceiling limit (or, as one would now say, "the envelope") is reached.

If there are no closed physical or ecological systems, one would need a "covering law" to provide a determinate explanation. In those instances, an explanundum is identified with a *class* of events whose occurrence follows (necessarily or probably) from the conjuncture of an initial condition with a relevant general law under which it is subsumed—as in Ernest Nagel's example of the recurrent condensation of moisture on the surface of a glass when there are differences in temperature.

I take it—I think the point is no longer debatable—that we cannot establish fully closed systems or "covering laws" in the social world. There does remain, however, the question whether one can *logically* establish unified fields or exhaustive general theory in the social sciences, for then one could "close" a system, and thus identify uniformities of behavior that would allow for prediction.

The physical model we have is classical mechanics, and the turn came with Galileo. In Aristotelian physics, objects sought their "natural ends." There were "higher forms of motion," as in the heavens and earthly sublunar motions of an inferior type. What Galileo did was to strip physics of the idea of purpose, of its normative and anthropomorphic concepts, and seek to establish exact mathematical laws of a unified field. Instead of considering a single or concrete falling body, he looked for its abstract properties[6]—mass, acceleration, velocity—as related variables that would apply to *any* falling body. The new physics of Galileo envisaged *homogeneization* of entities in a unified field, gauged by quantities rather than qualities, which could be (following Newton and Leibniz) measured as rates of change by the mathematical calculus. The unity of the physical world embraced the courses of the stars, the falling of stones, and the flight of birds, as a single gravitational field. And by the end of the nineteenth century, the laws of classical mechanics were axiomatized by Hertz and Mach.

The simple logic is followed by neo-classical economics. Instead of dealing with concrete entities, economics converts these through a metric, price, into homogeneous integers called "labor" and "capital," combines these in production functions, and seeks to establish the "optimal mix," at relative prices for *any* economic system that wishes to achieve maximum efficiency in the use of resources. In the unified field model of Walras, and later reformulated by Arrow and Debreu, all markets clear to achieve a general equilibrium. But this is an "ideal type" against which to measure the shortfalls of an economy. It is not a description of an economy.

Sociology has sought, at various times, to move to a general theory of society.[7] The first generation of sociologists rejected historical sequences such as slavery, feudalism, and capitalism, as too unilinear in their evolutionary development. They sought to move from history to *analytical* types, and bequeathed to us a set of distinctions that still govern most of social theory today. These are the typologies of *gemeinschaft* and *gesellschaft* of Tonnies, or the mechanical/organic types of societies of Durkheim, or the traditional/rational distinctions of Weber. But these distinctions were embedded historically in Western history and were derived from the experiences of industrialization and the move from rural to urban habitats. Increasingly one finds these limited in seeking to understand changes in Asia, or Africa, or the Middle East, often because, while dealing with types of social relationships, they ignore culture and politics.

A few sociologists went beyond these typologies to construct a "general theory" that would provide a unified framework to apply to any society. These have been notable efforts. The most sprawling, perhaps, was that of Vilfredo Pareto, in the four-volume (in English) *Mind and Society*. Trained as an engineer and mathematician, Pareto became an economist, and when he succeeded Walras in the chair at Lausanne, he set forth the first formalization of the general-equilibrium model. Having solved, he thought, the "circulation of goods," he would now deal with the "circulation of elites." For Pareto, economics was the model of logical or rational actions, and sociology the consequent study of non-logical actions. He created an elaborate system of sentiments, derivations and underlying residues, and grouped these into classes of residues that would embrace every kind of combination. But Pareto finally abandoned the effort. The work, thick as an olla podrida, simply falls apart under the weight of its illustrations.

Georg Simmel, the brilliant and dazzling sociologist of the first quarter of the twentieth century, realized that if one sought to deal with the extraordinary variety of "content" of human affairs, there could be no general ordering principle. His strategy, therefore, was to identify the *forms* of social relations both of structure (such as superordination/subordination) and of social interactions. It would never have occurred to Simmel to make a systematic, exhaustive catalogue of every possible social form—it would have gone against his temperament—but his writings, for example, influenced Robert Park, who thought that social life could be encapsulated by four major social processes—competition, conflict, accommodation, and assimilation. Park, and his student Ernest Burgess, shaped the Chicago school of sociology, with its theory of ecological and urban spatial changes. In Germany, the sociologist Leopold von Wiese, now largely forgotten, created a cumbersome sociological system of four basic concepts—social process, social distance, social space, and social formation, which together became "the geometry of social relations." Von Wiese's system was adopted and amplified by Howard Becker at Wisconsin, and became one of the sources of the study of German sociology by Becker's students.

The bravest attempt to create a vast architectonic structure, a general theory of action, was made, of course, by Talcott Parsons. The starting clue lies in a "Note on Gemeinschaft and Gesellschaft," which Parsons appended to his section on Weber's systematic theory in his *Structure of Social Action* (1936). Pointing out that these "are ideal types of *concrete* relationship," Parsons argued that they could not be the basis of a "general classification of social relationships," nor could such an effort "start from *any* dichotomy of only two types." Parsons, therefore, began his heroic effort to create a "formal/analytic" general system of sociology.

It would be foolhardy to attempt any summary of Parsons's work, but the logic is clear. In analyzing social structures, Parsons was attempting to construct the least number of terms—curiously always four—which could be applied, exhaustively, to *any* social structure or social relations. Thus, in positing the "functional requisites" of any society, Parsons argued, in his AGIL scheme, that all institutions need to have the Adaptive, Goal-Oriented, Integrative, and Latent management systems, for a society to function. (And within *each* of the systems there were, recursively, four sub-set boxes for each function.) In dealing with social relations, Parsons set forth his "pattern variables," in which he sought to classify all social relations by four sets of paired terms.

To illustrate:

Norms:	Universalistic	Particularistic
Status:	Achieved	Ascribed
Obligations:	Specific	Diffuse
Emotions:	Neutral	Affective

The confusion often arose because readers did not realize that Parsons did not mean these as *concrete* (or descriptive) but *analytical abstractions* which could be used, either along a single axis (so that some modern societies, such as that of the United States, would be universalistic, achievement-oriented, etc.), while others, by cross-classification, would be shown to be mixed. Few writers have used the pattern variable system. S. M. Lipset, in *The First New Nation*, made the scheme central to his effort to compare national *value* systems, adding to the Parsons scheme the dimension of elitism and egalitarianism. However, the effort to set rankings of the four English-speaking democracies (U.S., Australia, Canada, and Great Britain), on these dimensions, foundered because of the looseness of the terms. As Lipset writes: "It is obviously extremely difficult to be precise about such variations, and these should be considered at best as an informed guess."[8]

Parsons was following, self-consciously, the logic of exposition exemplified in classical mechanics or Walrasian general equilibrium theory, to its exhaustive end. And one must salute him for that extraordinary effort. Yet one must also say, sadly, that it is a failure. In understanding the reasons why, we may understand, as well, the limits of theory in sociology.

The Parsonian system is a huge ziggurat, a vast taxonomy of systems and relationships. But these are divorced from institutions, and there is no way of moving back from the classifications to the concrete (and historically embedded) situations. Classical mechanics has a metric—motions per unit of time—and a calculus for dealing with the rates of change. Economics has a metric, price, which allows for the homogenization of goods (a pound of potatoes and a pound of automobile) and a linear, aggregate combination in index numbers; and thus one can chart the ratios of exchange, or the total amounts of consumption, investments, etc.

But sociology has no such metric—though Parsons, at the end, sought to deal with the exchange of money and influence, but these were largely illustrative, not measured. How does one take wealth, power, and status and find "conversion ratios" whereby one transposes a position from one "scale" to another? Yet these strivings are the core of social mobility and social stratification, which are the distinctive subjects of sociology, as well as the stuff of literature from *The Red and the Black* to *The Great Gatsby*.[9]

But there is a larger theoretical difficulty with the effort to construct a general theory, which is my argument that society is *not* a "system," and that the classical efforts to conceptualize society in terms of "integration," "totality," or in "structural-functional terms" are misleading. Why?

IV

We are all bound to History. For Hegel, who is the source of our modernist preoccupation (as Nietzsche is of our post-modernist bricolage), History was divided into periods, which he called "moments," each held together by some *inner zusammenhängen*, an organic totality that defined each different epoch. Within that chambered nautilus was the *Begriff*, the principle of reason which made the world intelligible.[10] Each epoch had its own realization until broken by the world-historical figures—Alexander, Caesar, and Napoleon—the unwitting instruments of the cunning of reason.

For Marx, there was a similar principle of totality, except that *techne* not the *Begriff* was the driving force of change. Each historic epoch is marked off by its own mode of production. Every society is a structurally interrelated whole, and any aspect of that whole—legal codes, religion, art, and the like—cannot be understood by itself. Yet if, as Marx said in *Capital*, in changing the technical world, Man changes his own nature, then, as Sidney Hook once put it, "human nature under ancient slavery must have been different in some respects from human nature under modern capitalism." And if that is so, how is it possible to understand past historical experience in the same way as we understand present experience, since understanding presupposes an invariant explanatory pattern to encompass both?

Marx never answered that question directly, but in the *Nachlasse*, the posthumous writings edited by Bernstein, in responding to a question why the Greeks still retain such an appeal for us, he replied that the

Greeks are the childhood of the human race and therefore have all the artlessness of children. The answer is a cheat. Antigone, one has to say, in defying Creon to give decent burial to her brothers, was not a child.

Even when history is divided into radically different sociocultural systems, as in the theories of Pitirim Sorokin, each of these systems, such as the *sensate* and the *ideational*, possess a function unity, integrated by the leitmotif within each culture, so that the sensate principle operates like a ramrod from the area of material goods to that of the sensual culture, while in the ideational system, the ascetic principle runs like a plumb-line from work to the spiritual life.

Other sociological theories of "totality" sidestep the trap of historicism by adopting a structural–functional standpoint. Malinowski and the early Parsons grounded the explanation of any dimension of a society, from ritual to exchange, by reference to the system as a whole. Or, in the case of Durkheim, societies are "integrated" through the normative order, or the value system, which, through the setting of norms and the application of sanctions, "legitimates" behavior throughout the realms of the society.

The major theoretical difficulty is that social structures are not "natural," or, to put it in epistemological terms, constitutive of society. Those who see Marxism as a "general theory" of society have to show that the mode of production is constitutive and thus "determines" (in the first or the last analysis) all other dimensions of society. But this is not, historically, the case. The mode of production is a construct, a prism to be applied by the analyst to different historical societies, just as one can apply Weber's "modes of domination" (i.e., the patriarchal, patrimonial, and legal–rational forms) to societies, and the two modes are not homologous with one another. The choice of a prism depends upon the problem one seeks to explain or the different societal comparisons one wishes to make.

Equally one cannot escape continuities in one realm and disjunctions in others. How does one explain as a fundamental reference point the persistence of the great historic religions over millennia of time, when economic systems have disappeared and political empires have crumbled? Though these religions have changed in manifold ways, the great cores of belief—monotheism in Judaism, the savior figure of Jesus in Christianity, the karma and nirvana of Buddhism and Hinduism—and the great texts of the Upanishads, the Vedanta, the Old Testament and the New, the Koran, still compel belief today. Does a material explanation suffice? The powerful Enlightenment figures from Voltaire through Marx thought that religion, which they saw as fetishism or superstition, as "childhood" beliefs, would disappear with the spread of rationalism and science. Yet they have not.

I do not believe that religion is a "property" of the human mind. But every culture, every group, and every individual faces common existential predicaments and situations: the fact of death, the response of grief, the understanding of tragedy, the nature of obligation, the recognition of courage. The *answers* vary, for that is the history of human culture since men live in varied ways—and they seek coherent answers which are passed along from generation to generation. The great historic religions have been the most coherent responses, for they have fused cosmology and dogma, litany and liturgy, ritual and worship into powerful emotional forms.

The answers have varied but the questions are the same. Which is why, in the end, these meanings become understandable to one another, even when they become bitterly competitive for the allegiance of the faithful. And people respond not, perhaps, to a common human nature, but to the common predicaments of fate.

In culture, particularly in religion, there is no unitary principle of change. One can distinguish between changes in the nature of institutions, and changes in the character of beliefs. This is the prime reason, it seems to me, why the concept of secularization is wrong, for it conflates two different processes. Max Weber wrote of the *entzauberung der Welt*, the "demagification" of religion in the West. It is true, I think, that religion has lost institutional authority, in the sense of commanding behavior by prohibition or permission, especially in the area of morals. Fewer persons obey the prescription of the Church. But what we have also witnessed is the multiplication of faiths, of cults and new belief systems, as a recurrent feature of life. Belief and faith, again, are responses to the existential or non-rational demands for meaning, that life beyond the mundane seeks.

Do societies "cohere"? If so, change must be uniform throughout each sphere. Yet culture changes in radically different ways from other dimensions of society. In our economy, which is instrumental, when an invention or innovation is cheaper, better, or more efficient, then, subject to cost, it will be used. Change, thus, is one of substitution and tends to be "linear." But there is no such principle of change or principle of progress in culture. There is either tradition or syncretism. Tradition guards the portals of change, especially when undergirded by religion, while syncretism, often wildly as in the age of Constantine, multiplies the icons, or as today widens the moral and aesthetic repertoire of culture. One can borrow technology more easily than culture, unless culture itself becomes purely a commodity to be used for status purposes or to emphasize generational differences.

If one looks at the "structure" of a society, the different sectors do not hang together in any consistent set of ways over time. The society is not a "totality." The economy is more or less a system, in that there is a high degree of interrelatedness so that a change in one set of variables, and their magnitudes, has a more or less determinate effect on others. The polity is not a "system," but an "order," based on consent or coercion, and framed through a legal system which is a constructed set of arrangements. One cannot plot the changing valences in the alternations of power, as if the polity were a Calder mobile whose configurations change with the winds. Stability is rare in most systems, and disruptions—revolutions or civil wars—the more common norm.[11]

And culture is even less of a system. Historically, there have been different "styles," which are sometimes related to different historical times, such as mannerism or baroque in architecture and painting. But as one sees the profligate borrowings of contemporary syncretism, or the pastiche and parody of the post-modernist scene, in what way can one say that the culture and the polity and the economy cohere, either as responses to the modes of production or the alternation of sensate and ideational systems?

At limited historical times, there has been coherence of culture and character, usually when molded by strong religious influences, as in early Catholic or Puritan societies. Or today, as in the theocratic societies of Islam, where theology pervades all dimensions of life and prescribes one's behavior from family to commerce to culture. Or, as has been attempted in totalitarian societies, such as the Soviet Union, where *partinost* enforced an ideology in culture and polity and the economy.

But in modern Western societies we see, over the past two hundred years, radical disjunctions, so that in the culture we have a principle of self-realization, or being a "whole person," while in the economy one sees specialization and segmentation, and in the polity there are the principles of representation and participation. Inevitably, these *contrary norms* create built-in conflicts, since the work-place tends to emphasize hierarchy and specialization (the emphasis on "roles"), while the culture promotes the idea of gratification and permissiveness in the name of fulfillment or liberation or emancipation. (See table 1.)

What all this means, I would argue, is that it is difficult to think of history as holistic "periods," and that in the largest sense there cannot be a "general theory" of society, or a "general theory" of social change. It also makes more problematic our ability to forecast and to design institutions.

TABLE I.1.
The Disjunctive Realms of Modern Society

Realms	Axial Principles	Axial Structures	Central Value Orientation	Relations of individual to society	Basic processes	Structural problematics
Techno Economic	Functional Rationality	Bureaucracy	Material Growth	Segmentation into roles	Specialization Substitution	Reification of institutions and persons
Polity	Equality	Representation	Government by consent of governed	Participation in decisions, individual wealth and welfare	Negotiation-conflict co-optation	Entitlements. Meritocracy. Centralization of power
Culture	Realization of Self	The Production of "meanings" and artifacts	The virtue of the "New" and "original"	The emphasis on the whole Person	Break-up of genres & distinctions. Syncretism	"The democratization of Genius." The crisis of Judgment.

V

The fundamental sociological difficulty today, if one seeks to build theory, is the radical break-up of the institutional structures of society—in the economy and the polity—because of technology and telecommunications, and the changes in scale in the arenas where all these activities are played out.

Capitalism has become world-wide, but the industrial proletariat is shrinking everywhere, increasingly disunited and unable to cohere, from the Third World to the First. Markets are no longer places but networks, which enlarge the arenas in which exchanges take place, and multiply the number of actors, while the transactions take place in "real time," thus increasing the volatility of activities. Capital can now flow freely everywhere, to take advantage in differences in exchange rates or opportunities to invest, but people cannot.

Twentieth-century industrial America was framed by three corporate behemoths. U.S. Steel was the prototypical corporation of the first third of the twentieth century, because of the role of heavy industry. General Motors was the exemplar of the middle of the century, because of mass production and mass consumption. And IBM the paragon of the final third, because of its role in manufacturing mainframe computers. Yet the dominance of all three is "broken," shattered in great measure because of newer technologies they could not control, which made vertical integration and economies of scale dysfunctional, for example, in relation to the newer minimills, the flexible production, and the downsizing of the units of production. In the 1991–1993 recession, more than 45 percent of the unemployed were white-collar workers, or double the number of the previous recession of ten years before. There is a serious problem of the unraveling of the American middle class.[12] The large change in "materials revolution" means that increasingly, technological substitution (e.g., fiber optics for copper) means a lesser dependence on raw materials, and freedom from resource sites. This poses huge economic problems for Third World areas such as Africa, which are locked into "primary-product" production and, political and ethnic difficulties apart, find themselves increasingly locked out of the world economy.

Geo-economics is driven by markets which transcend national boundaries, while geo-politics becomes more and more reactive and dependent on "managed trade" to protect its people. But increasingly there is economic integration and political fragmentation.

In the effort to manage our large and complex economies we find that command systems and direct planning do not work, and even the macroeconomic management promised by Keynesian economics cannot finetune an economy. Given the facts and fears of inflation, people grow more distrustful of the political authorities. Any science depends on regularities, and in the social world those regularities depend on trust. Yet if the political distrust rate in a country is higher than the economic discount rate, a government is in trouble. Econometric models, which most firms and governments rely on for forecasting, depend, principally, on "lagged variables," that is, the assumptions that the behavior of three months or six months before will remain stable. Yet it has been the failure of those assumptions that has gotten these models in trouble. The newer methods of the Chicago economists, such as Robert Lucas, eschew lagged variables and use "future expectations," based upon the market choices individuals and firms will make. But how stable, even, are "rational expectations"?

The structural difficulty is compounded by the new scales of activities and the mismatched scales that increasingly occur. If one looks back to the United States in the 1930s, what is striking is the largely unplanned yet intelligent response by the New Deal to a change of scale. From 1900 to 1930, we saw the development of a national economy with national corporations. But the political power was still dispersed among the states. What the New Deal did was to create national political institutions (such as an SEC for financial markets, or an NLRB for collective bargaining by unions and employers) to match those new scales. Today, in the world economy, we have few political institutions to match the scale of economic activities. And the nascent political institutions, such as in Europe, encounter fears in the several countries of a new supra-national bureau-cracy.

Our major political institutions are lodged in the nation-state. This was not a "natural" institution (though the nation itself is based, culturally, on the language and history of a people) but was an adaptive device of the past 200 years to the new scales of economic activities and communica-tion. Yet increasingly the nation-state is in trouble for, as I put it more than fifteen years ago, "the nation-state is by now too small for the big problems of life, and too big for the small problems." It is too small for the large, swirling tides of demographic flows, capital and commodity flows, and the management of monetary policy; and too big for the vari-ety and diversity of local neighborhoods and communities.

These are all "structural" problems of institutional management. If one thinks of the adequacy of sociological theory, what can one say of the more intractable questions such as the resurgence of ethnicity, tribalism, fundamentalism, and racial conflicts? How does one explain fascism, with its heady mixture of atavism, "blood," and primal tribalism with the phil-osophical sophistries of a Martin Heidegger or a Carl Schmitt, and with the advanced technology of weapony and destruction? Or of Soviet Marx-ism and Chinese Maoism, with their original utopian visions, the vast transformation of the societies "from above," and the terror instruments of the Gulag and the Cultural Revolution? Does sociological theory know of radical evil?

Let us return, finally, to the mundane, and the world of practice: the relationship, in an old phrase of Walter Lippman's, of drift to mastery. The social world is, necessarily, one of *design*, even the design of a market to provide the rules of competition and the enforcement of contract. True, we cannot have a designated economy, commanding people what to do, since the multiplicity of interests and the unintended consequences will defeat any plan. But institutions as the rules of the game—legal rules under a Constitution, procedural rules for the acquisition and sale of property, competition for positions, whether electoral or educational—all involve design. And design necessarily implies purposes as well—of an educational curriculum and the creation of a health-care system which provides access for all. The rhetoric is one of community and the common good, or the reward for individual achievement even if the rewards are high. Yet different values and different interests are at stake, and there are no *unitary* designs which can satisfy conflicting ends.

Social science, at best, is the study of the variations in behavior of clus-ters of individuals and organized groups, for every society is a plural soci-ety with individuals occupying multiple and different positions, and identities whose interests vary and change over time. What a social science can try to do in these circumstances is to identify the *salient* interests and identifications of these clusters as they express themselves in the market or in the polity.

Social policy is the effort to express and negotiate these differences into design. But in such instances, social policy is more like medicine, for it does not deal with the theoretical, though it may seek to draw from them, but with the particular. And here we turn, again, to Aristotle. As he writes: "With a view to action, experience seems in no respect inferior to art, and men of experience succeed even better than those who have theory without experience. The reason is that experience is knowledge of individuals, art of universals . . . but the physician does not cure man . . . but Callias or Socrates. . . . If, then, a man has the theory without the experience, and recognizes the universal but does not know the individual included in this, he will often fail to cure."

Science and art come to men *through* experience ("experience made art," as Polus says), but theory arises from "connected experience," and thus, to the *why* as well as the *how* of things. In this relation of practice to theory, we have the alpha and omega, the *archai* and *telos*, of our imperfect art.

Notes

1. As Marx wrote in the Author's Prefaces to *Capital* (1873), responding to the question about the different economic development of England and Germany: "Intrinsically, it is not a question of the higher or lower degree of development of the social antagonisms that result from the natural laws of capitalist production. It is a question of these tendencies working with iron necessity toward inevitable results. The country that is more developed industrially only shows the less developed the image of its future." And as Marx remarks further on, his intention was "to lay bare the economic law of motion of modern society," to demonstrate "the natural laws of its movements."

2. As sociologists we have to note that the religious form of that kind of possession is called *charisma*, which in its earliest use, in Paul's Epistles to the Corinthians, is called "speaking with tongues," or the claim that the Word has entered directly into one's body, a phenomenon we know quite commonly as "holy roller" religious revivals in the United States. (In its media mania, or political form, it is called speaking with forked tongue.)

3. Whether the term paradigm—meaning a theoretical scheme expressed in axiomatic form whose system is "closed"—has validity in physics is a reasonable debate, yet its loose and indiscriminate use in other fields, particularly the social

sciences, gives thrust to the comment of a scientist friend that the use of the term "paradigm" is in inverse relation to the knowledge of the history of physics.

4. There is a crucial intermediate step, in the thinking of Kant, for whom Reason lies not in Nature, but in Mind. As Kant writes in the *Prolegomena*: "the understanding does not derive its laws (a priori) from, but prescribes them to, nature." In other words, it is the concepts we use, such as space and time, which order our experience and our understanding of nature. But the concepts derive from Mind. Yet what if Mind itself is not transcendental but has a history? This is the fateful question that Hegel asked. For Hegel, since all epistemologies are "incomplete," all knowledge itself is "incomplete" until History has realized its form. Thus too, no transcendental or even moral judgments can be made until the end of history. Thus it is for good reason that Marxist dictators fend off criticism by saying, "History will judge."

5. This is the abstract drama played out in the *Phenomenology*. When Hegel comes to give this a manifest form in his *Philosophy of History*, the crucial point is that Reason can begin in History only "where Rationality begins to manifest itself in the actual conduct of the World's affairs." Thus, for Hegel in the *Philosophy of History*, India, though it is rich in intellectual products and literature, has no History for given "the iron bondage of distinctions" (i.e., the caste system), it is incapable of development. And Africa, which is bound to fetishism and lacks moral scruples, is incapable of escaping from its brutal natural state. Rationality, says Hegel, begins in Asia and travels from East to West, "for Europe is absolutely the end of History."

6. In this, of course Galileo was following the track of the pre-Socratics. For the earliest Ionian philosophers, such as Thales of Miletus, the search was for the fundamental substances or "essences" of things, such as air, earth, fire, or water. But with Anaximander, the turn came to the definition of their properties, such as hot, cold, wet, and dry, and the combination of these properties with one another.

7. The condition of such a theory was laid out neatly by Karl Mannheim: "A systematic or general sociology must retrace the variability of social phenomena to those basic elements and basic concepts of a more or less axiomatic character which makes society possible at all." [In "The Place of Sociology," in *Essays on Sociology and Social Psychology*, edited by Paul Keskemeti (London: 1953), p. 204. The essay was written originally in 1936 and included in the posthumous volume.]

8. S. M. Lipset, *The First New Nation* (New York: 1963), chapter 7. The quotation is on p. 249.

9. In his autobiographical essay, "A Life of Learning," printed in this volume, Robert K. Merton writes:

> My prime theoretical aversion is to any extreme sociological, economic, or psychological reductionism that claims to account uniquely and exhaustively for patterns of social behavior and social structure. . . .
>
> Although much impressed by Parsons as a master-builder of sociological theory, I found myself [as a graduate student] departing from his mode of theo-

rizing (as well as his mode of exposition). I still recall the grace with which he responded in a public forum to my mild-mannered but determined criticism of his kind of general theory. I had argued that his formulations were remote from providing a problematics and a direction for theory-oriented empirical inquiry into the observable worlds of culture and society and I went on to state the case for "theories of the middle range" as mediating between gross empiricism and grand speculative doctrines. In typically civil fashion, Parsons paid his respects to my filial impiety and agreed that we both had cause to disagree.

[I have reversed the order of the sentences, to sharpen the point. See pp. 293 and 287]

10. Hegel was writing a total history to explain the structure of the world at all levels, from the inner design or the *Begriff* (or reason) to its phenomenological manifestations:

—Thought, or consciousness, which was the paleontology of mind

—Religion, the expressions of aesthetics, morality, and myth

—Economics, or labor, which was the "objectification" of nature

—The polity, which is the unifying principle on the social level.

11. In thinking of the relation of an economy (or the "substructure" of society, in Marxist terms) to a polity, consider the case of Germany from, say, 1880 to 1980. Throughout that century there was a capitalist economy, but four radically different political systems: Wilhelmian Germany, with limited suffrage and a parliamentary system subservient to the Kaiser; the weak and divided Weimar Germany, with a president and a parliamentary system of proportional representation; Nazi Germany, with a dictator ruling by decrees; and the Federal Republic, with a strong chancellor and a strong party system of government. For the communists, fascism was the "last stage of monopoly capitalism" and, given the economic crisis of capitalism, could not last. But in all these instances, one would have to say that "politics rules, okay."

12. For a detailed analysis of these structural changes, see my essay "The Fate of IBM and the Restructuring of American Capitalism," in *Dissent*, Summer 1993. And for an anticipation of the problems of the middle class, my essay "The World and the U.S. in 2013," in *Daedalus*, Summer 1987.

Toward a Broader Vision of Inner-City Poverty

William Julius Wilson

Research findings from the Chicago Urban Poverty and Family Life Study (UPFLS) suggested that current theories of inner-city poverty ought to be reexamined.[1] We need a broader vision of the processes that affect a poor person's chances in life. This is particularly true of studies that attempt to explain the experiences of inner-city residents in terms of a single variable (such as race or social structure or culture). Many of these studies ignore important aspects of reality that have shaped and continue to shape the lives of these residents because ideological concerns compete with theoretical consideration in the selection of key explanatory variables.

Thus, those who endorse liberal ideology have tended to emphasize social structural factors, including race. By social structure I mean the ordering of social positions (or statuses) and networks of social relationships that are based on the arrangement of mutually dependent institutions (economy, polity, family, education) of society. Race, which reflects both an individual's position (in the sense of social status defined by skin color) and network of relationships in society, is a social structural variable. Many liberal explanations of social inequality invoke race to the exclusion of other structural variables. So it is appropriate to list it separately as a major variable in liberal accounts of inner-city joblessness and poverty.

On the other hand, those who endorse conservative ideology tend to stress the importance of group differences in values and attitudes in explaining the experiences and behavior of the disadvantaged. According to

this view, group differences reflect differences in culture. Culture embod-
ies the "social processes of sharing modes of behavior and outlook within
the community" (Hannerz 1969: 184). To act according to one's culture
is to follow one's inclinations as they have been developed by learning or
influence from other members of the community to which one belongs
or identifies.

The UPFLS research demonstrates that social structural factors are important for understanding joblessness and other experiences of the inner-
city poor, but that there is a good deal such factors do not explain. Although race is clearly an important variable in the social outcomes of
inner-city blacks, much ambiguity remains about the meaning and significance of race in certain situations. At the same time, cultural factors
do play a role, but any adequate explanation of inner-city joblessness and
poverty has to include other variables. Also, even social psychological
variables—a set of factors generally absent from the current debate—must
be integrated with social structural and cultural variables to provide the
most complete explanation. To repeat, we need a broader vision, a vision
that includes all the major variables and, even more important, reveals
their relative significance in determining the experiences and life chances
of inner-city residents. Such a vision guides my interpretation and integration of the UPFLS research finding presented in this chapter. It also
reflects the policy recommendations I advance.

Inner-City Black Joblessness

Black males have been maligned in recent years. The negative and worsen-
ing image of these men exacerbates racial hostility because it lends itself
to overgeneralization about the entire black community. Regardless of
the image, the economic and therefore the social position of the black
male, particularly the inner-city black male, has deteriorated rapidly in
this country. In 1940 a typical black man would be employed for 37.8
years, unemployed (seeking but not finding a job) for 4.0 years, and out
of the labor force (no longer seeking a job) for 3.2 years from age 20 to
age 65. This was almost identical with the employment experiences of the
average white man in 1940. By 1985, as he aged from 20 to 65, the average
black man would be employed for 29.4 years, unemployed for 5 years,
and out of the labor force for 11 years. His white counterpart would
experience 35.6 years of employment, 2 years of unemployment, and 7
years of being outside the labor force. The greatest declines in years of
employment for both black and white men have occurred since 1970. The

expected years of employment for the typical white man decreased from 39 to 36 from 1970 to 1985. For the typical black man, it declined even more sharply—from 36 to 29 years (Jaynes and Williams 1989). Today, over half of all African American men between the ages of 25 and 34 are either not employed or do not earn sufficient wages to support a family of four above the poverty level. Today, nearly 70 percent of young black high school dropouts (between 16 and 24 years of age) are jobless.

Historically, white women have had lower rates of employment than black women. However, since the early 1980s, these statistics have changed largely because of increased unemployment among black women (Jaynes and Williams 1989). Although employment for black married women has increased over the past two decades, black unmarried women and black female high school dropouts have experienced a precipitous drop in employment since the 1970s.

The joblessness of black men and black women is severest in the inner-city, and some areas are worse than others. In 1987 the unemployment rate of black fathers from the inner-city neighborhoods of Chicago was 5.2 percentage points higher than the rates of urban black fathers nationally. The labor-force participation rate (employed or unemployed but still seeking work) was 9 points lower, and black fathers from poor areas of Chicago were three times more likely than their white counterparts to be unemployed in 1987. Also, whereas across the nation urban black fathers up to 44 years of age had worked approximately seven out of every eight years since age 18, their inner-city counterparts in Chicago had worked an average two of every three years; those ages 18 to 24 in Chicago's inner city had worked only 39 percent of the time. Women experienced a similar pattern. Urban black mothers nationally had worked more than half the time since age 18, whereas mothers from Chicago's inner city had worked only 39 percent of the time (Tienda and Steir 1991).

Why have conditions deteriorated so dramatically for black men and increasingly for black women since the early 1980s both in absolute terms and relative to that of other ethnic groups? I shall address this question based mainly on UPFLS data on the experiences of inner-city residents in Chicago. Let me first discuss and integrate the findings on the importance of social structural variables in the next two sections.

Economic Restructuring and Inner-City Employment

In 1974, 47 percent of employed black males ages 20 to 24 held blue-collar semiskilled machine operating and skilled-craft positions that typically earned wages adequate to support a family. By 1986 that figure plummeted to 25 percent. Industrial restructuring severely curtailed the occupational advancement of the more disadvantaged urban minority members. John Kasarda's research shows that "the bottom fell out in urban industrial demand for poorly educated blacks" (1989: 35), particularly in the goods-producing industries, in Northeast and Midwest cities.

Also, a recent study reveals that although black employment in New York City increased by 104,000 in public administration and professional services—industries whose workers are more highly educated—from 1970 to 1987, black employment declined by 84,000 in durable and non-durable goods manufacturing—industries whose workers have lower levels of education (Bailey 1990). Thus, although industrial restructuring has apparently improved opportunities for the more highly educated blacks, it has reduced opportunities for the least educated blacks.

Data from the UPFLS survey show that efforts by out-of-school inner-city black men to obtain blue-collar jobs in the industries in which their fathers had been employed have been hampered by industrial restructuring. "The most common occupation reported by the cohort of respondents at ages 19 to 28 changed from operative and assembler jobs among the oldest cohorts to service jobs (waiters and janitors) among the youngest cohort" (Testa and Krogh 1989). Fifty-seven percent of Chicago's employed inner-city black fathers (aged 15 and over and without undergraduate degrees) who were born between 1950 and 1955 worked in manufacturing industries in 1974. By 1987 industrial employment for this group had fallen to 27 percent. Of those born between 1956 and 1960, 52 percent worked in manufacturing industries as late as 1978. But again, by 1987 manufacturing employment for this group fell to 28 percent (Krogh 1993). These employment changes have accompanied the loss of traditional manufacturing and other blue-collar jobs in Chicago. As a result, young black males have turned increasingly to the low-wage service sector and unskilled laboring jobs for employment, or have gone jobless. The strongly held U.S. cultural and economic belief that the son will do at least as well as the father in the labor market does not apply to many young inner-city males.

Occupational shifts in Chicago reflect these changes. Over 10,000 manufacturing establishments operated within the city limits in 1954, employing a total of 616,000, including nearly half a million blue-collar or production workers. By 1982, the number of plants had been cut by half, providing a mere 277,000 jobs and fewer than 162,000 blue-collar employees—a loss of 63 percent. This is in sharp contrast with overall growth of manufacturing employment in the country, which added almost a million production jobs since the late 1950s. Substantial cuts in trade employment accompanied the decline of the city's industrial base. Retail and wholesale lost over 120,000 jobs from 1963 to 1982. The mild growth in service employment (excluding health, financial, and social services) created an additional 57,000. But this fell far short of compensating for the collapse of Chicago's low-skilled employment pool. The economic recovery from 1983 to 1987 was not sufficient to offset the devastating employment losses that occurred during the recession-prone years of the 1970s (Wacquant and Wilson 1989).

Manufacturing industries, a major source of urban black employment, particularly in the North, are especially sensitive to a slack economy. In recent years they have had to absorb the combined shock of increased foreign competition, stagflation, and technological upgrading. This has translated into massive employment cutbacks, wage cuts, and periodic layoffs—notably in older, central-city plants. Also, nonunion employees, low-wage workers, and newly hired workers in those industries, disproportionately represented by blacks, are most adversely affected by a recession-prone economy (Wacquant and Wilson 1989). In the UPFLS both black men and black women said that more of their friends have lost jobs because of plant closings than those indicated by Mexicans and the other ethnic groups. Moreover, almost half of black fathers and 40 percent of black mothers stated that they were at high risk of losing their jobs because of plant shutdowns. Only a third of Hispanic parents, and only a quarter of white fathers and 20 percent of white mothers felt this way (Tienda and Steir 1991).

Finally, a spatial mismatch between central-city residence and the location of employment has aggravated the employment problems of inner-city blacks. Although studies based on data collected before 1970 did not show consistent or convincing effects on black employment as the result of this spatial mismatch (see, e.g., Ellwood 1986), the employment of inner-city blacks relative to suburban blacks has clearly deteriorated since then. Recent research, conducted mainly by urban and labor economists, strongly shows that the decentralization of employment is continuing and that employment in manufacturing, most of which is already suburbanized, has decreased in central cities, particularly in the Northeast and Midwest. Blacks living in central cities have less access to employment, as measured by the ratio of jobs to people and the average travel time to and from work, than do central-city whites. Moreover, unlike most other groups of workers across the urban/suburban divide, less educated central-city blacks receive lower wages than suburban blacks who have similar levels of education. And the decline in earnings of central-city blacks is related to the decentralization of employment in metropolitan areas—that is, the movement of jobs from the cities to the suburbs (Holzer 1990).

In the UPFLS, both black men and black women saw greater jobs prospects outside the city. For example, only one-third of black fathers from areas with poverty rates of at least 30 percent reported that their best opportunities for employment were in the city. Over 60 percent of whites and Puerto Ricans and 54 percent of Mexicans living in similar neighborhoods felt this way (Tienda and Steir 1991).

Getting to suburban jobs is especially problematic for the jobless individuals in the UPFLS because only 28 percent have access to an automobile. This rate falls even farther, to 18 percent, for those living in extreme poverty or ghetto areas. In the lifestyle of two-car middle-class and affluent families, commuting is accepted as a fact of life, but it occurs in a context of safe school environments for children, more available and accessible day care, and higher incomes to support mobile, away-from-home lifestyles. In a multitiered job market that requires substantial resources for participation, most inner-city minorities must rely on public transportation systems that rarely provide easy and quick access to suburban locations. Blacks clearly see a spatial mismatch of jobs.

An economic structural argument is useful in helping to explain the loss of black and white jobs in manufacturing and changes in employment opportunities including spatial changes. But data from the UPFLS reveal that inner-city Mexicans have greater success than inner-city blacks in holding on to manufacturing jobs or in finding employment more quickly even though they have considerably less formal education. Moreover, inner-city whites who have also lost manufacturing jobs are more successful than blacks in finding other employment.[2] These outcomes *cannot* be accounted for by an economic structural argument. However, there are other social structural variables that pertain to neighborhoods, social networks, and households that have yet to be considered. Such variables are especially important in accounting for differences in the employment experiences of inner-city women.

The Relevance of Neighborhoods, Social Networks, and Households

Seven out of eight people residing in ghettos in metropolitan areas in 1990 were minority group members, most of them African Americans. But the figure also includes a significant number of Hispanics. This is not a monolithic socioeconomic group, however; the term embraces all the Spanish-speaking cultures of the New World, which vary broadly. For example, there are significant differences in the socioeconomic status of Mexicans and Puerto Ricans. The latter are largely concentrated in New York City and more closely resemble African Americans than Mexicans in terms of poverty concentration.

If comparisons are drawn only between the two largest minority groups in the United States—African Americans and Mexicans—some significant neighborhood differences can be noted. The Mexicans who reside in inner-city neighborhoods tend to be first-generation immigrants (i.e., they were not born in the United States). In the UPFLS, 85 percent of the inner-city Mexican random sample were first-generation immigrants. Nonetheless, their neighborhoods were on average less poor than those of Chicago's inner-city African American population. In 1980, 20.5 percent of blacks but only 7.9 percent of all Mexican immigrants lived in tracts with poverty rates of 30 to 39 percent. And over one-fifth (21.6 percent) of blacks—but only 2.1 percent of the Mexican immigrant population—resided in extreme poverty census tracts, those with poverty rates of 40 percent or more (Van Haitsma 1992).

Thus, whereas inner-city African Americans are overrepresented in areas of high to extremely high poverty concentration, inner-city Mexican immigrants are more likely to live in areas of moderate poverty (i.e., areas with poverty rates of 20 to 29 percent). More important, the Mexican-immigrant neighborhoods in the inner city feature lower levels of joblessness and higher levels of social organization than comparable African American neighborhoods. As Martha Van Haitsma, a member of the UPFLS ethnographic research team, puts it:

> Mexican immigrants living in Chicago poverty areas may well be residents of crowded and dilapidated buildings, but they are surrounded by small local businesses, many of them owned and operated by persons of Mexican origin, and by Mexican-targeted social service agencies. Poverty-tract blacks are more isolated from jobs and from employed neighbors than are Mexican immigrants. (1992: 31)

As time has passed, inner-city black neighborhoods have experienced increasing problems of social organization. For example, in the neighborhood of Woodlawn, located on the South Side of Chicago, there were over eight hundred commercial and industrial establishments in 1950. Today, it is estimated that only about a hundred are left, many of them represented by "tiny catering places, barber shops, and thrift stores with no more than one or two employees." As Loïc Wacquant, a member of the UPFLS research team, put it:

> The once-lively streets—residents remember a time, not so long ago, when crowds were so dense at rush hour that one had to elbow one's way to the

train station—now have the appearance of an empty, bombed-out war zone. The commercial strip has been reduced to a long tunnel of charred stores, vacant lots littered with broken glass and garbage, and dilapidated buildings left to rot in the shadow of the elevated train line. At the corner of Sixty-Third Street and Cottage Grove Avenue, the handful of remaining establishments that struggle to survive are huddled behind wrought-iron bars. . . . The only enterprises that seem to be thriving are liquor stores and currency exchanges, these "banks of the poor" where one can cash checks, pay bills and buy money orders for a fee.

Like many other inner-city neighborhoods of Chicago, Woodlawn first experienced a large outmigration of whites. A substantial exodus of black working- and middle-class families followed. These changes significantly altered the class structure of the neighborhood. I have advanced the theoretical argument that the outmigration of higher-income families increased the social isolation of inner-city neighborhoods (Wilson 1987). Social isolation deprives residents of certain inner-city neighborhoods not only of resources and conventional role models, whose former presence buffered the effects of neighborhood joblessness, but also of cultural learning from mainstream social networks that facilitates social and economic advancement in the modern industrial society.

Poor individuals with similar educational and occupational skills confront different risks of joblessness, including long-term joblessness, depending on the neighborhoods in which they reside, the formal and informal networks to which they have access, and the families or households to which they belong. Also, a social context that includes poor schools, inadequate job information networks, and a lack of legitimate employment opportunities creates two major problems—it gives rise to weak labor-force attachment, and it increases the probability that individuals will be constrained to rely on public assistance or seek income derived from illegal or deviant activities. This further weakens their attachment to the legitimate labor market.

Data from the UPFLS reveal that the nonworking poor black men and women "were consistently less likely to participate in local institutions and have mainstream friends [i.e., friends who are working, have some college education, and are married] than people in other classes" and ethnic groups (Fernandez and Harris 1991: 18). However, there are noticeable gender differences in the structure of interpersonal relations among the nonworking poor blacks in the inner-city neighborhoods of Chicago. Jobless black females (mostly mothers on welfare) were significantly more isolated from mainstream individuals and families than jobless black males. Welfare mothers interacted with other welfare mothers. "It is not simply poverty that isolates women, but being nonworking further increases isolation. This lends some credence to the imagery of AFDC [Aid to Families with Dependent Children] women being cut off from others" (Fernandez and Harris 1991: 18). Overall, the personal friendship network of blacks (both male and female) is more insular and less likely than those of the Mexican immigrants to have at least one employed close friend.

This form of social isolation operates in the inner-city black neighborhood through the lack of access to resources provided by stable working residents. Such resources include informal job networks. Analysis of the UPFLS ethnographic data reveals that "social contacts were a useful means of gaining informal work to help make ends meet but far less often successful in helping with steady employment; networks existed but largely lacked the capacity to help lift residents into the formal labor market" (Pedder 1991: 37).

Moreover, UPFLS data on job search behavior reveal that black men and women in the inner city are less likely than Mexican immigrants to report that they received help from a friend or relative in obtaining their current job. Recognizing the importance of the informal job network system, a 35-year-old welfare mother of two children in the UPFLS states:

A lot of people get good jobs because they know friends, and they work there. If you know somebody that's been working in an established company for a long time, and they tell you to come in and fill an application, you can get a job. It always pay to know somebody.

However, the job search strategies black inner-city residents most frequently reported using were filling out an application at a place of business and seeking assistance at an employment office (Laseter 1994). Also, both black men and women more often use the public transit system to get to and from work than Mexicans who rely more heavily on carpooling, itself an important network activity (Van Haitsma 1991).

In short, social isolation not only deprives inner-city residents of conventional role models, whose strong presence once buffered the effects of neighborhood joblessness, but also of the social resources (including social contacts) provided by mainstream social networks that facilitate social and economic advancement in modern industrial society.

Just as there are differences in neighborhoods and social networks between blacks and Mexicans, so too are there household differences. Black women face far greater challenges in the household. Black mothers in the inner city are far more likely to reside in households where no other adults are present and therefore face greater challenges in raising children. Whereas 44 percent of the black women living with their children in Chicago's inner city have no other adults in the household, only 6.5 percent of comparable Mexican women are the sole adults in their household. Also, inner-city black women whose children are under 12 years of age are eight times more likely than comparable Mexican women to live in a single-adult household (Van Haitsma 1991).

Analyzing data from the UPFLS, Van Haitsma found that "network differences translate into childcare differences. Mexican women with young children are significantly more likely than their black counterparts to have regular childcare provided by a friend or relative" (1991: 19). The high proportion of two-adult Mexican households with working fathers, particularly among the immigrant Mexicans, may be an important factor in the mother's greater access to network child care.

Also, the high percentage of black mothers who live with young children in a single-adult household is associated with problems of labor-force attachment. If a single mother in Chicago's inner city lives in a co-residential household—that is, one that includes at least one other adult—and receives informal child support, she significantly improves her chances of entering the labor force. Among the inner-city mothers who were not receiving AFDC, those who lived in a co-residential household and received informal child care had a 90 percent probability of labor-force activity. On the other hand, those who maintained sole-adult households and did not receive informal child care had only a 60 percent probability of working. Of the 12 percent of the inner-city women on AFDC who candidly reported that they worked at least part-time—probably in the informal economy—those who lived in a co-residential household and received informal child care were more than five times as likely to work as were those wo lived in single households and did not receive informal child care (Lundgren-Gaveras, 1991).

I noted in the previous section that recent economic structural changes have clearly had an adverse effect on the employment experiences of inner-city blacks, but that a purely economic structural explanation for black economic woes is not sufficient. "Were pure market forces responsible for the observed differences in employment statuses," Marta Tienda and Haya Steir argued, "Latinos should experience the highest levels of labor market hardship in Chicago, and particularly those of Mexican origin who, in addition to very low levels of education, often lack adequate language skills owing to the recency of their migration to the United States" (1991: 27).

The discussion in this section takes us beyond a consideration of pure market forces. They show that inner-city blacks reside in neighborhoods—and are embedded in social networks and households—that are not as conducive to employment as are the neighborhoods, networks, and households of the immigrant Mexicans. What has not been addressed is how the interpretation of these ethnic differences by mainstream society affects decisions about hiring, decisions that can reinforce or strengthen the economic marginality of inner-city blacks, including their high rate of joblessness.

The Meaning and Significance of Race

As one inner-city manufacturer from our study put it:

When we hear other employers talk, they'll go after primarily the Hispanic and Oriental first, those two, and, I'll qualify that even further, the Mexican Hispanic, and any Oriental, and after that, that's pretty much it, that's pretty much where they like to draw the line, right there.

Interviews of a representative sample of Chicago-area employers by our UPFLS research team show that many consider inner-city blacks—especially young black males—to be uneducated, unstable, uncooperative, and dishonest. The survey featured face-to-face interviews with employers representing 179 firms in the city of Chicago and in surrounding Cook County. The sample is representative of the distribution of employment by industry and firm size in the county. The survey included a number of open-ended questions on employer perception of inner-city workers that yielded views concerning job skills, basic skills, work ethic, dependability, attitudes, and interpersonal skills.[3] Of the 170 employers who provided comments on one or more of these traits, 126 (or 74 percent) expressed views of inner-city blacks that were coded as "negative." That is, they expressed views (whether in terms of environmental or neighborhood influences, family influences, or personal characteristics) that suggest that inner-city black workers—especially black males—bring to the workplace traits, including level of training and education, that negatively affect their job performances. For example, a suburban drug store manager said:

It's unfortunate but in my business I think overall [black men] tend to be known to be dishonest. I think that's too bad but that's the image they have. (Interviewer: So you think it's an image problem?) Yeah, a dishonest—an image problem of being dishonest men and lazy. They're known to be lazy. They are (he laughs). I hate to tell you, but. It's all an image though. Whether they are or not, I don't know, but it's an image that is perceived. (Interviewer: I see. How do you think that image was developed?) Go look in the jails (he laughs).

The employer survey data reveal that racial stereotyping is greater among those Chicago employers with lower proportions of blacks in their workforce, especially the blue-collar employers who tend to stress the importance of unobservable qualities such as work attitudes (Neckerman and Kirschenman 1991). As one respondent states: "The black work ethic. There's no work ethic. At least at the unskilled. I'm sure with the skilled . . . as you go up, it's a lot different." Another employer remarked:

I've never seen any of these [black] guys read anything outside a comic book. These Mexicans are sitting here reading novels constantly, even though they are in Spanish. These [black] guys will sit and watch cartoons while the other guys are busy reading. To me that shows laziness. No desire to upgrade yourself.

Given such attitudes, the lack of black access to the informal job networks is a particular problem for black males, as revealed in the following comments by an employer:

All of a sudden, they take a look at a guy, and unless he's got an in, the reason why I hired this black kid the last time is 'cause my neighbor said to me, yeah I used him for a few [days], he's good, and I said, you know what, I'm going to take a chance. But it was a recommendation. But other than that, I've got a walk-in, and, who knows? And I think that for the most part, a guy sees a black man, he's a bit hesitant, because I don't know.

How and why have such attitudes developed? The success that black men had in obtaining manufacturing and other blue-collar jobs in previous years suggests that these strong negative views have only recently emerged. UPFLS data show that of the employed men in the 1941–55 age cohort from poor Chicago neighborhoods, the proportion of blacks in manufacturing and construction was only slightly below that of whites and exceeded that of Hispanics in 1974. Also the proportion from the 1956–69 birth cohort was considerably above that of Puerto Ricans and whites and only slightly below that of Mexicans in 1978 (Krogh 1993).

Although the employers' perceptions of inner-city workers make it difficult for low-income blacks to find employment, it is interesting to consider that there is one area where the views of employers and many inner-city residents converge—namely in their attitudes toward inner-city black males. Inner-city residents are aware of the problems of male joblessness in their neighborhoods. For example, more than half the black UPFLS survey respondents from neighborhoods with poverty rates of at least 40 percent feel that very few or none of the men in their neighborhood were working steadily. More than one-third of the respondents from neighborhoods with poverty rates of at least 30 percent expressed that view as well. Forty percent of the black respondents in all neighborhoods in the UPFLS feel that the number of men with jobs has steadily decreased over the past ten years. However, responses to the open-ended questions in our Social Opportunity Survey and data from our ethnographic field interviews reveal a consistent pattern of negative views on inner-city black males, especially young black males.

Some provide explanations that acknowledged the constraints black men face. An employed 25-year-old unmarried father of one child from North Lawndale states:

I know a lot of guys that're my age, that don't work and I know some that work temporary, but wanna work, they just can't get the jobs. You know, they got a high school diploma and that . . . but the thing is, these jobs always say: "Not enough experience." How can you get some experience if you never had a chance to get any experience?

Others, however, express views that echo those of the employers. For example, a 30-year-old married father of three children who lives in North Lawndale and works the night shift in a factory states:

I say about 65 percent—of black males, I say, don't wanna work, and when I say don't wanna work I say don't wanna work hard—they want a real easy job, making big bucks—See? And, and—when you start talking about hard labor and earning your money with sweat or just once in a while you gotta put out a little bit—you know, that extra effort, I don't, I don't think the guys really wanna do that. And sometimes it comes from, really, not having a, a steady job or, really, not being out in the work field and just been sittin' back, being comfortable all the time and hanging out.

A 35-year-old welfare mother of eight children from the Englewood neighborhood on the South Side agrees.

Well, I mean, see you got all these dudes around here, they don't even work, they don't even try, they don't wanna work. You know what I mean, I wanna work, but I can't work. Then you got people here that, in this neighborhood, can get up and do somethin', they just don't wanna do nothin'—they really don't.

The deterioration of the socioeconomic status of black men may be associated with increases in the negative perceptions of both the employ-ers and the inner-city residents. Are these perceptions merely stereotypi-cal or do they have any basis in fact? Data from the UPFLS survey show that variables that measure differences in social context (neighborhoods, social networks, and households) accounted for substantially more of the gap in the employment rates of black and Mexican men than did variables that measure individual attitudes (Van Haitsma 1991). Also, data from the survey reveal that jobless black men have a lower "reservation wage" than the jobless men of the other ethnic groups. They were willing to work for less than $6.00 per hour, whereas Mexican and Puerto Rican jobless men expected $6.20 and $7.20, respectively, as a condition for working; white men, on the other hand, expected over $9.00 per hour (Tienda and Steir 1991). This would cast some doubt on the characterization of black inner-city men as wanting "something for nothing" of holding out for high pay.

But surveys are not the best way to get at underlying attitudes and values. Accordingly, to gain a better grasp of the cultural issues, I exam-ined the UPFLS ethnographic research that involved establishing long-term contacts and interviews with residents from several neighborhoods. Richard Taub, a member of our UPFLS research team, points out that

> Anybody who studies subgroups within the American population knows that there are cultural patterns which are distinctive to the subgroups and which have consequences for social outcomes. The challenge for those con-cerned about poverty and cultural variation is to link cultural arrangements to larger structural realities and to understand the interaction between the consequences of one's structural position on the one hand and pattern group behavior on the other. It is important to understand that the process works both ways. Cultures are forged in part on the basis of adaptation to both structural and material environments. (Taub 1991: 1)

Analysis of the ethnographic data reveals identifiable and consistent patterns of inner-city ethnic group attitudes and beliefs. The data, system-atically analyzed by Taub, reveal that the black men are more hostile than the Mexican men about the low-paying jobs they hold, less willing to be flexible in taking assignments or tasks not considered part of their job, and less willing to work as hard for the same low wages. These contrasts are sharp because many Mexicans interviewed are recent immigrants.

"Immigrants, particularly Third World immigrants," will often "tolerate harsher conditions, lower pay, fewer upward trajectories, and other job-related characteristics that deter native workers, and thereby exhibit a better 'work ethic' than others" (Aponte 1991: 41). The ethnographic data from the UPFLS suggest that the Mexican immigrants are harder workers because they "come from areas of intense poverty and that even boring, hard, dead-end jobs look, by contrast, good to them" (Taub 1991: 14). They also fear being deported if they did not find employment.

It should be emphasized, once again, that the comparison between blacks and Mexicans in the UPFLS ethnographic sample are sharp because most of the Mexicans in our sample were recent immigrants. Since our sample was largely drawn from poverty areas, it includes a disproportionate number of immigrants who tend to settle initially in such areas. As previous research has consistently shown, migrants who leave a poorer economy for a more developed economy in hopes of improving their standard of living initially tend to accept, willingly, the kinds of employment that the indigenous workers detest or have come to reject. Accordingly, it is reasonable to hypothesize that the more "Americanized" they become, the less willing they will be to accept menial low-wage and hazardous jobs.

The inner-city black men, on the other hand, complained that they get assigned the heaviest or dirtiest work on the job, are overworked, and are paid less than nonblacks. They strongly feel that they are victims of discrimination. "The Mexican American men also report that they feel exploited," states Taub, "but somehow that comes with the territory." Taub argues that the inner-city black men have a greater sense of "honor" and often see the work, pay, and treatment from bosses as insulting and degrading. Accordingly, a heightened sensitivity to exploitation increases anger and a tendency to "just walk off the job" (Taub 1991: 14).

One cannot understand these attitudes, and how they developed, without considering the growing exclusion of black men from higher-paying blue-collar jobs in manufacturing and other industries and their increasing confinement to low-paying service laboring jobs. Many low-paying jobs have predictably low retention rates. For example, one of the respondents in the UPFLS employer survey reported turnover rates that exceeded 50 percent in his firm. When asked if he had considered doing anything about this problem, the employer acknowledged a rational decision to tolerate a high turnover rather than increasing the starting salary and improving working conditions to attract higher-caliber workers:

"Our practice has been that we'll keep hiring and, hopefully, one or two of them are going to wind up being good" (Neckerman 1991: 7).

"This employer, and others like him, can afford such high turnover because the work is simple and can be taught in a couple of days," states Kathryn Neckerman. "On average, jobs paying under $5.00 or $6.00 an hour were characterized by high quit rates. In higher-paying jobs, by contrast, the proportion of employees resigning fell to less than 20 percent per year" (1991: 7). Yet UPFLS data show that the number of inner-city black males in the higher-paying positions has sharply declined. Increasingly displaced from manufacturing industries, their options are more confined to low-paying service work. Annual turnover rates of 50 to 100 percent are common in low-skilled service jobs in Chicago, regardless of the race or ethnicity of the employees (Neckerman 1991).

Thus the attitudes that many inner-city black males express about their jobs and job prospects reflect their plummeting position in a changing labor market. The more they complain and manifest their dissatisfaction, the less desirable they seem to employers. They therefore experience greater rejection when they seek employment and clash more often with supervisors when they do secure employment. For all these reasons, as Taub (1991) emphasizes, it is important to link cultural traits and structural realities.

Residence in highly concentrated poverty neighborhoods aggravates the weak labor-force attachment of black males. The absence of effective informal job networks and the availability of many illegal activities increase nonmainstream behavior such as hustling. As Sharon Hicks-Bartlett, another member of the UPFLS research team, points out, "Hustling is making money by doing whatever is necessary to survive or simply make ends meet. It can be legal or extra-legal work and may transpire in the formal or informal economy. While both men and women hustle, men are more conspicuous in the illegal arena of hustling" (1991: 33).

In a review of the research literature on the experiences of black men in the labor market, Philip Moss and Christopher Tilly point out that criminal activity in urban areas has become more attractive because of the disappearance of legitimate jobs. They point to a study in Boston that showed that while "black youth in Boston were evenly split on whether they could make more money in a straight job or on the street, by 1989 a three-to-one majority of young black people expressed the opinion that they could make more on the street" (Moss and Tilly 1991: 7).

The restructuring of the economy will continue to compound the negative effects of the perceptions of inner-city black males. Because of the increasing shift away from manufacturing and toward service industries, employers have a greater need for workers who can effectively serve and relate to the consumer. As revealed in the comments by the employers, inner-city black men are not perceived to have the character, traits, and personality to fulfill this role.

But the restructuring of the urban economy could also have long-term consequences for inner-city black women. Neckerman (1991) insightfully points out that a change in work cultures accompanied the transformation of the economy, resulting in a mismatch between the old and new ways of succeeding in the labor market. In other words, there is a growing difference between the practices of blue-collar and service employers and the practices of white-collar employers. This mismatch is important in understanding the labor market success of inner-city workers.

Low-skilled individuals from the inner city tend to be the children of blue-collar workers or service workers, and their work experience is thus largely confined to blue-collar or service jobs. What happens "when employees socialized to approach jobs and careers in ways that make sense in a blue-collar or service context enter the white-collar world" (Neckerman 1991: 27)? The employer interviews suggest that workers from blue-collar or service settings seek positions that carry high entry-level salaries, that provide all the necessary training on the job, and that grant privileges and promotion by both seniority and performance. But, in a white-collar setting, inner-city workers face entry-level positions that require more and continuous training and employers who are looking for energetic, intelligent people with good language skills. Promotions in this environment seldom depend on seniority. Accordingly, "their advancement may depend on fairly subtle standards of evaluation, and on behavior that is irrelevant or even negatively sanctioned in the blue-collar and service settings." Interviews with inner-city workers revealed that most recognize the changing nature of the labor market and that a greater premium is placed on education and training for success, but many "did indeed espouse blue-collar ways of getting ahead" (Neckerman 1991: 27).

In summary, the issue of race in the labor market cannot simply be reduced to discrimination. Although our data suggest that inner-city blacks, especially males, are experiencing increasing problems in the labor market, the reasons include a complex web of interrelated factors including those that are race neutral.

The loss of traditional manufacturing and other blue-collar jobs in Chicago resulted in increased joblessness among inner-city black males and a concentration in low-wage, high-turnover laborer and service sector jobs. Embedded in ghetto neighborhoods, social networks, and households that are not conducive to employment, inner-city black males fall farther behind their white and Hispanic counterparts, especially when the labor market is slack. Hispanics "continue to funnel into manufacturing because employers prefer Hispanics over blacks and they like to hire by referrals from current employees, which Hispanics can readily furnish, being already embedded in migration networks" (Krogh 1991: 12). Inner-city black men grow bitter and resentful of their employment prospects and often manifest or express these feelings in their harsh, dehumanizing, low-wage work settings.

Their attitudes and actions, combined with erratic work histories in high-turnover jobs, create the widely shared perception that they are undesirable workers. The perception then becomes the basis for negative hiring decisions by employers that increase sharply when the economy is weak. The rejection of inner-city black male workers gradually grows over the long term not only because employers are turning more to the expanding immigrant and female labor force, but also because the number of jobs that require contact with the public continues to climb.

The position of inner-city black women in the labor market is also problematic. Their high degree of social isolation in impoverished neighborhoods reduces their employment prospects. Although Chicago employers consider them more acceptable as workers than the inner-city black men, their social isolation is likely to strengthen involvement in a work culture that has few supports for a move into white-collar employment. Also, impoverished neighborhoods and weak network and household supports decrease their ability to develop language and other job-related skills necessary in an economy that increasingly rewards employees who can work and communicate effectively with the public.

Historic segregation in urban ghettos created the neighborhoods, households, and networks that handicap inner-city blacks. The significance of segregation for inner-city blacks has been increased because of the outmigration of higher-income working-and middle-class families from the most impoverished neighborhoods. All of these changes have had an effect on family formation, a subject to which I now turn.

The Effects of Race, Social Structure, and Culture on the Inner-City Black Family

Donna Franklin and Susan Smith (1991) present UPFLS data showing that never-married mothers from Chicago poverty areas tend to have lower rates of labor-force participation, experience longer periods of time on welfare, and live in more highly concentrated poverty neighborhoods.

"This suggests," they argue, "that the circumstances of the respondent's childhood probably also predispose her to early childbearing and, in turn, effect her economic well-being as an adult" (23). Franklin and Smith point out that it is often assumed that if a young woman plays by the rules of conventional middle-class society by staying in school and delaying parenting, she will significantly improve her chances for future economic success.

Yet their analysis of the data from the UPFLS survey suggests that if she is black and resides in the inner-city ghetto, "her decision to delay parenting may have only minuscule effect on her economic well-being" (25). Why? Because the strongest predictor of whether she will emerge from poverty is the economic stability of the man she marries. Unlike white and Hispanic women from Chicago poverty areas, the sharp decline in traditional labor market opportunities and the limited number of marriageable males severely circumscribe the options of the inner-city black mother. Franklin and Smith argue that the high percentage of inner-city black mothers who are on welfare, have never worked, and have never married reflect these conditions.

Consistent with the conclusions advanced by Franklin and Smith, data presented by Mark Testa (1991), a member of the UPFLS research team, estimate that only 6 percent of the single, inner-city expectant black fathers marry during the prenatal period (from conception to birth)—the period popularly dubbed the "shotgun wedding" interval. Testa furthermore found, after taking class background and economic status into account, that inner-city non-Hispanic white and Mexican single fathers are respectively 2.5 and 3 times more likely to marry one year after the birth of their first child than are their black American counterparts. This pattern of black fathers' separation from the family in the inner-city neighborhoods of Chicago, although extreme, represents a historic trend across the nation.

"Black men born in the early 1940s were twice as likely as [black] men born in the late 1950s to wed at a given age, and the rate has continued to fall for the post-baby boom cohort," reports Testa. "With fewer black men marrying prior to the women's pregnancy, the proportion of infants conceived in marriage dropped over time. The result is that in spite of near constant rates of nonmarital fertility [i.e., the number of pregnancies per 1,000 unmarried women], the out-of-wedlock birth ratio among African-Americans surged past 50 percent in the 1980s" (1991: 27).

Both nationally and in Chicago,'s inner city, non-Hispanic whites and Mexicans are much more likely than blacks to marry after the birth of their first child. In Chicago, for example, after class background and economic status are considered, inner-city Mexican and non-Hispanic white fathers are 180 percent more likely to marry after the birth of their first child than their black American counterparts. The notable exception is Puerto Rican fathers, who exhibit the same national and Chicago postpartum marriage rates as blacks even after class background and economic status are considered.

Analyzing survey data from the UPFLS, Testa found that in both the national and Chicago samples, if a male is employed the likelihood of marriage after the child's conception increases by more than 50 percent. If he is a high school graduate the rate of postpartum marriage also rises by between 40 and 60 percent. "But neither employment nor education differences between successive cohorts of black males can account fully for the secular decline in marriage rates," states Testa. In Chicago's inner city, African American men born during or immediately after World War II were more than 2.5 times more likely to marry after the conception of their child, regardless of their economic and educational background, than black men born in the late 1950s who became fathers at a similar age (Testa 1991). Marriage rates for inner-city black men after this period have continued to decline.

Although male employment status and marriage are strongly related, the growing male joblessness accounts for only a portion of the increase in levels of marital parenthood. Testa therefore hypothesizes that "variation in the moral evaluations that different sociocultural groups attach to premarital sex, out-of-wedlock pregnancy, and nonmarital parenthood affects the importance of economic considerations in a person's decision to marry" (Testa (1991: 16). The stronger the norms against premarital sex, out-of-wedlock pregnancy, and nonmarital parenthood, the less that economic considerations affect decisions to marry.

As I pointed out above, there are significant differences among inner-city blacks, whites, and Hispanics in the rate of nonmarital pregnancy and the timing of marriage relative to pregnancy (i.e., neonatal or postpartum marriage). Some of these differences can be accounted for by the higher levels of joblessness and concentrated poverty in the black community. But even when ethnic group variations in work activity, poverty concentration, education, and family structure are taken into account, significant differences still remain between inner-city blacks and the other groups, especially the Mexicans. Accordingly, it is reasonable to consider whether cultural variables should be included among the interrelated factors that account for these differences.

A brief comparison between inner-city blacks and inner-city Mexicans, many of whom are immigrants, and their perspectives on the family, provides some evidence for these cultural differences. Taub points out that marriage and family ties are subjects of "frequent and intense discourse" among Mexican immigrants. Mexicans come to the United States with a clear conception of a traditional family unit that features men as bread-winners. Although extramarital affairs are tolerated for men, "a pregnant, unmarried woman is a source of opprobrium, anguish, or great concern" (Taub 1991: 6). Pressure to get married is applied by the kin of both parents.

The family norms and behavior in inner-city black neighborhoods contrast sharply. The husband-wife relationship is only weakly supported. UPFLS ethnographic data reveal that the relationships between inner-city black men and women, whether in a marital or nonmarital situation, tend to be fractious and antagonistic. Both sexes typically avoid intense and meaningful relationships. Inner-city black women routinely indicate that they distrust men and feel strongly that black men lack dedication to their families. They argue that black males are hopeless as either husbands or fathers and that more of their time is spent on the streets than at home. The ethnographic data reveal that both inner-city black males and females believe that since most marriages will eventually break up and since marriages no longer represent meaningful relationships, it is better to avoid the entanglements of wedlock altogether. In other words, it is better to remain free than be trapped in an unhappy formal relationship. Men and women are extremely suspicious of each other and their concerns range from the degree of financial commitment to fidelity. For all these reasons, they often state they do not want to get married until they are sure it is going to work out.

Changing patterns of family formation are not limited to the inner-city black community. They represent extreme versions of the current trends in the society. A commitment to traditional husband-wife families and the stigma associated with out-of-wedlock births, separation, and divorce have waned significant in the United States. "The labor market conditions which sustained the 'male breadwinner' family have all but vanished, and have always been tenuous among blacks" (Breslau 1991: 11). This has gradually led to the creation of a new set of orientations that places less value on marriage and rejects the dominance of men as a standard for a successful husband-wife family.

The major argument advanced in this section is that inner-city black single parents, unlike their Mexican-immigrant counterparts, feel little pressure to commit to a marriage. They emphasize the importance of having secure jobs and financial security before seriously considering matrimony, attitudes that cannot be fully understood without considering the interaction between material and cultural constraints. It is one thing to note the differences in the cultural orientation between blacks and Mexicans, it is quite another thing to explain these differences.

The intensity of the commitment to the marital bond among Mexican immigrants will very likely decline the longer they remain in the United States and are exposed to U.S. norms, patterns of behavior, and changing opportunity structures for men and women. Nonetheless, cultural arrangements reflect structural realities. In comparison with African Americans, Mexican immigrants have a stronger attachment to the labor force, and stronger households, networks, and neighborhoods. Therefore, a real convergence between inner-city blacks and Mexicans in attitudes toward the family and toward family formation in the near future is unlikely.

Conclusion and Implications for Public Policy

At the beginning of this chapter I indicated the need for a broader vision to understand the complex processes that shape the experiences of groups in poverty. The UPFLS findings provide the basis for such a vision because they allow the integration or social structural, racial, and cultural variables. I demonstrated this point by addressing the question of why conditions have deteriorated so dramatically for black men and increasingly for black women since the early 1980s both in absolute terms and relative to that of other ethnic groups.

The findings from the UPFLS reveal that industrial restructuring has had a devastating effect on black males. Also, black men have been more adversely affected by these economic changes than either white, Mexican, or Puerto Rican men. Whereas black men were pushed out of manufacturing into personal service jobs, laboring jobs, and joblessness, Mexicans and Puerto Rican men held on to their manufacturing jobs more often and for longer periods of time. Whites were also forced out of manufacturing, but were more successful than blacks in obtaining higher-paying skilled trade and nonlaboring jobs. Swings in the business cycle also hit black men harder than white men, and black workers, male and female, seem to experience a greater spatial mismatch of jobs.

There are several reasons why blacks sustained greater losses from these economic changes. They reside in neighborhoods—and are embedded in social networks and households—that are less conducive to employment than those of the other ethnic groups. As these factors further weaken their ability to compete with the other groups they appear less attractive to employers whose views on inner-city black workers, especially males, tend to be negative. Black men's responses to declining employment prospects frequently served to reinforce the perception that they present special problems at work. Their exclusion from the labor market grows over the long term not only because employers are able to draw from the expanding immigrant and female labor-force pools, but also because a disproportionate number of new jobs require contact with the public, which is problematic for inner-city black men who are often perceived to be threatening.

Inner-city black women, although more acceptable to employers than black men, also experience problems in the labor market. Their high degree of social isolation in impoverished neighborhoods and restricted social networks strengthens involvement in a work culture more suitable to blue-collar and service work than to the expanding area of white-collar employment.

Finally, the UPFLS data show a strong relationship between male employment status and marriage. However, the data also suggest that the stronger the norms against premarital sex, out-of-wedlock pregnancy, and single parenthood, the less that economic considerations affect decisions to marry. UPFLS ethnographic data reveal that inner-city black single parents in Chicago feel little pressure to marry. They emphasize the importance of having secure jobs and financial security before seriously considering matrimony. Moreover, they have little reason to contemplate seriously the consequences of single parenthood because their prospects for social and economic mobility are severely limited whether they are married or not.

These responses represent a linkage between new structural realities, changing norms, and evolving cultural patterns. The new structural realities are seen in the diminishing employment opportunities for low-skilled workers. As employment prospects recede, the foundations for stable relationships become weaker over time. More permanent relationships such as marriage give way to temporary liaisons that result in broken relationships, out-of-wedlock pregnancies and births, and to a lesser extent, separation and divorce. The changing norms concerning marriage in the larger society reinforce the movement toward temporary liaisons in the inner city, and therefore economic considerations in marital decisions take on even greater weight. The evolving cultural patterns are seen in the sharing of negative outlooks toward marriage and toward the relationships between males and females in the inner city, outlooks that are developed in and influenced by an environment plagued by persistent joblessness. This combination of factors has increased out-of-wedlock births, weakened the family structure, expanded the welfare rolls, and as a result, caused poor inner-city blacks to be even more disconnected from the job market and discouraged about their role in the labor force.

The findings from the UPFLS suggest the need for public policies guided by a vision sufficiently broad to address simultaneously the complex and interrelated issues of social structure, race, and culture. From my perspective the most important social structural variable is to have a strong and competitive economy in which, as Michael Harrington used to put it, employers are looking for workers rather than workers looking for employers. This would certainly improve the situation of the groups most discriminated against in the labor market. I say this because in slack labor markets—labor markets with high unemployment—employers are—and indeed, can afford to be—more selective in recruiting and in granting promotions. They overemphasize job prerequisites and exaggerate the value of experience. In such an economic climate, disadvantaged minorities suffer disproportionately and the level of employer discrimination rises. In contrast, in a tight labor market, job vacancies are numerous, unemployment is of short duration, and wages are higher. Moreover, in a tight labor market the labor force expands because increased job opportunities not only reduce unemployment but also draw into the labor force those workers who, in periods when the labor market is slack, respond to fading job prospects by dropping out of the labor force altogether. Accordingly, in a tight labor market the status of all workers—including disadvantaged minorities—improves because of lower unemployment, higher wages, and better jobs (Tobin 1965).

The economic recovery during the first half of the 1990s lowered the unemployment rates among blacks in general. For the first time in more than two decades, the unemployment rate for African Americans dipped below 10 percent in December 1994. Indeed, "the unemployment rate for black adults dropped faster in 1994 than it did for white adults" (Holmes 1995: A8). This was in part due to a brief growth of manufacturing jobs. By contrast, the economy saw a slight decrease in manufacturing jobs during the economic recovery period in the late 1980s and more than 1.5 million positions disappeared from January 1989 to September 1993. However, 301,000 manufacturing jobs were created during the next sixteen months, significantly benefiting black workers who are heavily concentrated in manufacturing (Holmes 1995).

Nonetheless, the unemployment rate represents only the percentage of workers in the labor force—those who are actively looking for work. A more significant measure is the employment to population ratio, which is the percentage of adult workers aged 16 and older who are working. For example, whereas the unemployment rate for black youths 16 and older was 34.6 percent in December 1994, compared with a white youth unemployment rate of 14.7 percent, only 23.9 percent of all black youth were actually working, compared with 48.5 percent of white youths (Holmes 1995).

It would take sustained tight labor markets over many years to draw back those discouraged workers who have dropped out of the labor market altogether, some for very long periods of time. Developing policies to ensure a tight labor market is a long-term consideration. I would like to suggest some short-term and realistic policies based on several of the findings from the UPFLS.

One of the problems indicated by our research is the mismatch between inner-city residence and the location of jobs. This presents a special problem for blacks because they have less access to private automobiles and, unlike Mexicans, do not have a network system that supports organized carpools. Accordingly, they depend heavily on public transportation. As Sophie Pedder (1991) points out, "Chicago suffers from a weak and expensive public transportation system linking the central city to the suburbs, which reinforces physical isolation" (38). The creation of privately subsidized car pools to get inner-city residents to the areas of employment, particularly suburban areas, would be a relatively inexpensive way to significantly improve employment.

Our research suggests the importance of job referrals from current employees. Increased use of job referrals can be achieved by increasing employment in the neighborhood. However, the creation of job information centers in various parts of the inner city could significantly improve awareness of the availability of employment in the metropolitan area. These information centers could coordinate efforts with the car pool organizations to get the job applicants who lack private transportation to the employment sites.

Our research also indicates the need to consider ways to improve employer perceptions of public training programs (Royster 1991). One possibility is to increase the linkage between public training programs and businesses by involving representatives from the latter in the actual training of the participants. Another possibility is to enlarge the curriculum of the training program to address the problem of the blue-collar–white-collar work-culture mismatch. Also, the importance of work cultures in understanding patterns of schooling, occupational choice, and labor market success could be considered as a part of the basic curriculum in inner-city high schools.

Access to employment is of course related to areas of residence. The extremely high degree of housing segregation in Chicago contributes to the social isolation of inner-city residents, particularly black residents. American housing policies to promote home ownership have tended to benefit the working and middle classes, not the poor. "Direct financial housing subsidies for low income families, common in European welfare states, has been virtually non-existent in the United States" (Schmitter-Heisler 1991). The housing available for the poor tends to be confined to a limited number of public housing projects disproportionately concentrated in inner-city neighborhoods—neighborhoods that not only lack employment opportunities but that have few informal job information networks as well.

Our research suggests the need for a public housing program that does not reinforce the social isolation that exists in poor inner-city neighborhoods. One possible model is the Gautreaux program in Chicago. Under a 1976 court order the program has relocated more than 4,000 residents from public housing into subsidized housing in neighborhoods throughout the greater Chicago area. Careful research of this program reveals that the families who were relocated in housing in the suburbs experienced significant gains in employment and education.

The problem of housing segregation for low-income inner-city residents could also be alleviated by making it more difficult to manipulate zoning laws or make use of discriminatory land-use controls or site selection practices. This would clear the path for the construction of more affordable housing for low-income families or enable many poor families to secure residence in neighborhoods that provide desirable services (Taylor 1986).

Finally, our research also suggests the need, as shown by Lena Lundgren-Gaveras, "to promote accessible, reliable, child care for low-income single mothers in order to increase their labor force activity" (1991: 18). Lack of adequate child care is a major, if not the main, reason why many poor single mothers do not work and receive welfare. But considering the jobs that are accessible to low-income women, it is not just child care but flexible child care that is needed.

Lundgren-Gaveras reports that one of the mothers interviewed by the ethnographers "worked at night or early mornings as a waitress, another mother worked part-time and studied at night to finish her high school diploma, a third mother worked as a cleaner when work was available. Many of the mothers who worked relied on a combination of formal and informal support and labor-force activity" (19). It would be useful, she urged, to review the incorporation of flexible systems of child care in other countries such as Sweden and Denmark to see if they might have relevance for incorporation here.

None of these proposals is expensive. And most could be easily and quickly incorporated. Ideally they ought to be part of a more comprehensive program designed to combat poverty and social deprivation in the United States. But until such a program is developed we ought to take immediate steps to adopt these modest proposals.

References

Aponte, Robert. 1991. "Ethnicity and Male Employment in the Inner City: A Test of Two Theories." Paper presented at the Chicago Urban Poverty and Family Life Conference, October 10–12.

Bailey, Thomas. 1990. "Black Employment Opportunities," in Charles Brecher and Raymond D. Horton, eds., *Setting Municipal Priorities.* New York: New York University Press.

Breslau, Daniel. 1991. "Reciprocity and Gender in Low-Income Households." Paper presented at the Chicago Urban Poverty and Family Life Conference, October 10–12.

Ellwood, David T. 1986. "The Spatial Mismatch Hypothesis: Are There Teenage Jobs Missing in the Ghetto," 147–48, in Richard B. Freeman and Harry J. Holzer, eds., *The Black Youth Employment Crisis.* Chicago: University of Chicago Press.

Fernandez, Roberto M., and David Harris. 1991. "Social Isolation and the Underclass." Paper presented at the Chicago Urban Poverty and Family Life Conference, October 10–12.

Franklin, Donna, and Susan E. Smith. 1991. "Adolescent Mothers and Persistent Poverty: Does Delaying Parenthood Still Make a Difference?" Paper presented at the Chicago Urban Poverty and Family Life Conference, October 10–12.

Freeman, Richard B. 1991. "The Employment and Earning of Disadvantaged Male Youths in a Labor Shortage Economy," in Christopher Jencks and Paul Peterson, eds., *The Urban Underclass.* Washington, D.C.: Brookings Institution Press.

Hannerz, Ulf. 1969. *Soulside: Inquiries into Ghetto Culture and Community.* New York: Columbia University Press.

Hicks-Bartlett, Sharon. 1991. "A Suburb in Name Only: The Case of Meadow View." Paper presented at the Chicago Urban Poverty and Family Life Conference, October 10–12.

Holmes, Steven A. 1995. "Jobless Data Show Blacks Joining Economy Recovery." *New York Times,* July 29.

Holzer, Harry J. 1990. "The Spatial Mismatch Hypothesis: What Has the Evidence Shown?" Paper presented at a conference on The Truly Disadvantaged, Northwestern University, October.

Jaynes, Gerald David, and Robin Williams Jr., eds. 1989. *A Common Destiny: Blacks and American Society.* Washington, D.C.: National Academy Press.

Kasarda, John D. 1989. "Urban Industrial Transition and the Underclass," *Annals of the American Academy of Political and Social Science* 501 (January): 26–47.

Kirschenman, Joleen, and Kathryn Neckerman. 1991. " 'We'd Love to Hire Them, But . . .': The Meaning of Race for Employers," in Christopher Jencks and Paul Peterson, eds., *The Urban Underclass.* Washington, D.C.: Brookings Institution Press.

Krogh, Marilyn. 1991. "A Description of the Work Histories of Fathers Living in the Inner City of Chicago." Paper presented at the Chicago Urban Poverty and Family Life Conference, October 10–12.

———. 1993. "A Description of the Work Histories of Fathers Living in the Inner City of Chicago." Working paper, Center for the Study of Urban Inequality, University of Chicago.

Laseter, Robert L. 1994. "Young Inner-City African American Men: Work and Family Life." Doctoral dissertation, University of Chicago.

Lundgren-Gaveras, Lena. 1991. "Informal Network Support, Public Welfare Support and the Labor Force Activity of Urban Low-Income Single Mothers." Paper presented at the Chicago Urban Poverty and Family Life Conference, October 10–12.

Moss, Philip, and Christopher Tilly. 1991. "Why Black Men Are Doing Worse in the Labor Market: A Review of Supply-Side and Demand-Side Explanations." New York: Social Science Research Council.

Neckerman, Kathryn M. 1991. "What Getting Ahead Means to Employers and Inner-City Workers. Paper presented at the Chicago Urban Poverty and Family Life Conference, October 10–12.

Neckerman, Kathryn M., and Joleen Kirschenman. 1991. "Hiring Strategies, Racial Bias, and Inner-City Workers," *Social Problems* 38 (November): 433–47.

Pedder, Sophie. 1991. "Social Isolation and the Labor Market: Black Americans in Chicago." Paper presented at the Chicago Urban Poverty and Family Life Conference, October 10–12.

Royster, Deirdre A. 1991. "Social Isolation and the Labor Market: Black Americans in Chicago" Paper presented at the Chicago Urban Poverty and Family Life Conference, October 10–12.

Schmitter-Heisler, Barbara. 1991. "A Comparative Perspective on the Underclass," *Theory and Society* 20: 455–83.

Taub, Richard. 1991. "Differing Conceptions of Honor and Orientations Toward Work and Marriage Among Low-Income African Americans and Mexican Americans." Paper presented at the Chicago Urban Poverty and Family Life Conference, October 10–12.

Taylor, William L. 1986. "Brown, Equal Protection, and the Isolation of the Poor," *Yale Law Journal* 95: 1700–1735.

Testa, Mark. 1991. "Male Joblessness, Nonmarital Parenthood and Marriage." Paper presented at the Chicago Urban Poverty and Family Life Conference, October 10–12.

Testa, Mark, and Marilyn Krogh. 1989. "The Effect of Employment on Marriage

Among Black Males in Inner-City Chicago." Unpublished manuscript, University of Chicago.

Tienda, Marta, and Haya Steir. 1991. " 'Making a Livin': Color and Opportunity in the Inner City." Paper presented at the Chicago Urban Poverty and Family Life Conference, October 10–12.

Tobin, James, 1965. "On Improving the Economic Status of the Negro," *Daedalus* 94: 878–98.

Van Haitsma, Martha. 1991. "Attitudes, Social Context and Labor Force Attachment: Blacks and Immigrant Mexicans in Chicago Poverty Areas." Paper presented at the Chicago Urban Poverty and Family Life Conference, October 10–12.

———. 1992. "The Social Context of Nonemployment: Blacks and Immigrant Mexicans in Chicago Poverty Areas." Paper presented at the annual meeting of the Social Science History Association, Chicago, November 5–8.

Wacquant, Loïc J. D., and William Julius Wilson. 1989. "Poverty, Joblessness and the Social Transformation of the Inner City," in D. Ellwood and P. Cottingham, eds., *Reforming Welfare Policy*. Cambridge: Harvard University Press.

Wilson, William Julius. 1980. *The Declining Significance of Race: Blacks and Changing American Institutions*. Chicago: University of Chicago Press.

———. 1987. *The Truly Disadvantaged: The Inner City, the Underclass, and Public Policy*. Chicago: University of Chicago Press.

Notes

This essay is based on a larger study, *When Work Disappears: The World of the New Urban Poor* (New York: Knopf, 1996).

1. This study includes a survey of 2,495 households in Chicago's inner-city neighborhoods conducted in 1987 and 1988; a second survey of a subsample of 175 respondents from the larger survey who were reinterviewed solely with open-ended questions on their perceptions of the opportunity structure and life chances; a survey of a stratified random sample of 179 employers, designed to reflect the distribution of employment across industry and firm size in the Chicago metropolitan area, conducted in 1988; and comprehensive ethnographic research, including participant observation research and life-history interviews conducted in 1987 and 1988 by ten research assistants in a representative sample of black, Hispanic, and white inner-city neighborhoods.

The UPFLS was supported by grants from the Ford Foundation, Rockefeller Foundation, Joyce Foundation, Carnegie Corporation, Lloyd A. Fry Foundation, William T. Grant Foundation, Spencer Foundation, Woods Charitable Fund, Chicago Community Trust, Institute for Research on Poverty, and U.S. Department of Health and Human Services.

2. For a discussion of these findings see Krogh (1993).

3. Some of the results of this survey were published in two earlier papers by Kirschenman and Neckerman (1991) and Neckerman and Kirschenman (1991).

Race, Localism, and Urban Poverty

Margaret Weir

One of the greatest strengths of William Julius Wilson's work is to take a broad perspective on the development of inner-city poverty in the United States. Wilson takes us beyond the often circular arguments about the respective roles of structure and individual behavior to show how impersonal structural forces—both economic and social—interact with distinctive group histories. Yet most fundamental in his analysis of the emergence of contemporary black ghetto poverty are the broad-scale economic shifts caused by industrial restructuring. Wilson argues that the shift from a manufacturing-based economy to one organized around services and the deconcentration of industry from urban centers to suburban locations have destroyed the traditional channels of mobility for the urban poor, sharply restricting opportunities for economic advancement.

And indeed, economies across the industrialized world have been transformed over the past twenty years, shifting the basis of economic activity and encouraging the adoption of new forms of industrial organization. In Western Europe as well as the United States, these transformations have had significant spatial and social repercussions, as some regions have sunk into decline, economic inequalities have grown, and concentrations of poverty have emerged. But only in the United States has industrial restructuring been associated with the emergence of the distinctive form of racially identified deep poverty and social isolation, described so well by Wilson.

The few studies that we have of the consequences of industrial restructuring on the poor in Europe suggest that inequality has increased but that poverty is not as deep nor are the poor as socially and spatially isolated as in the United States.[1] And even though the presence of nonwhite immigrants and their children in European cities has provoked concerns about the emergence of an American-style convergence of race and poverty, nowhere is "the new poverty" as racially identified as in the United States. Those who apply the label "underclass" in Britain, for example, define a group far more heterogeneous than is identified in the United States. In his warning that Britain is developing an underclass, Labour Member of Parliament Frank Field has pointed to the growing poverty and exclusion from the economy of three groups including elderly pensioners, the long-term unemployed, and single-parent families.[2] The conservative analyst Charles Murray, who has sought to export his analysis of an American underclass to Britain, has limited his argument to warning about potential dangers.[3]

There are other indicators that neither poverty nor social isolation is as severe in the European context. Loïc Wacquant's work on housing projects in the Paris suburb of La Courneuve describes an area saturated by government programs rather than one abandoned by public and private institutions as are inner cities in the United States.[4] Brixton, a poor area of South London with a significant population of Afro-Caribbeans, was the site of riots in 1981 but today it resembles a bustling immigrant community—poor but functioning. There is little resembling the devastation and absence of public life that characterize American inner cities.

What accounts for the depth of poverty and isolation in American cities? I consider that question by focusing on the role of American politics and policy, concerns often implicit in Wilson's work but not directly addressed. The distinctive feature of American politics most relevant to ghetto poverty today, I argue, is a tradition of localism, deeply etched in American politics and law, and developed in the context of racial antipathies and racial discrimination. This combination of localism and racism has had profound effects on the development of social policy in the United States; it has also influenced the way we draw political boundaries and define subnational political jurisdictions. In the process, it has deeply affected the definition of political community in America.

Localism, Race, and Social Policy

Localism has long been a defining feature of American politics. In the 1830s, Alexis de Tocqueville described municipal independence as the "natural consequence" of the sovereignty of the American people.[5] Considerable local independence persists nearly two centuries later despite the formal subordination of localities to state government and the growth of federal government and national policy unimagined by the Founders.

From a cross-national perspective, American municipalities enjoy substantial autonomy. They have the power to determine their own budgets as well as considerable freedom to raise revenues with taxes and bonds. Since the turn of the century, localities have used zoning to regulate what activities—and often what people—fit within their boundaries. And even as the federal government has grown in the past half-century, local autonomy has been supported and enhanced in a variety of ways by an emerging body of local government law.[6]

Despite its celebrated virtues, localism has always had a more troubling side. In a nation divided by race, local autonomy may serve to reinforce racial divisions. This potential became the underlying principle of metropolitan development after World War II as cities across the United States absorbed the flow of black migrants from the South. Racial antipathy and racial discrimination had created a distinctively American organization of space and politics: by the late 1960s, metropolitan America had become a mosaic of distinct political jurisdictions segmented by race and income.

This form of racialized localism was supported and reinforced by a variety of federal policies. The role of the federal government in supporting suburban development after World War II is well known. Less often highlighted is the federal role in ensuring that the benefits of suburban living would not be available to black citizens: the federal government sanctioned discrimination in housing markets by promulgating rules that prevented blacks from receiving Federal Housing Administration mortgages. Similarly, the federal government bowed to local opposition to subsidized housing that might increase integration; federal housing policies were predicated on local acceptance.

The American combination of localism and fragmentation has created structural pressures against generous public provision at the local level.[7] Instead it creates incentives for cities to compete against one another and for cities and suburbs to compete, each seeking to attract business and high-income populations and to avoid the burden posed by needy populations.

Party Politics and Urban Policy

From the 1930s to the 1980s, however, national partisan politics and the policies they gave rise to helped temper these structural pressures against public provision. The centrality of cities—their poor and working-class citizens—to national political outcomes during that time period provided the political support for a system of intergovernmental grants that cushioned local inequalities. The grants were of two distinct types: the first focused on individuals, the second on places.

The first inkling of the importance of cities in national politics occurred in 1932, when urban immigrants helped sweep Franklin D. Roosevelt into power. The significance of the urban vote increased as the New Deal drew a whole generation of voters into politics. By the 1944 presidential election, place of residence had surpassed economic class as a determinant of voting behavior; in seven key states, Democratic support in the largest city was sufficient to overcome Republican support in the rest of the state.[8] By 1960, politicians of both parties viewed urban support as a decisive precondition for winning national power.

The political importance of cities in national politics was reflected in a range of intergovernmental grants that marked a new activist role for the federal government in the realm of social welfare. The first set of grants, focusing on individuals, was launched during the New Deal. These grants supported programs that have become the mainstay of the American welfare state: under the rubric of Social Security, the federal government supported old age pensions, unemployment insurance, and Aid to Dependent Children. Pathbreaking though these federal commitments were, they remained limited. Only the contributory pension program was fully federal; state (and to a significant extent, local) control over unemployment insurance, old age assistance, and Aid to Dependent Children made for wide variations in benefit levels and in access to benefits. As several students of the New Deal have stressed, the power of the South in national politics had stymied the most sweeping impulses of the New Deal. Central to Southern objections to more generous social policies was the desire to maintain the political, economic, and social subordination of the black population.

In the 1960s and 1970s, a second wave of intergovernmental grants was launched. This time, however, a new type of grant, focusing on places, was added to the federal repertoire. Under the name of urban policy and the War on Poverty, these grants sought to address the shortcomings of American social policy by recognizing the spatial dimension of poverty and social need. As blacks had moved North and concentrated in central cities just as whites were departing for the suburbs, cities became the most visible representatives of poverty and social inequalities.

Together, the individual- and place-oriented intergovernmental grants helped to mitigate the inequalities that existed across spatial and political boundaries. They were not, however, sufficient to overcome the economically and socially divisive consequences of localism. The limits of inter-governmental grants as organized are particularly evident in two critical areas of social policy that remained strongly tied to local prerogatives and local capacities: housing and education; and in one, employment, that remained within the province of the private market.

Housing policies not only failed to provide much support for city residents, they also reinforced the divisions between city and suburb. The centerpiece of American housing policy, the tax deduction for interest on mortgages, was of little use to the majority of poor urban dwellers, who were far more likely to be renters than owners. Even during the 1960s and 1970s, the federal government devoted relatively few resources to low-income housing or to support for rental housing. Perhaps most crucially, the construction of public housing remained contingent on local acceptance; middle-class communities could and did reject publicly subsidized low-cost housing in communities across the United States from the 1930s on. The federal government had limited power to challenge such local preferences and in the early 1970s, it quickly retreated when its efforts provoked opposition.[9]

The local provision of public education has been a cornerstone of American democracy. Largely funded by local property taxes, the quality of local education is deeply connected to local financing capacities despite considerable expansion of state funding for education since the 1960s. As metropolitan areas have segmented by income, deep inequalities in the provision of education have emerged across localities.[10]

Finally, the absence of a national employment policy, providing public jobs, training, or even sufficient job information left the new urban migrants to make their own way in the labor market. Their success was mixed; although some unionized industries hired significant numbers of black workers, discrimination by the craft unions limited access to other jobs. Public employment marked the area of greatest employment gain for African Americans during the 1960s. By the late 1960s, Labor Department officials had identified underemployment as a central problem of inner-city minority neighborhoods but they were able to do little to address it.

Where racial discrimination and racial antipathy had once given rise to regional politics based on race, by the 1950s, it created the foundations for a metropolitan politics based on race. The individual and place-based politics of the 1930–80s helped to cushion some of the sharpest inequalities between cities and suburbs.[11] But the rules governing local autonomy and political incorporation combined with the structure of taxation and social policy benefits to encourage a separation of the population along race and income lines. It would be only a matter of time until these pressures fed back into national politics, stripping cities of their pivotal position and jeopardizing these policies.

Industrial Restructuring and the Urban Poor

Given these specific political conditions and policy arrangements, industrial restructuring had particularly devastating effects on minorities in inner cities. As urban manufacturing declined and surviving industries relocated to the suburbs, metropolitan fragmentation combined with the specific features of individual- and place-oriented policies to create a group of people deeply impoverished and increasingly detached from the rest of society.

Wilson highlights the difficulty that blacks who reside in the inner city have in securing suburban employment; such difficulties cannot be understood without considering housing policies that prevented black citizens from moving to the suburbs in the 1950s when such housing was plentiful and cheap. Likewise, policies that continue to discourage the construction of low-income housing in suburban areas make access to employment more difficult.

Similarly, with regard to education, the closing off of most metropolitanwide solutions to educational problems with the *Milliken v. Bradley* Supreme Court decision in 1974 has left urban areas on their own to educate an impoverished and isolated population. This task is especially difficult because it comes at a time when we are asking public schools to do more than ever before. As Patricia Albjerg Graham has pointed out, not only do we expect schools to retain students, but we expect them to ensure that students have gained skills relevant to their future work lives—a qualitatively new function for the public schools.[12] As education has become virtually the only way to secure good jobs, the American version of localism in education serves to restrict life chances based on place of residence.

Urban Isolation

The social policies of the 1980s and 1990s have sharpened economic inequalities and deepened the isolation of the poor by making place of residence even more important for well-being. Decisions to lodge responsibility for social policy in lower levels of government have strained the capacities of states and municipalities with concentrations of poor people, forced as they are by political and economic pressures to keep tax rates low.[13]

Students of American social policy have noted that the cuts in social policy made during the Reagan administration fell far short of the administration's aims and that social policies were too deeply entrenched to be cut substantially. This is largely true of grants to individuals, such as Social Security and even Aid to Families with Dependent Children. The dynamics of congressional politics were critical in preserving these individual-based grants from the significant cuts proposed.[14]

The same is not true of grants to places, which were sharply cut or eliminated altogether in the 1980s. The Comprehensive Employment and Training Act, which provided local public jobs and served as a subsidy for local employment, was one of the few federal programs discontinued in 1981. By 1990, revenue sharing had been eliminated, as had local development programs funded by Urban Development Action Grants (UDAG). As Demetrios Caraley has shown, grants to programs that benefited city governments were cut by 46 percent between 1980 and 1990.[15]

Behind these policy changes is a new era of American politics in which cities no longer occupy a pivotal political role. Many commentators have noted that the presidential election in 1992 was the first in which suburbs formed an absolute majority of the electorate. But in an important sense, Ronald Reagan was the first "suburban president": his electoral and policy strategies were both premised on the political insignificance and isolation of cities.

American politics and policy can now be described as one of "defensive localism" in which the aim is to reduce domestic spending by the federal government, push responsibilities down to lower levels of government, and contain social problems that are the by-products of economic restructuring within defined spatial and political boundaries.

Because questions about local political boundaries are not part of American national politics, there is little room within national debates to consider the problems that arise from the resource fragmentation at the local level. In this context, it is easier for those seeking to limit the government's role in adjusting to economic change to blame local politicians for mismanagement or to point to individual deviant behavior as the cause of the cities' social problems.

Are Alternative Scenarios Possible?

This is a fairly dismal scenario and I'd like to conclude by considering how inserting the political dimension might positively affect the way we think about policy solutions to urban poverty. Most central, I think, is the need for regional approaches to urban poverty, which would begin to break down the political boundaries that presently divide city and suburb. This approach differs from urban policies of the past, which promoted local dependence on federal largesse and did little to encourage city-suburban cooperation.

This orientation is implicit in many of Wilson's own policy recommendations, including the call to expand Gautreaux housing, improve transportation from city to suburb, and establish job information networks in inner cities.

For several reasons, this regional approach to urban poverty is not as politically far-fetched as it may seem. The spillover effects of inner-city poverty—most notably crime and drugs—have deeply affected some inner suburban areas. Moreover, suburbs are not all of a piece. The 1950s image of suburbs is undifferentiated middle-income sanctuaries is no longer accurate. Like cities, suburbs have been affected by economic changes and the effects of aging. The ensuing problems they are experiencing give them potential points of cooperation with cities on issues of economic development and infrastructural development. Finally, employers in both the central city and the suburbs are concerned as never before about the quality of the labor force. The unprecedented interest in this issue provides an opening for human resource development and labor market policies, which were the missing component of the American welfare state from the 1930s on.

One of the central contributions of Wilson's work on urban poverty has been to highlight the importance of place and spatial patterns of residence. What I have suggested is that we now need to take into account the way politics map onto these spatial patterns because these patterns have important implications for the politics of poverty in the United States. They also offer telling clues about how social and economic policies can reinforce poverty and isolation and how they can help to overcome it.

Notes

1. See, for example, Ceri Peach, "Immigration and Segregation in Western Europe Since 1945," in *Foreign Minorities in Continental European Cities* (Stuttgart: Franz Steiner Verlag Wiesbaden GMBH, 1987); Hilary Silver "National Conceptions of the New Urban Poverty," *International Journal of Urban and Regional Research* (1993): 336–54; and Karen Gibson and Peter Hall, "American

Poverty and Social Policy: What Can Be Learned from the European Experience?" Background Memorandum Prepared for the Social Science Research Council Policy Conference on Persistent Poverty, Washington, D.C., November 9–10, 1993.

2. See Frank Field, *Losing Out: The Emergence of Britain's Underclass* (Cambridge: Basil Blackwell, 1989).

3. Charles Murray, "The British Underclass," *The Public Interest* 99 (Spring 1990): 4–25.

4. Loïc J. D. Wacquant, "Urban Outcasts: Stigma and Division in the Black American Ghetto and the French Urban Periphery," *International Journal of Urban and Regional Research* (1993): 366–83.

5. Alexis de Tocqueville, *Democracy in America* vol. I (New York: Vintage, 1945), 67.

6. See Richard Briffault, "Our Localism: Part II—Localism and Legal Theory," *Columbia Law Review* 90, 2 (1990): 346–454.

7. Paul Peterson, *City Limits* (Chicago: University of Chicago Press, 1981).

8. Richard Polenberg, *War and Society: The United States, 1941–45* (New York: Lippincott, 1972), 212–14.

9. See Richard Briffault, "Our Localism." Michael Danielson, *The Politics of Exclusion* (New York: Columbia University Press, 1976).

10. Ira Katznelson and Margaret Weir, *Schooling for All: Class, Race and the Decline of the Democratic Ideal* (New York: Basic Books, 1985), chap. 8.

11. Advisory Commission on Intergovernmental Relations, *Fiscal Disparities: Central Cities and Suburbs, 1981* (Washington, D.C.: August 1984), 15.

12. Patricia Albjerg Graham, *S.O.S.: Sustain Our Schools* (New York: Hill and Wang, 1992).

13. See E. Blaine Liner, *A Decade of Devolution: Perspectives on State–Local Relations* (Washington, D.C.: Urban Institute Press, 1989). After the election of a Republican Congress in 1994, individual entitlements for the poor also became the target for cutbacks. The 1996 Personal Responsibility Act substantially reduced spending on food stamps, abolished the federal guarantee of cash assistance, and imposed time limits on benefits that will further reduce federal assistance in the future.

14. John Chubb, "Federalism and the Bias for Centralization," in John E. Chubb and Paul E. Peterson, eds., *The New Direction in American Politics* (Washington, D.C.: Brookings Institution, 1985).

15. Demetrios Caraley, "Washington Abandons the Cities," *Political Science Quarterly* 107, 1 (1992): 1–30.

Inner-City as Place

Michael Katz

I will begin these comments by setting William Julius Wilson's paper in the context of his contribution to the analysis of inner-city poverty. I then turn briefly to two other issues. The first is novelty: whether contemporary conditions within inner-cities are unprecedented. The second is how to frame discussions of inner-city poverty: I want to suggest the importance of complimenting the prevailing "people"-centered approach with one that focuses on "place."

William Julius Wilson is the most influential contemporary writer on inner-city poverty. His book, *The Truly Disadvantaged*,[1] set the agenda for the recent upsurge of research on urban poverty, stimulated especially by the Social Science Research Council's Committee on the Urban Underclass, launched officially in 1988. As archivist to the SSRC committee, I observed his book influence the committee's initial formulation of its task. Indeed, never have I seen a book so clearly and powerfully shape a national research agenda.

Wilson deserves special credit for his willingness to publish a book of bold hypotheses about a crucial, controversial issue and then to mount a major research project to test them. It was a singular act of intellectual bravery. His contribution to this discussion synthesizes the results of the research projects gathered under the umbrella of his Chicago Urban Poverty and Family Life Study (UPFLS).

His emphasis on black male unemployment constitutes Wilson's single most important substantive contribution to discussions of inner-city poverty. By placing black male unemployment at the center of inner-city poverty, Wilson advanced it to a prominent place on the agenda for re-

163

search and public policy. In fact, it is now difficult to remember how little research and policy focused on black male unemployment as late as 1987. His essay here continues his emphasis on the issue. He begins by documenting the detachment of African American men from the labor force and then works outward to show the relevance of the UPFLS findings for interpreting the patterns he describes. One could ruminate on many of his essay's specific findings, but I want to concentrate on two issues they raise that seem particularly appropriate for a historian's attention.

The first of these is the question of novelty. Wilson's argument assumes the novelty of contemporary inner-city poverty. We confront a situation, his argument implies, for which there are no real precedents. The combination of industrial restructuring with the historic forces of discrimination has produced something new in American history.

Not everyone would agree. An alternative argument contends that poverty and racism form continuous threads in American history. Perhaps they have intensified in the present, but they are not fundamentally new. Even more, the argument for novelty reflects a conservative attempt to stigmatize inner-city poor people, especially African Americans, and to frighten the public into backing punitive, mean-spirited policies.

Perhaps paradoxically for a historian, I think the argument for continuity is wrong and misdirects the analysis of the problem. Here is a summary of the case, which I lay out in greater length in the conclusion to my edited volume, *The "Underclass" Debate: Views from History.*[2]

The case for continuity has several components of which the first is ideology. Common themes and preoccupations have run through American discourse on poverty since the early 1800s. Poverty emerges as a moral problem with its roots in the misbehavior of flawed individuals, perpetuated from one generation to another by inadequate families. Poor people fall into two groups, the worthy and unworthy, the deserving and undeserving, or the working poor and the underclass. Even for the deserving, responses to poverty require discipline and restraint more than sympathy and compassion because they interfere with the market and because welfare undermines the incentives for work and family life. At the same time, the limits of our social obligations—what we owe each other—remain unclear, partly because wealth reflects achievement and merit, partly because taxation for redistribution is a form of theft.

The case for continuity draws also on the pervasive poverty in America's cities throughout their history. In earlier times, huge numbers of city people suffered absolute poverty. Probably around half the population of any large city in the nineteenth century would be considered poor by almost any standards. Nor, of course, is racism new. African Americans have experienced severe discrimination in work, housing, schools, public facilities, and political life throughout the history of the nation. Nor is the higher incidence of single-parent families and out-of-wedlock births among them novel. Rates among them have always been higher than among native-born whites.

Despite these persistent patterns, the case for discontinuity remains strong. It begins with the observation that the key concepts—poverty, racism, social disorganization, even family—are social constructions, not fixed, objective categories. They express relations among individuals, groups, and their settings. They take their meaning from their contexts, and with the emergence of postindustrial cities, their context has been transformed.

Since the end of World War II, a series of economic, demographic, and spatial changes have produced an urban form unlike any other in history. Inner-cities can only be understood in terms of this new situation. Let me highlight a few of the changes of special relevance. First is the new mobility context. Earlier urban poverty coexisted with urban growth and with the expansion of opportunities for unskilled and semiskilled work. Prospects for modest social or economic mobility, especially for one's children, remained widespread. As a result, poverty existed within a context of hope. Now, with deindustrialization, depopulation, and declining opportunity (situations described by Wilson) all that has changed and urban poverty increasingly exists within a context of hopelessness.

The labor market: early twentieth-century black migrants to industrial cities became wage-workers; a process of proletarianization (described particularly well by the historian Joe Trotter) accompanied their urbanization. Often paid badly, theirs was primarily the poverty of the working poor. Today, African Americans, in the phrase of Thomas Sugrue, experience "deproletarianization"; they suffer chronic detachment from the labor force. Their problem is not just bad jobs but no jobs at all.

Space: Nineteenth- and early twentieth-century cities were less segregated than today's. Their small black populations were less spatially concentrated than European immigrants, who, themselves, never experienced levels of segregation comparable to those among African Americans now. Indeed, modern American cities reveal the highest levels of racial segregation in the nation's history, and the vast districts of concentrated poverty, documented by Wilson and others, constitute a new feature of America's social landscape. This concentration of poverty and the social isolation it creates influence the lives of the inner-city poor in unprecedented ways, as Wilson describes. In fact, as Douglas Massey and Nancy Denton show in their stunning book, *American Apartheid*,[3] segregation itself sustains, reproduces, and intensifies poverty.

The special features of contemporary inner-city poverty highlight the limits in the way current researchers frame their questions. These focus for the most part on individuals and groups, their labor market experience, family situation, and social behavior. Deindustrialization and discrimination enter as backdrops or background explanations, but they are not by and large the central concerns. Despite the relevance of families and behavior, research and public discussion remain incomplete because they neglect politics and institutions and because they focus more on people than on places.

Take politics: The situation within inner-cities did not just happen. It is not the inevitable result of inexorable forces. Rather, it is the legacy of policy and action, of choices and human agency. Urban history, in fact, is importantly a story about contests over the definition, ownership, and transformation of space. Urban renewal, highway construction, the underfunding of public transportation, segregation, redlining, disinvestment: all these policies manifest the politics that reshaped inner-cities.

As a consequence, districts of inner-city poverty now lie outside the market. Within them, neither housing nor jobs function on normal market principles, and market-based policies are unlikely to bring about their transformation. They also lack effective institutions, other than those of repression or custody. Both private and public institutions have abandoned them, destroying the basis of civil society and degrading the public sphere. (In this, as in so many other ways, inner-cities are metaphors for conditions eroding public and private life throughout American society; only their residents lack the means with which to buffer their effects.) Without satisfactory institutions and civil society, family and community become ever more difficult to sustain and poverty more difficult to overcome.

For these reasons, poverty research and policy need refocusing on places. Contemporary districts of inner-city poverty require reconstruction and regeneration if individuals within them are to lead more satisfying and productive lives. Indeed, without their regeneration and renewed attention to the public sphere, policies directed at individuals, families, and collectivities (such as gangs) will have only the most limited success.

Notes

1. Wilson, Julius William, 1987. *The Truly Disadvantaged: The Inner City, the Underclass, and Public Policy.* (Chicago: University of Chicago Press)

2. Katz, Michael, ed. 1993. *The "Underclass" Debate: Views from History.* (Princeton: Princeton University Press)

3. Massey, Douglas and Nancy A. Denton, 1993. *American Apartheid: Segregation and the Making of the Underclass.* (Cambridge: Harvard University Press)

Social Science and Social Policy: A Case Study of Overreaching

Daniel Patrick Moynihan

Politics is almost always in some measure an argument about the future, and people claiming to be knowledgeable in this regard will almost always find an audience among politicians.

The collapse of Marxist-Leninist doctrine in Central and Eastern Europe and elsewhere, involving as it did the most audacious claim not only to know but to possess the future, is a useful reminder of how precarious such claims generally are. But it also reminds us how much a demand—you could almost say need—there is for any seeming guide to the unknown.

Even as we observe the demise of the nineteenth-century vision of "scientific socialism," we do well to remind ourselves that in the eighteenth century the Framers of the American Constitution were no less firmly advocates of what they called the "new science of politics." Given what James Madison termed "the fugitive and turbulent existence of . . . ancient republics," they had a lot of convincing to do as they expounded the advantages of their proposed form of government. This they did in terms of psychological realism adapted to Newtonian physics. Men were not angels, but they were *predictable*. In their selfishness. Hence, a system of government that allowed "opposite and rival interests" to offset one another would go far to make up for the "defect of better motives."

Thus there began a tradition of pragmatic social inquiry—what Benjamin Franklin called "useful knowledge"—which has flourished in the United States. At the turn of this century, much seemed possible. Thus, in

1908, writing in the *Columbia Law Review* on the subject of "Mechanical Jurisprudence," Roscoe Pound declared:

> We have . . . the same task in jurisprudence that has been achieved in philoso-phy, in the natural sciences, and in politics. We have to . . . attain a pragmatic, a sociological legal science.

By mid-century, the political scientist Peter Odegard, among others, was less buoyant, perhaps because more experienced. He lamented "the monumental accumulation of data and the meager crop of significant con-cepts." The sociologist Edward Shils put it that "social research in the present century has been characterized by an extraordinary scattering of attention over a great variety of uncoordinated problems which were in-vestigated at a very concrete level." Precious little, in Leonard Cottrell's phrase, being in any sense "additive."[1]

And yet it may be argued that the tradition of psychological realism so evident in *The Federalist* has proved more than a little productive, and could have been of some service to the state had "they" but known it. An instance, verging on the prophetic, will be found in an obscure article, "Nationalism or Class?—Some Questions on the Potency of Political Symbols," which the then-28-year-old Daniel Bell published in 1947 in *The Student Zionist,* a journal based at the University of Chicago. He begins:

> The basic political question in Palestine, apart from the immediate issue of immigration, is quite obviously the prospects of Arab-Jewish relations. The strategical policy of every Jewish political group is based on some perspec-tive regarding the nature and direction of Arab thinking, ranging from the bi-nationalism of Hashomer Hatzair and Ichud to the violent Jewish particu-larism of the Irgun.
>
> In the last analysis, each position is based on some estimation of the po-tency of certain symbols of identification. For the Hashomer, class con-sciousness in the Marxist sense is a strong enough cement to weld lower-class Arabs and working class Jews into a common front. For the Ichud, the liberal utopianism of peace and fellowship is of sufficient appeal to unite all men of good will. For the other Zionist groups to a lesser extent, and for the Revisionists to a greater extent, the emotions of nationalism are the most potent in creating group solidarity.

The Hashomer Hatzair were, as Bell indicates, bi-nationalist Marxists; they looked to an Arab-Jewish worker state. The Ichud group, associated with Rabbi Judah Leon Magnes, chancellor and first president of the Hebrew University, were middle-class intellectuals and also bi-nationalists. What were the prospects of such a society? None, thought Bell. Not least because Arabs were unlikely to "achieve that state of maturity which allows them to recognize a sense of class interest and rational cooperation with Jews."

Whereupon? Whereupon the idea of a *Jewish* state would prevail, and that Jewish state would seek alliances abroad.

> If nationalism is still the key to political action, then a policy of national alliances may be necessary for survival. This would involve an effort toward closer affiliation with Great Britain or the United States.

Which, I dare to think, meets William of Occam's, or for that matter, Jim Tobin's standard of parsimony.

Indeed, there is a succession of American social scientists going a long way back who have been remarkably acute in perceiving the sociological inadequacy of Marxism-Leninism as it confronted what was known as The National Question. In 1931, Carlton Hayes remarked on the paradox "that political nationalism should grow stronger and more virulent as economic internationalism increases. . . ."[2] Paradoxical, that is to say, if you put much store in the Marxist prediction of the emergence of proletarian internationalism. In our time, that prediction was severely questioned by a school of ethnic studies that we associate with such eminences as Milton Esman, Milton Gordon, Nathan Glazer, Walker Connor, Donald Horowitz, and of course, John Dollard of Yale. Indeed, I have taken to observing that what Karl Marx wrote in the British Museum Nathan Glazer disproved in the New York Public Library, but that while you see, or used to see, statues of Marx all over the place, one hardly ever sees a statue of Nathan Glazer.

To tarry just a moment on the topic of social science and *foreign* policy, this line of inquiry made it possible in the late 1970s to forecast with some accuracy that the Soviet Union, that great Marxist-Leninist construct, would disintegrate in the late 1980s.

I say this now because I did then. I have set forth the details in *The National Interest*, and will confine myself here to three citations. In 1979, *Newsweek* had a forum on "The Eighties." What will happen? I wrote that in the 1980s the Soviet Union could blow up, and the world with it! (Those tactical nuclear warheads.) Then, this on the Senate floor, January 10, 1980:

> The Soviet Union is a seriously troubled, even sick society. The indices of economic stagnation and even decline are extraordinary. The indices of so-

cial disorder—social pathology is not too strong a term—are even more so.
The defining event of the decade might well be the break-up of the Soviet
Empire. But that . . . could also be the defining danger of the decade.

And, finally, this at a press meeting in Buffalo, New York, October 15,
1984:

> There is a basic fact, so elemental, why do we have difficulty understanding
> it: The Cold War is over. The West won. . . . The Soviet Union is a failed
> society and an unstable one. . . . The place has collapsed. As a society, it just
> doesn't work. Nobody believes in it any more.[3]

Let us now turn to the present decade and to social policy in the 1992
presidential election. The economy was experiencing a protracted and
fairly deep recession. Unemployment had once again become a prominent
issue. But also, and for the first time in our history, the issue of welfare
dependency had been raised to the level of presidential politics. Not, that
is, the issue of people who are out of work, but people who, typically, are
not in the workforce. The number of AFDC cases grew by 11.5 percent
over the period January 1991 to January 1992.[4] In the latter month, there
were 4,719,000 AFDC cases with a total of 13,527,000 AFDC recipients.
By contrast, in January there were 8,929,000 people unemployed, of
which some 3,294,000 were receiving unemployment benefits.

President George Bush set the pattern in his State of the Union address
of January 28, 1992:

> Ask American parents what they dislike about how things are in our coun-
> try, and chances are good that pretty soon they'll get to welfare.
>
> Americans are the most generous people on earth. But we have to go back
> to the insight of Franklin Roosevelt who, when he spoke of what became the
> welfare program, warned that it must not become "a narcotic" and a "subtle
> destroyer" of the spirit.
>
> Welfare was never meant to be a lifestyle; it was never meant to be a habit;
> it was never supposed to be passed from generation to generation like a
> legacy.
>
> It's time to replace the assumptions of the welfare state, and help reform
> the welfare system.

As we later learned in *Roll Call*, the Capitol Hill newspaper,[5] out in
Arlington Heights, Illinois, White House strategists assembled a focus
group with hand-held Perception Analyzers, each hooked up to a computer. Viewers were told to turn a dial up to 100 or down to 0 as they
approved or disapproved parts of the speech.

There were two big scores. "This government is too big and spends too much," came in at 94. "Welfare was never meant to be a lifestyle . . . passed from generation to generation like a legacy" hit 91. Had the president declared, "This government is too big and spends too much on welfare," the Perception Analyzers might have gone into meltdown.

The following month Bush made welfare a principal feature of his television advertising. The president was declared to have "an agenda to strengthen . . . and make America more competitive in the world. . . ." The first specific was "to change welfare and make the able-bodied work. . . ."

The appearance of this television spot prompted this exchange on the *Today* show between two thoughtful and restrained political analysts, Tim Russert, NBC Washington Bureau Chief, and Al Hunt, Bureau Chief of the *Wall Street Journal:*

> Russert: . . . it's only February and they're playing the race card. This is serious business. He talked about "Now I have an agenda." He didn't mention health care, he didn't mention the environment, drugs, the unemployed. You know what he mentioned? Welfare. I called the Department of HHS yesterday. There's no new welfare plan. One out of seven kids in this country is on welfare, 96 percent are women and children, and George Bush is going after that as if it's an expensive program that can somehow alter the economic state of this country. . . . Mark it down. In 1988 it was Willy Horton, in 1992 it's going to be Willy Welfare. They're going to try to distract this country off the real issue of the economy.
>
> Hunt: But Tim, you shouldn't be surprised. This was a guy who last month said he would do whatever it takes to get reelected. If there's trouble they're going to make Willy Horton look like Saint Francis of Assisi, I agree.
>
> Russert: It is cynical, it is outrageous.[6]

The association of welfare dependency both with urban violence and with race soon was a fixture of the 1992 campaign. In New Haven, a few days before the Connecticut presidential primary in March, the Reverend Jesse Jackson led the two remaining Democratic candidates, Governor Bill Clinton and former Governor Jerry Brown, in prayer at a Stop the Violence rally that, according to the New Haven *Register,*

> was organized by community activists alarmed by a recent acceleration of city violence, including six young black men shot to death between Feb. 27 and March 16. Much of the violence has centered around young people with guns.[7]

On the occasion Jackson observed: "If this many blacks had been killed by whites, there would be riots. . . . If this many whites had been shot by blacks, there would be portable electric chairs." On the subject of dispari- ties between suburban and urban school expenditures, he continued, "One child is programmed for Yale, one programmed for jail."[8]

A few days before this, H. Ross Perot, running as a third-party candi- date for president, addressed the National Press Club in Washington. He ended the question and answer session with a cautionary tale of the fate of the American Indians. "Nothing ever stopped them," he said, "until we put them on a reservation." Then this:

> Don't ever put anybody on the reservation again. Our current welfare sys- tem puts people on the reservation.[9]

It is probably fair to state that this is the first time in our long history that these issues of caste and class—I adopt, of course, Dollard's usage— have come to such national prominence in such ominous terms. This bids fair to be a defining issue of social policy for the period now in prospect.

In social science terms, this was foreseen. In the U.S. Department of Labor in 1965 we sent to the president a policy paper that began with a one-sentence paragraph:

> The United States is approaching a new crisis in race relations.

The crisis would be associated with the social structure of inner-city black communities. This was in March. In September, in the Jesuit journal *America,* I put the proposition more graphically.

> From the wild Irish slums of the 19th-century Eastern seaboard, to the riot- torn suburbs of Los Angeles, there is one unmistakable lesson on American history: a community that allows a large number of young men to grow up in broken families, dominated by women, never acquiring any stable rela- tionship to male authority, never acquiring any set of rational expectations about the future—that community asks for and gets chaos. Crime, violence, unrest, disorder . . . that is not only to be expected; it is very near to inevita- ble. And it is richly deserved.

Let me set forth the simple background of the report, entitled "The Negro Family: The Case for National Action." I was, at this time, assis- tant secretary of labor for policy planning and research. This was a new position—part of the style of government in the New Frontier. I had a small but exceptionally able planning staff, some half-dozen people in all.

I also had a nominal supervisory relationship to the Bureau of Labor Statistics, then as now an elite corps of American government statisticians, and wholly supportive of our fledgling enterprise.

In 1963, I had set about trying to develop correlations between unemployment data of various sorts and other indicators of social disorder. We began to find strong correlations between "manpower" data, as we would have said at that time, and family indices of various kinds. Most striking was the relationship between the nonwhite male unemployment rate and the number of AFDC cases opened. Between 1948 (when the present unemployment data series begins) and 1961, we found a correlation, as I recall, of .91. Whereupon, the correlation, having already weakened, went negative. The unemployment rate went down, the number of new AFDC cases went up. James Q. Wilson has called this "Moynihan's scissors."

As I later showed in an essay in the *Annals of the American Academy of Political and Social Science,* these "scissors" occurred over a considerable range of subjects. *Something* was happening.[10]

I must be clear. I did not know *what.* I was well beyond my methodological depth. Thus the Nobel laureate Hans Bethe testified before the Committee on Foreign Relations:

> In 1945, I wrote that the Soviets could have the bomb in five years. They got it in four.

Even that was a bit of guesswork. But guesswork by a theoretical physicist who had already helped design the first bomb, and who was on hand at Alamogordo to watch it go off! My surmise was concocted of much thinner stuff.

You ought to have known a lot more than I did to feel comfortable in telling the president of the United States that his nation was "approaching a new crisis in race relations." True, the report was fairly careful about the limits of the available data and the techniques of interpretation, explicitly warning that

> Data are few and uncertain, and conclusions drawn from them, including the conclusions that follow, are subject to the grossest error.

Nor were we alone in sensing trouble. At this time, for example, Kenneth Clark was writing of the "massive deterioration of the fabric of society and its institutions," "the tangle of pathology" in what we would come to call the inner city, "protest masculinity," hardly something new to urban historians, and so on. What we added was the sense of impending instability, as I would write in 1967, *"The possibility . . . that the situation had begun feeding on itself."*[11] In any event, as President John F. Kennedy would say, to govern is to choose. If we were wrong, no great harm could come of it; I chose to think we were right.

As it turned out, we were right enough in our forecasts. Let me be spare in the particulars. Something did snap in the early 1960s. The illegitimacy rate among African Americans rose from 24 percent to 63.5 percent. (This figure is for 1988, the most recent available.) Of African American children born in the cohort 1967–1969, 72.3 percent were on "welfare" (AFDC) before having reached age 18. (Which is to say they were paupers; not a pretty word but not a pretty condition.) The latest Census data show that in 1964, some 75 percent of black children under age 6 were living in a married-couple family. By 1989—in a steady des·ent—this had dropped to 39 percent.[12] By the 1990s, this overall situation had come near, as stated, the top of the agenda of presidential politics.

However, I was absolutely wrong in thinking that no harm would come of this work. Possibly great harm was done. This was not clear at the outset. Rather the contrary. In a hurried sequence in early June 1965, President Lyndon Johnson decided to make the strengthening of the black social structure, specifically family structure, the theme of a major address at Howard University. I wrote a first draft on a Thursday, overnight the White House turned out a second draft, and the speech was given on Friday afternoon, June 4. The response was overwhelmingly positive. The policy paper remained well in the background.

The paper became public in the aftermath of the urban riots in the Watts section of Los Angeles some three months later. On August 17, 1965, Bill Moyers, then presidential press secretary, gave out copies to a baffled White House press corps. The next day, August 18, those ever flourishing commentators, Evans and Novak, recounted the findings in a column entitled "The Moynihan Report."

The "report" soon became available and evoked, for the most part, indignation and denial. In retrospect, it is not hard to see why. Social science is not rocket science. No one would launch a space craft on the basis of an engineering report that warned of the possibility of "the grossest error" in design. There was, and is, no institutional capacity to review the data and the conclusions, such as exists, let us say, for papers published in the *New England Journal of Medicine.* The report should have been published, but the thesis ought never to have been raised to the level of presidential pronouncement. Even so, to repeat with a measure of insistence, we turned out to be accurate in our forecast.

Lee Rainwater, one of the premier sociologists of our age, along with a young colleague, William Y. Yancey, undertook to examine the ruckus. *The Moynihan Report and the Politics of Controversy* was published two years later, in 1967, by the MIT Press. It was and is a fascinating narrative, which opens with this passage from Louis Wirth's preface to Karl Mannheim's *Ideology and Utopia, which first appeared in 1936:*

> The distinctive character of social science discourse is to be sought in the fact that every assertion, no matter how objective it may be, has ramifications extending beyond the limits of science itself. Since every assertion of a "fact" about the social world touches the interests of some individual or group, one cannot even call attention to the existence of certain "facts" without courting the objections of those whose very *raison d'etre* in society rests upon a divergent interpretation of the "factual" situation.

In feverish times—and those *were* feverish times—this normal disposition can become pathological in itself. One is reminded of Hannah Arendt's observation that the tactical advantage of the totalitarians in Europe in the 1920s and 1930s derived from their ability to turn every statement of fact into a question of motive. I was everywhere attacked in this mode, being charged with "blaming the victim."

One of the questions Rainwater and Yancey addressed was: Why all the fuss when what I had written was "nothing new"? The publisher featured this theme in the jacket copy:

> The authors begin with two observations: first, the content of the Report was neither new nor startling; and second, it was instantly the focus of intense political debate, with presidential endorsement on one hand and important administration and academic objection on the other. How does "nothing new" generate such heat?

Later I spoke with Professor Rainwater (then productively engaged with the Luxembourg Income Studies) and he agreed that by "nothing new" they were referring to the standard statistics on AFDC caseloads and such like that I had cited. If no one else knew of them, he and his fellow researchers in the Pruitt-Igoe housing project in St. Louis knew them all too well. Rainwater agrees, however, that soon after the report appeared, "something happened."

My assessment would be that had the policy paper never been written, or never raised to the level of presidential pronouncement, the social changes it forecast would have come about in any event, and would have gradually been recorded and acknowledged. That would have made it easier for the changes to be accepted in the political world, and might have given social scientists the opportunity to sort it all out.

As it turned out, however, the subject was banished from the academy. At the risk of pressing my luck, let me say that this, too, was forecast. Following the 1968 congressional elections, I wrote in *Commentary* that the prospect of any serious social intervention was finished for the foreseeable future. Nature would take its course.

> If at the moment educated, middle-class Negroes are much in demand and doing nicely, this is not so for the lower class and is likely never to be. This country is not fair to Negroes and will exploit any weaknesses they display. Hence they simply cannot afford the luxury of having a large lower class that is at once deviant *and* dependent. If they do not wish to bring it into line with the working class (*not* middle-class) world around them, they must devise ways to support it from within. It is entirely possible that this could happen, and it might be an eye-opener for all concerned. In all events . . . [a]n era of bad manners is almost certainly begun. For a moment it had seemed this could be avoided, that the next two decades could be bypassed in a sweep of insight and daring. But destiny reasserted itself. The Physiocrats never did have much luck.[13]

Mind, that era of bad manners may now be easing. The work of William Julius Wilson comes immediately to mind. In 1984—twenty years later, but even so—he and Kathryn Neckerman picked up those "scissors" and began to puzzle over the subject. In 1986 they published an analysis that shows that the crossover disappears when the number of AFDC cases is charted against the nonwhite male labor-force *nonparticipation* rate.[14] This and other work led Wilson to exceptionally fruitful insights into the role of male employment and earnings in the central city, issues that were at the heart of our research in the Department of Labor a generation ago.

Here we come to the crux of the issue of social science and social policy. We are at the point of knowing a fair amount about what we don't know. The past quarter-century has been on the whole productive in this regard. On the other hand, our social situation is vastly worse. In 1965 we probably had at most a slight purchase on the issue as it was then. Which is to say, the employment nexus. Further, the federal government, along with state and local governments, was solvent. Indeed, over a fifteen-month period from early 1969 to mid-1970 I took part in a fierce debate within the Nixon White House, joined in by just about every cabinet department and, of course, the then-Bureau of the Budget, over the desirability of the president proposing to the Congress that the federal government establish a guaranteed annual income. This became known, in the event, as the

Family Assistance Plan. With Arthur F. Burns as my principal antagonist, you can be assured that nothing of importance was overlooked in the debate. On the other hand, the subject of cost *scarcely* arose. I later published a 559-page book recounting the event. In all, some 34 lines deal with the subject of cost of the proposal, which is described throughout as "relatively *inexpensive.*"[15]

It was simply a given that if the idea was defensible on its merits, the money would be found. It will be a generation, if ever, before any such assumption will again be possible within the counsels of the presidency. That's a pity, for such a measure would be much welcomed today by those political tendencies—they can no longer be called movements, much less organizations—that opposed the proposal when it came, on grounds that it was insufficiently generous. An era of bad manners was indeed upon us. George Will, not entirely approvingly, observed that "Nixon's administration was the second most liberal administration since the New Deal, second only, and not by much to Lyndon Johnson's."[16] But the proposal was dismissed as inadequate or worse by people who will never see its like again.

And then there are the epidemics. First heroin, then AIDS, then crack (which first appeared in the Bahamas in 1983).[17] In 1989, at Brown University, I offered the thought that

Just as heroin in the 1960s contributed to the rise of the single-parent family, so will crack soon give us the no-parent child as a social problem.[18]

A few years later, a front-page story in the Sunday *New York Times* declared:

Collapse of Inner-City Families
Creates America's New Orphans

Death, Drugs and Jail Leave Voids in Childhood[19]

We have no cure for AIDS, no pharmacological treatment for cocaine dependency, although there is reasonable hope that medical science will produce some therapies. As for social science, however, there would seem to be less confidence than ever. This pessimism is in ways a legacy of the Great Society. In the late 1960s, the American Academy of Arts and Sciences sponsored a long and fruitful seminar on the subject of poverty. I began my presentation, "The Professors and the Poor," by telling of a

lady who had come to see me at the Joint Center for Urban Studies seeking support for a federal antipoverty grant and complaining that none
were being given out in her neighborhood in Boston. I demurred: Rox-
bury was being deluged with programs. "Exactly," came the retort from
my visitor, "but do you notice they only fund programs that don't succeed."[20] A decade later, Peter H. Rossi would distill this insight in "Rossi's
Iron Law":

> If there is any empirical law that is emerging from the past decade of wide-
> spread evaluation research activities, it is that the expected value for any
> measured effect of a social program is zero.

This is not a counsel of despair. It is, again to cite Franklin, useful
knowledge. As recently as 1960, Loren Baritz noted in his study, *The
Servants of Power:* "Intellectuals in the United States have long bemoaned
the assumed fact that they are unloved and unappreciated by their society."[21] The last three decades have seen a role reversal in this regard. Especially in foreign policy, intellectual academics assumed awesome powers.

Much simpler applications come to mind, as for example, a 1992
address by President Bush to the National League of Cities. His
speechwriter got so far carried away as to assert that family breakdown
"endangers our position in a world increasingly driven by economic competition." But then this:

> The urgency is clear. We all know the statistics, perhaps you know them
> better than most Americans, the dreary drumbeat that tells of family break-
> down. Today, one out of every four American children is born out of wed-
> lock. In some areas, the illegitimacy rate tops 80 percent. A quarter of our
> children grow up in households headed by a single parent. More than two
> million are called latchkey kids who come home from school each afternoon
> to an empty house. And a large number of our children grow up without
> the love of parents at all, with nobody knowing their name.

The president, or someone such, might usefully note that illegitimacy ratios are rising in most, if not all industrial countries. The 1969 Canadian
proportion of 9.2 percent had risen to 23.1 percent by 1989.

So far as I can learn, no president of the United States has ever made
such a statement; ever come close to such a suggestion. And there was no
objection. It was a statistic. No small achievement of social science, those
numbers, but not seen as mysterious or arbitrary. If some overnight opinion poll had told the speechwriters they could or even should use such
materials, well, chalk up another social science achievement—the opinion

poll. But again, nonjudgmental, and by now well accepted. Surely, the public learned from what the president said, becoming in consequence more amenable to thoughtful action, whatever that might be. No small achievement.

This willingness—call it courage—was much in evidence in an extraordinary speech on "Race and the American City" delivered on the Senate floor, also in 1992, by Senator Bill Bradley of New Jersey. Here is a sample.

> In politics for the last 25 years, silence or distortion has shaped the issue of race and urban America. Both political parties have contributed to the problem. Republicans have played the race card in a divisive way to get votes—remember Willie Horton—and Democrats have suffocated discussion of a self-destructive behavior among the minority population in a cloak of silence and denial. The result is that yet another generation has been lost. We cannot afford to wait longer. It is time for candor, time for truth, and time for action.

The speech was extraordinary not only in its explicitness, but also in its reception. It was the subject of a lead editorial in the *New York Times* the following Sunday, and the *Washington Post* reprinted part of the text the following Monday. The "new crisis in race relations" of which we wrote a generation ago is now with us, and in a worse form than even we fully comprehended. And yet we seem no longer quite so willing to deny it.

What is more, something we have known for some time, demographics are at last turning our way, if I may use that term. The proportion of 15-to-24-year-olds as a percent of the total population has been declining since the mid-1980s and we forecast that it will continue to do so well into the next century. The size of the cohort most at risk grows smaller, after near to overwhelming social institutions in the 1950s and 1960s.[22]

This is surely the case in the world of the social sciences that is in the main politically liberal, and went through an awful period of silence and denial. Or rather, denial and denunciation. A striking feature of the 1960s was that just as a large consensus in favor of social science-oriented social action took shape, a considerable body of social science appeared, which said in effect, don't expect too much. Think, for example, of the writing in the early editions of *The Public Interest*, a journal of great influence founded by Irving Kristol and Daniel Bell. Almost without exception, the authors were political liberals who had stumbled upon things that weren't entirely pleasing to them but that could not be denied. I have referred to this as the Reformation. Not a few of the heretics were burned at the stake, and more than a few left the true church for good. But their witness prevailed. I take it as no coincidence that 1992 saw James Q. Wilson inducted as president of the American Political Science Association and James S. Coleman as president of the American Sociological Association. Their influence has in the end proved immensely important, and so might their example. For while each has ever sought to make social science available to social policy, each has kept his distance from government. They and their contemporaries and equals (few though they may be) have brought social science closer to the point where it does no harm in the realm of social policy. If we think only of the era of "scientific socialism," we can take the measure of such an achievement. It is not unlike the revolution in medicine that Lewis Thomas describes so well. Which is to say that by the beginning of the twentieth century, at long last, medical doctors had ceased doing harm to their patients.

And so I conclude on a note of modified optimism. The proper realm of social science, as with any mode of disciplined anticipation, is that of the culture itself. Knowledge for its own sake. But there are applied uses: in small amounts and if at all possible, at several removes from the political arena.

Notes

1. See Daniel P. Moynihan, *Came the Revolution—Argument in the Reagan Era* (New York: Harcourt Brace Jovanovich, 1988), 297.

2. Quoted in Walker Connor, "Ethnonationalism in the First World," in Milton J. Esman, ed., *Ethnic Conflict in the Western World* (Ithaca: Cornell University Press, 1977), 33.

3. "Soviet Union Is 'Failed Society' in Need of Clear Policy From U.S., Moynihan says," *Buffalo News* (October 15, 1984).

4. This figure was obtained by averaging AFDC caseload in the four months, October (1991)–January (1992), and comparing the result with the corresponding four-month average for the preceeding year.

5. Morton Kondrake, "Pennsylvania Avenue," *Roll Call* (February 3, 1992), 6.

6. NBC, *Today* (February 26, 1992).

7. "Rally's Cry: 'No More,' " *New Haven Register* (March 23, 1992), 1.

8. "Clinton, Brown Lock Arms with Jackson," *New London Day* March 23, 1992), A5.

9. H. Ross Perot, National Press Club (March 18, 1992).

10. "Urban Conditions: General," in Bertram M. Gross, ed., *Annals of the*

American Academy of Political and Social Science: Social Goals and Indicators for American Society I (May 1967), 159.

11. Daniel P. Moynihan, "The Press and the Negro: The Moment Lost," *Commentary* (February, 1967), 36.

12. Bureau of the Census, *Trends in Relative Income: 1964 to 1989,* Current Population Reports, Series P-60, No. 177, Table F.

13. Moynihan, "The Press and the Negro," 45.

14. William Julius Wilson and Kathryn Neckerman, "Poverty and Family Structure: The Widening Gap between Evidence and Public Policy Issues," in Sheldon H. Danziger and Daniel H. Weinberg, eds., *Fighting Poverty: What Works and What Doesn't* (Cambridge: Harvard University Press, 1986), 232–83.

15. Daniel P. Moynihan, *The Politics of a Guaranteed Income: The Nixon Administration and the Family Assistance Plan* (New York: Random House, 1973), 129, 146, 162, 188.

16. George Will, "Vacuum vs. Resentment," *Newsweek* (March 9, 1992).

17. James F. Jekel et al., "Epidemic Free-Base Cocaine Abuse: Case Study from the Bahamas," *The Lancet* (March 1, 1986).

18. Daniel P. Moynihan, "Toward a Post-Industrial Social Policy," *The Public Interest* (Summer 1989) 16.

19. *New York Times* (March 29, 1992), A1.

20. Daniel P. Moynihan, "The Professors and the Poor," *On Understanding Poverty: Perspectives from the Social Sciences,* (New York/London: Basic Books, 1968), 3.

21. Ibid., 18.

22. Daniel P. Moynihan, "Peace," *Coping* (New York: Random House, 1961). See also "Women in Management: The Spare Sex," *The Economist* (March 28, 1992), 17.

Epilogue: Sociology as a Discipline[1]

Paul DiMaggio

Sociology was founded, or at least named, a century and a half ago by Auguste Comte, a French intellectual who placed it atop the hierarchy of knowledge and believed that it would serve both as a positive science of morality and as the basis for a new secular faith. Sociologists were to be the priests of this faith ("sociolatry"), designing religious rituals and institutions to convince the masses of the righteousness of the moral principles that their scientific labors revealed. Comte thus not only crowned sociology (or "social physics") the queen of the sciences; he anticipated that sociologists would be leaders in the coalition of intellectuals and industrialists that would displace clerics and generals as rulers of an ever more civilized world.[2]

How times have changed. Few now believe that positivism can reveal moral truths, and many sociologists, as the essays in this volume confirm, question the utility of at least some tenets of positivism for the social scientific enterprise itself. Far from retreating before a secular juggernaut, resurgent clerics exert far more political influence in the contemporary United States than do social scientists of any persuasion.[3] The Defense Department's budget exceeds that of the National Science Foundation by two orders of magnitude. Even in the universities, which would seem to be its natural domain, sociology is just one, often the least well staffed and occasionally the most beleaguered, of several specialties in the human sciences, which together compete for resources and esteem on more or less equal footing with the natural sciences and the humanities.

Yet if sociology's trajectory has been less singular than its founder predicted, the discipline has nonetheless accomplished much since its incep-

185

tion, casting light on a range of phenomena that transcend all limits of time, space, and subject matter. This volume reflects much of this diversity of interest—from European revolutions to contemporary American families—and much of the field's diversity of opinion. And it vibrates with the enormous intellectual energy that has marked sociology's effort to comprehend the forces that shape the human condition.

Sociology's prospects look better at this writing than when Kai Erikson organized the conference from which this volume takes its title. Most departments then under fire have rebounded and few if any new crises have erupted. Undergraduate enrollments have increased at most institutions and the quality of graduate students has risen (if that can be divined from standardized test scores). To be sure, changes in state and federal policies confront universities with serious financial challenges; consequently, the line between research universities and others may become more sharply drawn, and institutions that cannot sustain a research mission may merge departments and reduce offerings in many specialties. But as universities like Yale and Duke that once questioned sociology's role benefit from their renewed commitment to the field, and even the two institutions that eliminated departments in the 1980s try to recruit through back doors representatives of the discipline they kicked out the front (Washington University in St. Louis and the University of Rochester), sociology's place among the modern university's core disciplines seems secure.

At the same time, sociology continues to suffer internal doubts (expressed most sharply in this volume by Alan Wolfe) and external challenges. As Neil Smelser notes, both doubts and challenges reflect the curious melding of science, humanities, and art in a discipline that sometimes seems, even to those who love it, to have been assembled by committee. Perhaps because they have internalized these diverse views, sociologists are congenitally self-critical, reluctant to take for granted the convenient research conventions that permit disciplines with firmly established paradigms to speed efficiently, if myopically, down science's main highways. Typically, the authors of essays in this volume reflexively challenge the very epistemological bases of their enterprise: not, for the most part, to question its value, but in a relentless effort to sharpen their analytic tools and increase the power of their accounts and explanations.

One finds in these essays a sociology that is at once robust and vulnerable. Sociologists have never understood more about human social organization, grappled more closely with fundamental questions of explanation and causality, or deployed a wider array of methods with more catholicity in pursuit of knowledge. Yet many sociologists are deeply concerned by the field's failure to adopt a single understanding of its mission, much less a shared paradigm, and frustrated by the fact that they are neither understood nor appreciated by the public (as are, for example, historians) nor admired for their command of mysteries the public cannot grasp (as are physical scientists).

The contributions to this volume address these issues, and others, with extraordinary clarity and acuity. I shall organize the thoughts these chapters provoked around a gaggle of Gs that frame several characterizations of sociologists at century's end—generalists, generalizers, and guardians of the general good.

Much of sociology's vitality and many of its difficulties can be attributed, I shall argue, to the fact that it is a *generalist* science in a specialized world. Although Comte's dream that social physics would unify the sciences was chimerical, his heirs pursue many more topics in more directions than do their colleagues in other disciplines. This generalism has both benefits and costs.

One of the benefits is that sociologists have a rich and complex view of explanation, at least party because they study subjects for which different approaches to explanation are appropriate. For example, some of them study topics that lend themselves to the scientific quest for the accretion of interrelated generalizations, while others address questions for which the natural science model of inquiry serves poorly. Essays like Charles Tilly's and Viviana Zelizer's demonstrate that the once sterile debate between *generalizers* and *particularists* has matured into a more productive, less polarized dialogue.

The ability of the social sciences to put advances in knowledge and new ways of knowing to use depends on much that is outside their control. Many of this volume's essays address eloquently sociologists' role as *guardians of the general good.* Sociology, the only discipline that takes as core topics social and economic inequality, crime and deviance, and the nature of community, is a natural, indispensable asset for the formulation of public policy. Between the 1930s and 1970s, sociology's policy relevance paid the rent, as it were, representing the prime basis for the field's claim on public resources and attention. In the final section I consider the social and political conditions necessary for that role to be a viable and rewarding one.

Sociology as a Generalist Discipline

Sociology is a generalist field in several senses. First, as Erikson notes in his prologue, it covers an enormous topical terrain. When you are a sociologist, the world is your oyster. Second, as Smelser notes, it embraces a broad range of perspectives, including those ordinarily associated with the two cultures of science and the humanities, leading to diverse interpretations of the purpose of the enterprise. Third, and only partly related to the second, sociologists employ a wide range of research methods, from several brands of field observation, in-depth interviews, and archival inquiry, to computer simulation and survey research. Moreover, once they get their data, they subject them to techniques as different from one another as multidimensional scaling, least-squares analyses, dynamic models, network analyses (of numerous kinds), sequence analyses, stochastic models, and Boolean truth tables. Although this catalog may seem arcane, this third kind of diversity is important, for methodology is the gymnasium of theory, in which broad but flabby intuitions get worked into the hard muscle of social discovery, and behind these techniques lie different theoretical presuppositions, different metaphors for thinking about the connectedness of social life.

Although I use the term "generalist" loosely, ecologists use it in a far stricter sense, describing generalism and specialism as alternative strategies that have important implications for a species' fate (or an organizational form's or, by extension, an academic discipline's fate).[4] Generalist forms do many things and are therefore capable of drawing on many different kinds of resources for sustenance: they are said to occupy broad "niches." Specialists do just one or two things, and exploit a very narrow range of resources, but do so very efficiently. Sociologists, for example, receive research support from the National Science Foundation (NSF), from the National Endowment for the Humanities (NEH), and from many private foundations, but they don't receive as much from NSF as astronomers do, for example, or as much from NEH as classicists do.

Whether it is better (from a purely material standpoint) to be a generalist or a specialist depends on the state of the world. In moderately fluctuating environments, generalists ordinarily fare better, because they can draw on more varied resources. In sharply fluctuating environments, forms that are specialized to new conditions will outperform generalists, who are slower to adapt. (Of course, specialists who are *not* adapted to the new environment do very badly indeed!) If NSF were to expand dramatically, it would help specialist astronomy a lot and generalist sociology only a little. (Researchers committed to the kinds of work NSF likes would do very well, but others would be unaffected.) Similarly, if NSF were abolished, astronomy might be cast into crisis, while at least some sociologists would be able to tap into other kinds of grant support. Thus generalism in scientific disciplines, as in blue chip stock portfolios, tends to moderate the ups and downs of fortune under most conditions.

Of course, if change is sufficiently dramatic, generalists may lose their edge. If support from both NSF and NEH were eliminated (as one budget proposed by the House of Representatives in 1995 mandated), for example, sociology's generalism would prove less useful, just as the diversity of climates to which dinosaurs were well adapted didn't matter once some dramatic events (paleontologists argue endlessly over whether these were meteoric collisions, volcanic eruptions, or droughts, but agree that *something* earthshaking occurred) wrecked almost all of those environments simultaneously. Yet although elimination of NSF and NEH might hurt sociology more severely than it would harm economics (which has more private sources of research support) or psychology (which, itself a generalist discipline, has greater claim on military and medical research funding), the discipline's generalism would still pull it through, as sociologists could employ more research methods that do not require large grants than could their neighbors in disciplines that, like most of the natural sciences, have come to depend on a relatively few costly experimental technologies.

Sociology's generalism would therefore appear advantageous to its survival, and it probably is. At the same time, the ecological analogy, while revealing in some ways, is imperfect for several reasons. First, a generalist discipline is very different from a discipline of generalists. Particular sociologists are typically quite specialized in their research interests, perhaps not as much so as natural scientists, but probably to the same degree as their colleagues in economics or political science departments. Strictly speaking, sociology is a "polymorphic" population (a population consisting of notably different types or subdisciplines) as much as a generalist one. For the most part, these subfields are connected only loosely to one another, leading many observers to believe that sociology is a "disintegrated" discipline without a "core."[5]

Second, sociology is in many ways a very strange "generalist." Whereas generalist organizational forms often tend to be large and relatively well financed, sociology is far smaller, by any measure, than psychology, political science, or economics. As a result, sociology tries to penetrate a broader frontier with far fewer troops. Thus what Michael Hannan and John Freeman describe as the typical dilemma of even resource-rich generalists—the "obvious tradeoff between tolerance of widely varying conditions and capacity for high performance in any particular situation"— strikes sociology with double force.[6]

Third, the analogy between disciplines and species directs our focus to rivalry among the disciplines. Yet the very notion, promoted by Comte and (as Robert Merton and Gerald Holton tell us in Part II) Mary Somerville, that the sciences represent a cohesive system of thought and inquiry, calls our attention to the symbiotic relationship—in intellectual matters, if not at budget time—between sociology and its sister disciplines. It also reminds us of the special role of a generalist field as a bridge between subject matters and systems of thought that may otherwise suffer individually from myopia and collectively from fragmentation.

The Advantages of Generalism

Sociology's generalism gives its practitioners several advantages in their struggle for understanding. The multiplicity of topics sociologists address makes collective illusions relatively difficult to sustain, at least insofar as specialists talk to one another (which, perhaps because of the field's relatively small numbers, they often do). Social mechanisms that can be overlooked in studying the operation of small groups in the contemporary United States, for example, are likely to be glaringly evident to students of political conflicts in medieval Europe (and vice versa).

Sociology's methodological diversity is equally salubrious in this regard. Most social science disciplines do certain things very well and other things rather badly, often polishing their strengths to a bright sheen while turning a collective blind eye to their characteristic deficiencies of method. For example, experimental psychologists (at least those who work with college-student volunteers) can be masters of measurement and scaling, but are often cavalier about sampling. Economists tend to excel at devising statistical models, but are ordinarily less interested in measurement. If one takes the leading journals as evidence, standards in most other fields are higher than those in sociology for the aspects of method in which they excel, and lower for those that they choose to discount. If sociology's small numbers keep it from routinely inculcating the highest levels of technical expertise in its Ph.D.s, its diversity requires scholars whose methodological styles favor, for example, network analysis to run the gauntlet of reviewers who specialize in dynamic modeling, scaling, or even (in some fields) comparative historical techniques. In epistemology, as well as methodology, the field's diversity makes it difficult to take very much for granted for very long.

The advantage of diversity to scholarship is not limited to the policing function, however. A wide range of scholars, from fields as diverse as ego psychology, cultural anthropology, and the study of technical innovation, have noted that many of the richest and most exciting developments—in personal development, culture, and science—occur at the boundaries of life, when things that have been separated are juxtaposed.[7] (This is what people mean when they suggest that social marginality hones the ethnographer's eye or permits the data analyst to detect patterns that the less alienated might have ignored.) Sociology's diversity means that it is a discipline of ceaseless juxtaposition. Many of sociology's most productive insights emerge from the comparison of institutional settings too different to fall jointly within any other discipline's purview: take for just one example, Harrison White's striking observations about structural similarities between the contemporary system of scientific disciplines and the Indian caste system.[8] Moreover, the cross-cutting of method and topic places most sociologists in invisible colleges that include peers whose interests or styles of research are diametrically opposed to their own. This persistent boundary-dwelling gives sociologists an advantage—Paul Starr has referred to it as "the edge of social science"—that scholars in more paradigmatic disciplines often lack.[9]

If sociology's generalism is productive from the standpoint of the field's own intellectual vitality, it is indispensable from the standpoint of the social sciences as a whole. Sociology contributes to intellectual diversity within the social sciences in the same way that rain forests contribute to biodiversity—and for much the same reason. Sociology keeps alive elements of a conceptual gene pool the other social sciences almost certainly will need some day, nurturing temporarily unfashionable ideas and methods that its specialist, paradigm-toting neighbors discard.

There are many examples of this, both substantive and methodological. Sociology kept the notion of "institution" vital in the social sciences long after economists had decided it was of little value; now institutional economics is all the rage and its practitioners draw deeply on sociological insights. Sociologists, who, as Erikson and Smelser both note, are attracted to pattern and affinity, played key roles in developing formal methods of network analyses, which have increasingly entered the repertoires of other disciplines. Looking ahead, we can anticipate that sociology's sister fields will soon rediscover the importance of role structure analysis, which social anthropologists joined sociologists in pioneering but in which they now show little interest; and that sociological work on comparative analysis (methodological and theoretical) will ultimately be exploited by scholars in other fields. In thus surveying and maintaining the back roads of the social scientific imagination, sociology ensures that undervalued but potentially significant intellectual terrain is, if not fully explored, at least charted.

The Burdens of Generalism

Despite its advantages, generalism places heavy burdens on sociology. The first derives from the combination of diverse topics and approaches that sociologists pursue, on the one hand, and their small numbers, on the other. Given these two conditions, it is virtually impossible for sociologists to get up the critical mass of investigators required for "big science": sociologists have no Human Genome Project. Theoretical research programs extending even to three scholarly "generations" can probably be counted on one hand. Progress takes place, but at a pace so deliberate that changes in research fashion frequently leave lines of inquiry abandoned long before they are fully developed, much less exhausted. As Merton reputedly put it once, sociology suffers from too many new departures and too few arrivals.

A second, related, burden is structural. Generalism and small numbers together weaken structures that could provide internal social control. The intellectual organization of most other sciences is hierarchical: people's work is organized around broad problem areas, and within each area smaller clusters of workers pursue particular subproblems, often with characteristic techniques. Practitioners ordinarily have their work evaluated by researchers familiar with both their substantive focus and the methods they use to study it. By contrast, sociology's intellectual architecture resembles what management consultants refer to as a "matrix." Relatively few fields within the discipline have a critical mass of scholars who share both a subject matter and a method of investigation. More commonly, scholars are evaluated by technical experts who know nothing about the substance of their research and area specialists who may not understand their approach. This gives the individual much freedom, but also renders the review process vulnerable to what statisticians call Type 1 and Type 2 errors and makes it difficult for sociologists to build consensus about critical research questions. Sociology does have a core, as I shall argue, but its gravitational pull is sufficiently weak that chunks of the field sometimes spin into eccentric orbit, disengaged from their planet of origin and occasionally devoid of intelligent life.[10]

Generalism is also related to the difficulties, to which both Erikson and Smelser allude, that sociologists have in identifying the "core" of their discipline. Sociologists disagree about whether their discipline has a core, as about many other things. Those who believe it does not, note that introductory sociology textbooks organize material in more varied ways (and differ more in the material they include at all) than do textbooks in more paradigmatic disciplines. They also observe that there is little standardization of requirements for the Ph.D. in graduate-training departments.[11]

Sociology's putative corelessness is customarily attributed either to the differentiation induced by rapid growth in the late 1960s or to the supposed "fragmentation" (political and epistemological) caused by intradisciplinary conflicts of the same era. Yet a study carried out in the 1950s by the American Sociological Society (not yet an association) failed to discern a core in that golden era. Asked to recommend a "central core of knowledge that all candidates for advanced degrees should possess," the committee mentioned several methodological tools, all of which were "taught in other academic departments" and failed to "arrive at any formulation of strictly sociological requisites."[12] The timing is important, for if sociology lacked a core in the 1950s, events of the 1960s cannot be blamed for its subsequent coreless state. And if sociology's corelessness has been chronic rather than variable, we cannot blame the discipline's tribulations of the 1980s on a state that was in evidence at least three decades earlier.

Not all evidence supports the no-core view, however. When sociologists *do* try to characterize the discipline's substantive core, they tend to come up with similar formulations. And consensus is almost certainly greater among active research scholars at graduate-training institutions than in the field at large. For example, when such researchers evaluate grant proposals and papers submitted to leading journals, they display about as much agreement as do scientists in more paradigmatic disciplines.[13]

I believe that sociology *does* have a core: the study of social organization from a comparative perspective. By social organization, I refer to the forms (bureaucracies, networks, families, status groups, hierarchies), processes (stratification, group formation, demographic mechanisms, and social control), and cultural meanings that combine to shape the human terrain. This definition is reasonably comprehensive and it may even be one with which many sociologists can agree. But it does not trip off the tongue as do such phrases as "we study politics" or "the human mind" or even "choice under conditions of scarcity," because it consists of terms that require yet further elucidation.

Sociology's antagonists delight in asking if sociology truly has a "core," no doubt because they are aware of the discomfort the question inspires. But even colleagues of goodwill wonder what sociology is all about. Their perplexity directly reflects the discipline's generalism: Sociologists study so many things in so many ways that as soon as outsiders fix a mental image of the field they encounter instances that seem inconsistent with it. Because observers from other disciplines naturally associate the field with *the subject matter* it studies rather than the underlying conceptual framework that knits together work on diverse topics, their bewilderment is natural.[14]

This puzzlement also reflects the field's generalism *indirectly.* First, because of the difficulty of exerting social control noted above, a few sociologists (and outsiders who call themselves sociologists) do things that hardly any sociologist would recognize as sociology, and often attract much attention for doing it. (If public understanding of sociology can be measured by the proportion of publications in bookstore "sociology" sections that are actually written by sociologists, we are in trouble.) A second indirect effect of generalism, through its centrifugal impact on cognitive networks, as Smelser perceptively notes, is the tendency of most sociologists, even prominent and celebrated ones, to consider themselves closer to the margins than to the mainstream of the field. When even those who are in fact contributing directly to the discipline's cognitive core envision themselves at the margin, it is understandable that outsiders may wonder if there is a core at all.

But if you doubt that sociology *does* have a core set of concepts and abstract generalizations capable of guiding inquiry and producing hypotheses across many concrete phenomena, just consider the foregoing discussion. Where did our hypotheses come from about the structural conditions that produce disciplinary cores and about the conditions under which practitioners and observers will recognize that such cores exist? They came from the application of fundamental principles—core sociological insights about social structure, networks, and identities—to the familiar case at hand, generating distinctly sociological explanations unlikely to occur to observers who are not equipped with the sociologist's repertoire of analytic concepts and strategies.

The third burdensome consequence of sociology's generalism is simply the converse of the great self-reflexivity, the internalization of insight-producing juxtapositions, that I have already chalked up to the credit side of the ledger. More than any other discipline, sociology is defined by a series of tensions—between scientific and humanistic self-image, between the urge to predict and explain and the awareness of particularity, and between formalism and cultural analysis. These tensions, along with cognitive networks that make it difficult for sociologists to avoid them, are the source of sociology's strength; yet they also contribute to the recurrent "crisis of identity and self doubts" of which Smelser writes. Many, if not most, of these tensions concern the purposes of the enterprise: whether or, as I suggest below, in what ways sociology is to be a generalizing science.

Sociology as a Generalizing Science

The real question is not whether sociologists are scientists, but rather what kind of scientist they are. My definition of "scientists" here follows the admirably simple one that Merton quotes from William Whewell: "students of the knowledge of the material world"—but, in keeping with our Comtean tradition, it replaces the modifier "material" with "social" as a description of science's terrain. We must further qualify this definition to point out that scientists not only study knowledge, but also try to increase it through systematic effort. It is this systematic effort, along with a commitment to critical verification of one's claims with respect to empirical data (quantitative or qualitative), that defines the scientific enterprise, rather than the particular form of the principles to be educed— although, as Erikson notes, some greater concern with *"general tendencies* than with *particular events,"* a preference for more general rather than less general principles of explanation, insofar as these can be verified empirically, is implied.

Such a characterization captures the essence of science, I think, distinguishing it from the humanities without excluding much of what goes on in fields that everyone agrees are "scientific." Our definition does not require quantification: observational methods, fieldwork if you will, are important in biology, which is surely a science, as well as in sociology.[15] Nor does it require a faith, which even some natural scientists have lost, in the discoverability of universal covering laws. It decisively excludes as defining criteria lab coats, horn-rimmed glasses, and the opposition of reason to faith and intuition, all staples of imaginative accounts of the scientific enterprise.

But it does distinguish what most sociologists do from two of humanists' favorite preoccupations: establishing the details of historical record and interpreting objects, in each case *for their own sake.* To be sure, interpretation and getting history right are essential for a lot of sociology. But from the standpoint of the enterprise as a whole, they are steps toward explanation, and not the culminating moments of scholarship, as they are for most humanities scholars. Note that this point is not inconsistent with Smelser's illuminating account of sociology's rootedness in both science and the humanities. Sociology's object, to explain the social world, requires both historical scholarship and interpretive vision, for which the field has its humanistic lineage to thank.

General Explanation versus Human Agency: A False Opposition

So far, most readers should find little to object to in this description of sociology as a science, except perhaps its blandness. But I expect that some readers *may* object for the relationship of sociology to science is as much a matter of identity as of definition. Within this volume, Alan Wolfe is most dismissive of the "natural science approach," which he defines by its tools: "the experimental method, the verification of hypotheses, the accumulation of data, the interlinking of confirmed propositions into a theory about the world. . . ." Whereas Smelser describes a discipline poised at the intersection of science, the humanities, and art, Wolfe seems to think that until the rhetorical turn introduced "a much needed note of skepticism," the "belief that a rigorous, almost algorithmic, understanding of human behavior is possible" was hegemonic. The result, he contends, is "the failure of a scientific model based on the natural sciences to predict much more than the obvious. . . ."

This is not the place to recite all that sociologists (much less the social sciences together) have learned about the world. Suffice it to say that an inventory of well-supported explanatory propositions would be lengthy indeed, and the record of important descriptive findings would be far longer. (There would be fewer predictions, and many sociologists committed to the scientific method question prediction, as opposed to explanation, as a viable goal. But as David Patrick Moynihan and Daniel Bell demonstrate in their contributions to this volume, a happy conjuncture of good theory, acute observation, and keen intuition may make it possible to predict events as disparate as the crisis of the African American family and the fall of the Soviet Union.)

Do social science explanations simply report the obvious? Again, I think not. As Erikson tells us, sociology's subject matter "is really *not* the obvious, but the familiar—an important difference." People know a lot about what sociologists study because "the cultures they are a part of have already given them answers." But many of these answers are wrong, and almost all the rest are simplistic, which is precisely why the capacity of sociologists to engage in what humanists call "defamiliarizing discourse"—argument that makes us see the familiar in new and more accurate ways—is so essential.[16]

What Wolfe objects to is not science, at least as I have defined it, or even empiricism. (He calls on sociologists to collect what he calls "real world facts" and study "real world people.") His major complaint appears to be that insofar as it models itself on the natural sciences, sociology pays insufficient homage to human agency, to the capacity of people to interpret and shape their environments in ways that make prediction impossible. This capacity will not come as news to mainstream empirical sociology: there is a long tradition of interest, originating in Merton's observations about self-fulfilling prophecies, in the tendency of social scientific research to alter the very behaviors social scientists wish to predict.[17] Nonetheless, Wolfe blasts sociology's positivists for perceiving "no sharp break between natural and social phenomena" and criticizes Walter

Wallace, a distinguished positivist, for arguing that "the scientific analysis of social phenomena follows exactly the same general principles whether the objects of that analysis are human or nonhuman organisms. . . ." In Wolfe's view (and it is a position shared by many) this notion is inherently dehumanizing, as it represents a brazen disregard for the very creativity and volition that make us human.

There are several defects to this line of criticism. At best, it is overbroad. Although much of what sociologists try to understand requires an appreciation of human choice and meaning, some of it does not: Peter Blau's famous principle that the average minority-group member spends more time interacting with members of the majority than the typical majority-group member spends interacting with members of the minority, a principle that applies ineluctably across the full range of human preferences and persuasions, is a fruitful case in point.[18] So is Scott Feld's explanation of why most people will always feel that their friends are more popular than themselves.[19] It seems unwise to deny ourselves the benefits of such insights out of a mistaken fear that to acknowledge them detracts from human dignity.

Second, Wolfe's criticisms ignore much of what science-identified sociologists do.[20] There is little determinism is sociology: our most frequently employed statistical models are probabilistic, taking for granted the role of chance and choice in human affairs. And far from resting comfortably in a naive faith in prediction, scholars in the field's science-identified wing (where quantitative modeling and theory are most closely aligned) conduct many of the most searching and critical explorations of such notions as causality, explanation, and prediction.[21]

Wolfe betrays a similar misunderstanding of the work of science-identified sociologists when he writes that "Even when people's behavior is in general predictable, not everyone's is, and it ought to be just as much a goal of science to understand those who deviate from the statistical norm as it is those who do not." Statistically oriented sociology, at its most routine, focuses not upon documenting the typical or the average, but upon explaining variance, almost obsessively so. (Indeed, there is perhaps more justice to the opposite criticism: that sociologists who use least-squares statistical methods are often so preoccupied with explaining relatively small amounts of variation that they ignore striking and theoretically unanticipated commonalities.) Sophisticated social statisticians have devoted considerable attention both to "outlier analysis" (intensive investigation of cases that do not conform to one's models) and to the problem of population heterogeneity (how to make sure that one does not generalize about processes that work differently for different groups as if they operated uniformly for everyone).[22]

Third, Wolfe conflates the substance of what is studied with the approach one takes to studying it. Few sociologists would disagree that "unlike the natural sciences, [sociology] must account for the interpretive capacities of those it studies." But that does not mean that one cannot use certain natural science tools to study the ways in which humans impute meaning and make sense of the situations they encounter. Much cognitive psychology does this (e.g., Daniel Kahneman's research on routine errors in reasoning). So do sociological analyses of public symbol systems, civic and religious.[23] The problem is not that culture and interpretation are more difficult to measure than structural concepts, but that they require more concrete indicators, which therefore tend to limit the scope of explanatory models.[24]

Finally, and most important, Wolfe's critique fails because it conflates ontological with epistemological and tactical aspects of science. As Erikson puts it, "Few sociologists would insist that human gatherings are *like* galaxies or molecules, but we would all insist that the eye one trains on human social life is disciplined in the same way as the eye one trains on the things of the physical world." Even Comte, that tireless promoter of positivism, recognized the complementarity of scientific and humanistic ways of knowing, granting "the impossibility of obtaining absolute truth" through scientific means.[25] Reduction in sociology is a matter not of faith but of tactics: one provisionally blinds oneself to a portion of the world's "blooming, buzzing confusion," as William James put it, reducing this complexity in order to apprehend some small part of it. Thus calls for "multidimensional" theory, while an indispensable defense against the reification of opportunistic disregard into long-term blindness, should not be granted absolute authority. As is often the case, sociology's advantage lies not in one or another epistemological stance, but in the tension between them—in this instance, the dialectic between strategic multidimensionality and tactical reductionism.

Bell identifies the crux of the matter when he asks: "Are man and society part of nature; i.e., is the social order, such as the family and polis, 'natural,' or is there some qualitative change in a move from nature to culture . . . ?" Wolfe takes men and women outside of nature: so far outside that reflexivity and free will render explanation impossible. Rational-choice theory, one of the most "scientific" regions of sociology, highlights human volition even more dramatically than does Wolfe, but by placing human choice within nature, it treats agency as the primordial stuff out of which explanation is constructed. While less extreme, most other efforts to make of sociology a generalizing science deal with agency not by dishonoring it, but by placing it, as part of nature, within a system of probabilistic explanation.

Can Sociologists Produce General Explanations?

I have argued vigorously that nothing in the humanistic critique of scientism effectively challenges the ability of sociology to explain structure and change in human societies. In this section I suggest that what *is* problematic is the extent to which such explanations and principles can be general in scope.

The issue is not, I think, whether we should *try* to produce general explanations. The operations of science—defining constructs, deciding how to make them operational, designing and testing hypotheses—exercise a wholesome influence on theory construction, permitting one to hone arguments to a clarity that is otherwise elusive. At issue is the extent to which the value lies in the discipline itself (subjecting ourselves, as it were, to a zen of science) or in its results.

Charles Tilly and Viviana Zelizer pose this dilemma extraordinarily well in their two chapters. Although neither would go so far as William Blake ("To Generalize Is to Be an Idiot: To Particularize Is the Alone Distinction of Merit"[26]), both are skeptical about the prospects for generalization. Both Tilly and Zelizer find pattern in social life, but in the context of broader forms of particularization: for both, the pattern lies in mechanisms that produce the particulars, not in the outcomes themselves. Explanation, then, entails deploying structural principles in order to account for particular events, rather than predicting large numbers of those events in a probabilistic fashion.

Tilly's essay makes clear just how much sociology has made common cause with history in recent years. Comparativists absorb vast and multiple national historical literatures, often contributing to them as well. Institutionalists plumb the archives to examine the social construction of organizational forms. Dynamic models and sequence analyses engage the attention of the statistically and mathematically inclined. Still others plumb the implications for sociology of narrativity by means both formal and discursive.

History holds two lessons for sociology. One is that our causal models should be temporal and focus on the order in which things occur; generalization must incorporate sequence in order to be powerful. The other lesson, quite different, is that the objects or units of which we write are so thoroughly reconstituted by history, and the interaction of historical agents is so complex, that we search in vain for explanatory generalizations. Although, as Ira Katznelson notes, both points can be found in Tilly's essay, I think that his major thrust is the latter, and that his critique of predictive generalization is relevant well beyond comparative historical sociology.

In a sense, however, generalizability is not itself the issue. Rather the prospects for generalization rest on three separate matters: specificity, complexity, and scope.

Specificity

At the root of the problem is the ubiquitous tension between structure and specificity, between the shape and the feel of social life, which is built into sociology's subject matter. That tension is faced and resolved in different ways by all of the human sciences but, as usual, sociology's solution reflects its generalism. Economists and (only slightly less) psychologists have opted for abstraction, the former treating concrete tastes and preferences as exogenous and the latter measuring aptitudes rather than orientations. Anthropologists and historians have chosen specificity. By contrast, sociologists try to have it both ways and sometimes succeed, developing methods and ideas and theoretical approaches out of the confrontation between their generalizing aspirations and the "irreducible differentiae" (S. F. Nadel's term) of concrete human societies and cultural systems.[27] Nonetheless, there is often an uncomfortable fit between structural and formal categories (e.g., size, number), which lend themselves to great abstraction, and substantive categories (e.g., individualism, gender) which frequently reflect locally variable systems of meaning and classification.

As one moves from contemporary research in one society to historical comparative work, even structural categories lose their generalizabilty. Merton's essay on science in Part II contains two quotes from Lewis Carroll: one, which Carroll put in Humpty-Dumpty's mouth in *Alice's Adventures in Wonderland,* reflecting the scientist's devotion to precise (if in Humpty's case capricious) denotation, and one, above Carroll's own name, representing the humanist's appreciation of connotation and ambiguity. Where do sociologists fall along this continuum? Tilly and Zelizer question the nature of the units about which sociologists often hope to generalize: are such constructs as the family, money, classes, or the state fixed enough in time (or across space) to make generalization meaningful? Or do our constructs, like Alice's croquet gear, unfurl themselves into different forms as the game proceeds?

Complexity

Tilly criticizes what he calls monadism: the belief that history is driven by the behaviors of self-directing monads, that these behaviors create recurrent structures and processes, and that sociology's job is to develop models that explain the largest number of invariant outcomes. "[R]eal history," Tilly argues, "carefully observed, does not fall into neat, recurrent chunks; it winds and snarls like a proliferating vine. . . . [S]ocial processes follow strong regularities yet do not repeat themselves; the regularities lie in causal mechanisms, not in recurrent structures or sequences."

Tilly identifies two problems here. The first you will recognize as the problem of specificity. The second is that of complexity: even if one could treat units as comparable from case to case, the interactions that produce historical outcomes become more numerous and more complex as the scope of one's attention increases. Therefore, even if one grants that there are generalizable principles of social interaction at the level of the dyad or small group, the processes that Tilly studies are driven by repeated interactions among thousands, even millions, of dyads and groups, rendering the general principles of microanalysis more useful for interpreting history than for explaining it probabilistically. The concurrent operation of many social mechanisms, each lawful in its own right, can only be captured by reference to multiway interaction effects (statements that describe the effect of one variable on an outcome as contingent upon the state of a second, itself perhaps dependent upon the condition of a third). General propositions may be possible in theory, but generalization is unattainable in practice, first, because the complexity of the causal interactions that must be specified to create an exhaustive model overwhelms the cognitive limits of the human mind and, second, because even if such a model *can be* developed, it will *seem* historicist rather than general.

Are there any ways out of this dilemma? The simplest, favored by a few structuralists, is to deny it: rather than view the behavior of states or classes as aggregating out the activities of the people they comprise, one can treat all units as comparably subject to similar natural laws, and largely independent of processes operating at more micro levels of analysis. Although this position has had vigorous champions it is not one that many sociologists are prepared to embrace.

The notion of *historical path dependence*—the dependence of outcomes not simply upon the social conditions with which they are proximately associated, but upon the precise sequence of events that have preceded them—provides a second kind of resolution. Potentially, one can build history into explanatory generalization directly by treating the nature and order of events (e.g., the stages of revolutionary organization or the jobs in a person's career) as variables in a model[28] Third, one can at once acknowledge complexity and preserve generalization by developing models that divide societies, groups, industries, or organizations into different types and posit different causal mechanisms shaping the behavior of lower-level units in each.

The second and third solutions are really the same: developing general models with lots of interaction effects. Indeed, Tilly's critique of the insufficient complexity (though not of the insufficient specificity) of "invariant" models is met once we introduce these perturbations, for they demonstrate that "generalization" and "historicism" are not mutually exclusive: the more complex the interaction effects, the more consistent is explanatory generalization with an appreciation of historical particularity. We can find general principles, but the ones we find are not likely to be highly abstract or elegant.

Moreover, such principles are not likely to feel very "scientific." The trouble is that at some very finite point a model's complexity outdistances the capacity of our minds to grasp it. Imagine, for example, a statistical model that purports to explain political violence in urban electoral campaigns with recourse to five variables, each of which (for simplicity's sake) can assume one of three values. Imagine that this model explains 80 percent of the variance in violence as a function of interaction effects among these variables. Although models with that much explanatory power are rare in sociology, it is unlikely that it would be hailed as a breakthrough. For one would have to understand the connection between at least 243 distinct types of campaign and the extent of mob violence in order to get the point.[29] Readers would lose track of such a typology by the sixth or seventh type and dismiss its authors as hopeless historicists soon after. By contrast, a researcher who succeeded in explaining 80 percent of the variance as a result of the main effects of five variables, without interactions, *would* impress people, but that is precisely the kind of highly abstract general explanation ordinarily rendered unattainable by the complexity Tilly describes.

Scope

Some of the debate over generalizability reflects the laxity of many scholars in specifying the scope conditions to which their generalizations pertain.[30] From this perspective, the question before us is not, "can sociologists create scientific generalizations," but rather to what scope of generalization should we aspire. The most eloquent argument for generalizations of rather modest scope is Merton's classic essay on theories of the middle range; on this, as on so many other matters, the Mertonian position has won the day.[31] Tilly reminds us of this when he writes that "To rediscover history is not to fit singular models, huge or modest, to great slabs of time and space."

Reduction of explanatory scope is a solution to the problem of specificity and complexity: the units to which uniform constructs apply become more similar, and the number of interactions that must be taken into account becomes fewer, as we restrict generalizations to smaller swathes of time and space. And scope conditions can themselves become parameters of more general (if less elegant) models that specify the ways in which causal mechanisms are themselves contingent upon temporal or spacial environments.

To complicate matters further, sociology as a discipline has been wrestling with the notion of causality, upon which the efforts to construct systems of general propositions are premised. Such efforts have hit off in two rather different directions. On the one hand, "agency" has become the apple pie of contemporary grand theories (from structuration theory to rational choice), which emphasize the capacity of human beings to determine their fates in defiance of (and perhaps in reflexive reaction to) regularities that social scientists have uncovered from past experience. In this volume, Wolfe's essay exemplifies this position. On the other hand, middle-range theory has become increasingly relational, viewing society as a network or field of relations in which units are "embedded" in different ways, and depicting relations rather than actors as the key units for purposes of explanation. (In this volume, Tilly's and Zelizer's essays speak for relational thinking: William Julius Wilson's essay also exemplifies it, when he depicts poverty as constituted by relations between people in low-income communities and between communities in the larger society; and Erikson captures it best when he writes that sociologists train their eyes "on the *spaces between* intersecting individuals. . . .")

Agent-centered and relational approaches are rather strange bedfellows, given the strong Durkheimian tradition in network analysis that views pairwise relations as aggregating to superordinate structures that constrain the actors whose relations constitute them. What binds them together is their shared rejection of the view, long prominent in sociology, that explanation consists of statements about the statistical effects of one attribute or characteristic of a person or collectivity on some other attribute, a view that Andrew Abbott has described as "ordinary linear reality."[32] The development of such positions, and of methods of research and data analysis that embody their presuppositions, enriches and complicates the question of generalizability still further.

A Question of Balance

I have argued that sociology is a science, broadly defined, oriented to the production of lawful generalizations about the social world. But I have also argued that there are reasons to doubt the extent to which our generalizations are likely to be both elegant and of very extensive scope.

How scientific, in any of that term's various senses, can sociology be? Ultimately, as sociologists like to say, it is an empirical question. The goal of generalization is a noble one, but if abstract principles are the aim of the scientific process, there are key moments in that process that require the tools of humanistic inquiry and critical, even deconstructive, thought. Often, it seems, the appropriate methodological stance is neither scientific nor humanistic, but *contrarian*. If case studies have proliferated in a research area and metatheoretical reflection has begun to overwhelm research-based conclusions, it is probably time to refine concepts, work on measurement issues, compile a few huge data sets, and start testing hypotheses. If by contrast, a subfield has become paradigmatic, and research consists of hypothesis-testing aimed at qualifying or elaborating upon established principles, it is probably time for case studies to offer a defamiliarizing submersion in the bath of lived experience, perhaps with a theoretical polemic or two to shake things up. From this perspective, the fact that sociology has witnessed both the development of increasingly sophisticated approaches to quantitative data analysis *and* a revitalization of the case study fieldwork approach is a sign not of fragmentation but of good health.[33]

What is clear, I think, is that we should not seek some harmonious mean or sociological third way between the humanities and the natural sciences, but should welcome (within reason) the clash of epistemologies and the pursuit of different ways of knowing. If sociology is the illegitimate issue of a union between science and the humanities, it should celebrate its bastardy, recognizing that in the tensions between the humanistic and science-identified wings of the field lies the source of its generalist advantage.

Sociologists as Guardians of the General Good

If sociologists have often been scientists pursuing knowledge for its own sake, they just as frequently have sought to turn their craft to public purposes, linking (as C. Wright Mills put it) private problems and public issues—diagnosing social ills, testing the presuppositions of proposed policy solutions, and evaluating the effectiveness of government programs. This role is well represented here in the contributions by Wilson, Moynihan, and Bell.

The manner in which sociologists have conceived of their public personae has varied over time. In Comte's vision, their role was to be quite literally priestly, practicing statecraft as they presided over the new religion of humanity. Others, like Karl Marx or, more modestly, such transitional figures as Pitirim Sorokin and J. L. Moreno, were prophetic in style. Sorokin believed social scientific insights would usher in an era of world peace; Moreno (who reported communicating directly with God) thought that utopia could be reached by the deliberate application of sociometry and psychodrama, both of which he invented.[34]

As Max Weber (one of the first to write about the tension between scholarly detachment and civic engagement, and to transcend that tension) would have predicted, a more modest, secular vision of the priestly persona prevailed. In the United States, at least, sociologists were central to the development of public policy from the 1930s through the 1970s. When Herbert Hoover asked Charles Ogburn to direct a commission on recent social trends, the significance of social science for public policy making was ratified. By the late 1960s, an expanding federal government engaged in large-scale social experiments as part of a commitment to ongoing institutional learning. For a while, it appeared that Comte's vision would be realized.[35]

More recently, the momentum of state expansion, and with it the rise of the policy sciences, has been slowed. When public discourse identifies citizens as part of a common community, portrays the state as a source of solutions, and aspires to make social learning routine, sociology's claims to public attention and support rest on its contribution to policy analysis. When the commons is shrinking, however, and social problems are defined as individual discontents beyond government's reach, sociology becomes less a partner to power than a potential source of embarrassment and reproach, with predictable consequences for the field's prosperity.

Policy Analysis and the Problem of Prediction

What was not apparent at the height of the romance between big government and social science was the fragility of the relationship. Some sources of this fragility resided in the nature of social science. As Bell notes, one can be as sophisticated as one wants about the difference between explanation and prediction, but ultimately, responsible politicians and policy makers must look into the future and develop programs on the basis of what they see.

But, as we have seen, sociology is not well equipped to generate confident predictions about most of the events that policy makers wish to divine. Sociologists and other social scientists are adept at predicting the response of individuals to changes in material incentives at any moment. They are less effective at predicting such things as massive economic restructuring, religious revivals, or geopolitical dislocations, which alter the calculus by which individuals make their choices. And they are usually even less good at predicting the contours of political or institutional change. (To be sure, a few farsighted social scientists like Moynihan and Randall Collins predicted the fall of the Soviet Union, but many more social scientists were on hand to explain why they had to be wrong.[36]) The villain, as usual, is the complexity of social life and the interaction effects one must take into account in order to make any predictions, not to mention the purely stochastic intrusions that intervene to divert even the swiftest and straightest currents from their path.

Wisdom, then, prevents us from pretending we can predict the future (for the same reason it makes us cautious about the prospects of abstract generalization), at the same time that policy relevance requires us to anticipate it. Most sociological interventions do not require great precision: the premises behind many public policies these days are so defective that we know all we need to explain why those policies are doomed to failure. When policy is more closely aligned to social science principles, Bell's distinction between scientific knowledge, intuitive divination, and prophecy by ambiguity offers a solution to this dilemma. At some point, propelled by hope or hubris, the engaged social scientist must take a leap of faith (as Moynihan describes his own choice to call attention to changes in African American families) and push science as far as it will go, leaving intuition to take one the rest of the way.

Sociological Progress and Public Discourse

Even when sociology is generating usable knowledge, it may be difficult to get policy makers to pay attention. As David K. Cohen and Michael Garet observed two decades ago, good research generates the opposite of the sound bites that pass for political discussion in much of our polity. In general, the better the research, the less conclusive the results, for good scholarship makes distinctions that reflect the complexity and contingency of the world itself.[37] This is more of a problem for sociology than for economics, our sometime partner, sometime rival, in policy debate. Economics has two advantages. First, it has a powerful modeling framework in which aggregate outcomes are driven by individual choices, which make its behavioral presuppositions relatively easy to understand. Second, it has an ideology (radical individualism) that is consonant with the ideology of American political elites, which makes its mistakes easier to overlook.

By contrast, sociologists interpret the world as it is. Wilson finds that African American poverty has been exacerbated not only by structural economic changes, but also by the concentration of the poor in particular neighborhoods (which in turn affects the resource networks to which poor people have access) and by the negative psychological impacts of racism and downward mobility. Try getting that sentence on the seven o'clock news! It would be a lot easier to lay poverty at the door of racism, culture, or economic change, but none of these sound bites alone would provide an adequate explanation of the problem or useful direction as to its resolution.

Clearly the research program that Wilson describes has produced much usable knowledge. His results enable policy makers to understand poverty well enough to model it and thereby to predict the results of policy interventions (at least insofar as experience, skill, and knowledge enable them to implement such measures adequately). Wilson's own policy recommendations comprise a mosaic of small, relatively inexpensive pieces—car pools, job information centers, reforms in job training programs—rather than (except perhaps for dispersed housing assistance) bold, costly initiatives. But his complex diagnosis does not (nor could it or should it) lead to a single transparent prescription that could help to resolve the crisis of political will brought about by conservative government bashing and the "reformation" of social scientific hubris about which Moynihan writes in his chapter.

The Social Preconditions for Sociological Policy Analysis

The partnership between social scientists and public policy makers is fragile in large part because it rests on a series of assumptions that are unexamined until they are violated. A first, and rather simple assumption, is that there are facts about the social world that remain to be discovered. When Sociology was on trial at Yale, elements in the administration (though few elsewhere on campus) were unreceptive to the argument that the field made a fundamental contribution to policy analysis because they seemed to think that anything one needed to know about the human condition could be found in the works of Aristotle and Cicero (and perhaps Cato the Elder).

A second, equally basic, assumption is that government should try to solve social problems. Arthur Stinchcombe has noted that sociologists tend to be interested in "facts about things the government and the economy do not have under control."[38] Political leaders who profess that the economy, or "the market," can satisfactorily resolve all of our problems or that government is incapable of solving any of them (or both) find sociologists about as useful as plastic flamingos, and about as welcome in public debates as fire ants at picnics.

A third, related, assumption is that effective government action requires organizational learning: that social programs must be implemented, studied, and then reformed on the basis of evaluation before they are likely to work. When a plan to vaccinate poor children can be slated for elimination by Congress because the responsible agency had not gotten it right within eighteen months of the passage of legislation, the idea of systematic learning has taken a serious hit.[39]

These points are straightforward. A more elusive, but equally important precondition for a productive relationship between social science and public policy is the notion of community that animates public discourse. The pronoun "we" often appears in the prose of sociologists who write about policy issues (though less often now, perhaps, than in the past). Sometimes "we" describes a set of publics who know something about the world as a result of social science research, as in "we are well aware of the costs of crime to residents of poor neighborhoods." At other times it refers to members of a polity taking collective responsibility for some public good: "we have new ways to prevent the degradation of our environment." At still other times, the first-person plural represents a commitment to an inclusive sense of social membership, as in "all of our children must have the opportunity to receive a first-rate education." Sometimes social scientists operate at all three levels at once: "we know we cannot ensure that poor mothers will find jobs simply by throwing them off welfare, and we must not let our children go to bed hungry at night."

A certain definition of community, a shared sense of collective identity, is necessary to make such first-person pronouns plausible and persuasive. What do we mean by "we"? What are the boundaries that place some people inside, and some people outside, our definition of community? The ways that social scientists use the term "we" begin to sound a little awkward when identity politics on both right and left challenge assumptions of common fate and purpose; when distrust of cultural authority and rejection of science from both poles erode the ability of social scientists to represent themselves as carriers of social knowledge; when political leaders first shrink the criterion of social membership from propinquity to formal citizenship, and then appear to embrace triage as a governing principle. Without a "we" about which to speak, sociology loses the rhetorical ground for its moral influence and the idea of "society" itself has less meaning, as either a subject of inquiry or an object of action.

A distinguished line of sociological scholarship, beginning with Weber, reflects upon the connections between Protestant religious faith and the emergence and expansion of rationality. In this volume Smelser notes the prominent role Protestant Christianity played in the emergence of sociology in the United States. Although his comments address the past, they also may be germane to the present. Smelser describes sociology's reformist tradition as the basis for its policy interventions, and notes that this thrust entails an identification with the oppressed and a commitment to describing the particulars of their lives. The affinity between this mission and the witnessing tradition in liberal Protestantism is self-evident. In recent years, the evangelical movement has grown mightily and liberal denominations have diminished in size and influence. To what extent has the "plausibility structure," as Peter Berger would put it, which sustained sociology's credibility as a policy science, been fundamentally weakened by the decline of the liberal Protestantism (with its notion of witness and its capacious definition of the human family) out of which sociology emerged?

Jean Bethke Elshtain raises the issue of community in a related way in her discussion of the roles of rhetoric (persuasive discourse) and dialectic (a collaborative search for truth) in intellectuals' interventions in policy matters. Elshtain eloquently defends rhetoric as "part and parcel of any coherent attempt to arrive at the truth," but she qualifies her comments as applying to "attempts to persuade *within a particular language community*" (italics added). Most policy analysts, I suspect, see little tension between rhetoric and dialectic, because they believe that a disinterested search for truth will reinforce their own preferences. But this is only true, first, if everyone agrees to use words in the same way, and second, if the truth one seeks is about the means rather than the ends of policy. Once dialectic and rhetoric are no longer embedded in a community of shared meanings and values, policy analysis becomes a much less comfortable activity.

Does this mean that sociologists can no longer perform a significant public role? Of course not. The work of sociologists and their colleagues in the policy-oriented regions of economics and political science continues to play an important part in policy formation in many areas. There will always be periods in which politicians are more or less attentive to the insights that the social sciences have to offer, and more or less interested in using government to solve the problems our research reveals. If sociology is a key element in the learning society for its ability to illuminate the means of public policy, it is perhaps even more indispensable as a guilty conscience when political commitment to resolving social problems fades.

None of this is to suggest that the public role of sociologists is a simple one. Whether writing memos to political appointees or drafting legislation or writing op-ed pieces expressing outrage at Congress's latest offense, that role is fraught with moral ambiguities too familiar to warrant our attention and too complex for brief discussion to be of value. Ultimately, however, we must agree with Weber that whatever the temptations attendant to sociologists' participation in policy discourse, the dangers of a policy enterprise uninformed by the values, methods, insights, and research findings of the social sciences would be far worse.

Conclusion

At 1995, the U.S. Congress is attempting to alter the understanding of government's purpose that emerged during the second and third quarters of the twentieth century, and similar if less radical currents affect policy making in the Western social democracies. Such changes, if they are brought to fruition, are certain to change the role of the social sciences in contemporary societies, as they will alter almost all of our political and social institutions.

But if sociology, like everything else, is vulnerable to sharp swings in its environment, it is also robust. A small, diverse set of scholars pursuing a quixotically vast object, sociology is prone to crises of faith and to external criticism. But its very diversity, or generalism as I have called it, lends it a resilience and capacity for growth that many disciplines and institutions lack. Recent political developments (it is still too early to assess their implacability) may jeopardize the market but augment the need for sociology's contribution to public understanding.

Internally, the field bristles with vitality. Sociologists still argue with one another about method and epistemology, but in general, the conversations are more sophisticated and less antagonistic than they were two decades ago. The results of sociological research—on inequality, the family, crime and punishment, poverty—provide far more purchase on these matters than was available even ten years ago, at least for those policy makers and citizens who care to consult them.

There will always be the doubtful and the disillusioned. But when Wolfe writes that "sociologists are no longer certain they have anything to offer the world," one doubts that he speaks for many of his colleagues. The conceptual and methodological diversity that sociology provides is as vital to the social scientific enterprise as cultural diversity is to society and as biological diversity is to the ecosystem. Sociology continues to produce metaphors to think with, facts to reason with, and an understanding of the social world that, while imperfect, provides a better compass than anything else available. The pursuit of knowledge and understanding is more difficult, and sociology's position is more humble, than Comte anticipated. But there are victories, and the excitement of the chase is undiminished.

Notes

1. I am very grateful to Kai Erikson for sensitive and helpful editorial criticism.

2. Gertrud Lenzer, ed. *August Comte and Positivism: The Essential Writings.* New York: Harper, 1975. Comte introduced the term "sociologue" at roughly the same time that Whewell introduced the term "scientist." As Robert Merton and Gerald Holton note in Part II, the function of Whewell's neologism was related to Mary Somerville's call for unification of the sciences, a concern at the heart of Comte's writings as well. Is it possible that John Stuart Mill, who gave critical support to Comte at key junctures in the latter's career, represented a link between the two efforts to achieve scientific unification, and between the terms, "sociologist" and "scientist," that emerged from them?

3. After reviewing some seventy-five areas of policy making, Steven Brint concluded that "the influence of experts in policy making is of distinctly secondary importance." Steven Brint, *In an Age of Experts: the Changing Role of Professionals in Politics and Public Life* (Princeton: Princeton University Press, 1994), 18, 135–44.

4. I draw here on the discussion of generalism and specialism in chapter 5 of *Organizational Ecology* by Michael T. Hannan and John Freeman (Cambridge: Harvard University Press, 1990).

5. For a graphic representation of this disintegrated quality, based on the analysis of cocitation data, see Diana Crane and Henry Small, "American Sociology Since the Seventies: The Emerging Identity Crisis in the Discipline," in Terence C. Halliday and Morris Janowitz, eds., *Sociology and Its Publics: The Forms and Fates of Disciplinary Organizations* (Chicago: University of Chicago Press, 1992).

See also Arthur L. Stinchcombe, "Disintegrated Disciplines and the Future of Sociology," *Sociological Forum* 9 (1994): 279–91.

6. Hannan and Freeman, ibid., 105.

7. See Eviatar Zerubavel, *The Fine Line: Making Distinctions in Everyday Life* (New York: Free Press, 1991).

8. Harison C. White, *Identity and Control* (Princeton: Princeton University Press, 1994), 118–26.

9. Paul Starr, "The Edge of Social Science," *Harvard Educational Review* 44 (1974): 393–415. The natural sciences have recognized this by adopting interdisciplinary approaches so thoroughly that in many medical schools, departmental titles are little more than a fiction, at least with respect to research activities. In general, however, the social sciences have remained more parochial.

10. I am indebted to a remark, on which this phrasing draws, that John Simon once made about the universe of philanthropic foundations. On structural factors influencing the capacity of disciplines to police their boundaries, see Stephen Fuchs and Jonathan Turner, "What Makes a Science 'Mature'? Patterns of Organizational Control in Scientific Production," *Sociological Theory* 4 (1986): 143–50; Mark A. Schneider, *Culture and Enchantment* (Chicago: University of Chicago Press, 1983); and Thomas F. Gieryn, "Boundary-Work and the Demarcation of Science from Non-Science: Strains and Interests in the Professional Ideologies of Scientists," *American Sociological Review* 48 (1983): 781–95.

11. For assertions that sociology lacks a core, see Crane and Small, op. cit.; Jonathan Turner and Stephen Turner, *The Impossible Science: An Institutional Analysis of American Sociology* (Newbury Park, Calif.: Sage, 1990); and Stephen Cole, "Why Sociology Doesn't Make Progress Like the Natural Sciences," *Sociological Forum* 9 (1994): 133–54. On textbooks and curricula, see, respectively, Barbara Levitt and Clifford Nass, "The Lid on the Garbage Can: Constraints on Decision-Making in the Technical Core of College-Text Publishing," *Administrative Science Quarterly* 4 (1989): 190–207; and Joan Huber, "Institutional Perspectives on Sociology," *American Journal of Sociology* 101 (1995): 194–216, 209.

12. Elbridge Sibley, *The Education of Sociologists in the United States* (New York: Russell Sage Foundation, 1963), 114.

13. See Huber, op cit., p. 204, for a characterization of the core similar to, if more concise than, the one offered here. On evaluation, see Michael Cole, *Making Science: Between Nature and Society* (Cambridge: Harvard University Press, 1992), ch. 5. Cole argues that sociology has consensus at its frontier without a core in its heartland.

14. The comparatively high ratio of research topics to sociologists makes cumulation of substantive findings difficult. James Davis asks: "Why are there no conflicts over priority in sociology? Because sociologists are nice? Nope, because no two sociologists ever study the same thing. . . ." James Davis, "What's Wrong with Sociology?" *Sociological Forum* 9 (1994): 179–97.

15. Of course, observation and quantification are not mutually exclusive; systematic field observation can yield valuable quantitative data. On this point, see

Albert J. Reiss Jr., "Trained Incapacities of Sociologists," in Halliday and Janowitz (eds.), op. cit., 297–316.

16. Moreover, as is often noted, the things that sociologists learn, or even the concepts they construct, often find their way into common language and understandings rapidly, adding to the sense that sociology teaches what we knew all along. Occasionally this reacts back upon sociological research itself. In my first year in graduate school, I spent several days reading over field notes from Richard P. Coleman and Bernice L. Neugarten's broad-ranging study of Kansas City (*Social Status in the City* [San Francisco, Jossey-Bass, 1971]), which was an effort to study the social structure of a large metropolis using methods similar to those employed in the classic community studies of the Yankee City series. Men and women interviewed in those studies often employed such colorful phrases as "rich people on the hill" or "people who live like animals" to describe the groups in their midst, and the researchers processed their accounts into the familiar analytic typology of upper, upper-middle, middle-middle, and so on. By the late 1950s, when Coleman and Neugarten conducted their Kansas City interviews, middle-class Americans had so assimilated this line of scholarship that when asked for their folk categorizations of the Kansas City social structure, many regurgitated Warner's typology, which they apparently had learned in school or through the media. Thus the apparent banality of social science findings is in part a consequence of the substantial power social science wields over the way we understand the world about us.

17. Robert K. Merton, "The Self-Fulfilling Prophecy," in *Social Theory and Social Structure* (New York: Free Press, [1948] 1968).

18. Peter Blau, *Inequality and Heterogeneity* (New York: Free Press, 1977).

19. Scott L. Feld, "Why Your Friends Have More Friends Than You Do," *American Journal of Sociology* 96 (1991): 1464–77.

20. I use the term "science identified" to describe that wing of the field that identifies most closely with the natural sciences, relies heavily on statistical tools, cares deeply about such issues as measurement and model specification, and for the most part, adopts a Popperian rhetoric and view of science. This term, though awkward, seems preferable to the simpler "scientistic" (many more sociologists are scientific in the broader sense), the pejorative "scientific" (which is unfair), or the catchier "pro-science" (which would include science fans who are not strongly identified, themselves or by others, with natural science approaches).

21. See, e.g., Michael E. Sobel, "Causal Inference in the Social and Behavioral Sciences," in Gerhard Arminger, Clifford C. Clogg, and Michael E. Sobel, eds., *Handbook of Statistical Modeling for the Social and Behavioral Sciences* (New York: Plenum Press, 1995). Also, Otis Dudley Duncan, *Notes on Social Measurement: Historical and Critical* (New York: Russell Sage Foundation, 1984); Joel H. Levine, *Exceptions Are the Rule: An Inquiry into Methods in the Social Sciences* (Boulder, Colo.: Westview Press, 1993); Stanley Lieberson, *Making It Count: The Improvement of Social Research and Theory* (Berkeley: University of California Press, 1985).

22. John W. Tukey, *Exploratory Data Analysis* (Reading, Mass.: Addison-Wesley, 1977); Herbert F. Weisberg and Charles E. Smith Jr., "The Advent of Dynamic Graphics Statistical Computing," *Political Science and Politics* 26 (1993): 228–32; Bruce Western and Simon Jackman, "Bayesian Inference for Comparative Research," *American Political Science Review* 88 (1994): 412–23.

23. Daniel Kahneman, Paul Slovic, and Amos Tversky, eds., *Judgment under Uncertainty: Heuristics and Decisions* (New York: Cambridge University Press, 1982); Robert Wuthnow, *Meaning and Moral Order* (Berkeley: University of California Press, 1987); Guy E. Swanson, *The Birth of the Gods* (Ann Arbor: University of Michigan Press, 1960).

24. Ronald Jepperson and Ann Swidler, "What Properties of Culture Should We Measure," *Poetics* 22 (1994): 359–71.

25. Comte, Auguste, *Introduction to Positive Philosophy*, edited with an introduction and revised translation by Frederick Ferré (Indianapolis: Bobbs-Merrill, 1970), 2.

26. Blake's annotation to *The Works of Sir Joshua Reynolds*, quoted in Steven E. Weil, *Rethinking the Museum and Other Meditations* (Washington: Smithsonian Institution Press, 1990), xiv.

27. S. F. Nadel, *Theory of Social Structure* (London: Cohen and West, 1975), 28. To be sure, there is a distinguished and fruitful generalizing tradition within structuralist sociology (Bell mentions Georg Simmel in this regard). But in recent years, leading structuralists (see Tilly's discussion in this volume of repertoires of action, or Harrison White's *Identity and Control*, op cit.) have increasingly taken culture and meaning into account.

28. Andrew Abbott, "Sequences of Social Events: Concepts and Methods for the Analysis of Order in Social Processes," *Historical Methods* 16 (1983): 129–47.

29. 243 = 3 [values] to the 5th [variables] power. Of course, in real life such a model would almost certainly contain 2-, 3-, and 4-way interaction effects as well, making it even more complicated.

30. Henry Walker and Bernard P. Cohen, "Scope Statements: Imperatives for Evaluating Theory," *American Sociological Review* 50 (1985): 288–301.

31. Robert K. Merton, "On Sociological Theories of the Middle Range," in *On Theoretical Sociology: Five Essays, Old and New* (New York: Free Press, 1967 [1949]).

32. Andrew Abbott, "Transcending Ordinary Linear Reality," *Sociological Theory* 6 (1988): 189–96, A third perspective, not represented in this volume, links these perspectives by focusing on the way that agency generates embedded structures. In this view, sociologists explain structures when they can identify rules of social interaction and create mathematical representations of such rules in the form of models that can generate macro-structures to which existing structures can be compared. See Bruce H. Mayhew, "Baseline Models of Sociological Phenomena," *Journal of Mathematical Sociology* 9 (1984): 259–81; and Thomas J. Fararo, *The Meaning of General Theoretical Sociology: Tradition and Formalization* (Cambridge: Cambridge University Press, 1989).

33. On quantitative approaches, see Gerhard Arminger, Clifford C. Clogg, and Michael E. Sobel, eds., *Handbook of Statistical Modeling for the Social and Behavioral Sciences* (New York: Plenum Press, 1995). On case study approaches, see Michael Burawoy, *Ethnography Unbound: Power and Resistance in the Modern Metropolis* (Berkeley: University of California Press, 1991) and Charles C. Ragin and Howard S. Becker, eds., *What Is a Case? Exploring the Foundations of Social Inquiry* (New York: Cambridge University Press, 1992).

34. Pitirim A. Sorokin, The Crisis of Our Age: *The Social and Cultural Outlook* (New York: E. P. Dutton, 1941). My remarks on Moreno are based on memory of a long-playing record, which I think was titled "J. L. Moreno Speaks," which Professor Ron Breiger shared with his social networks seminar at Harvard in the mid-1970s, in which Moreno recounted his personal conversations with God. Although the record has passed into history and precise information is not available, Breiger recalls that it was produced by the Sociometric Research Institute in Dobbs Ferry, N.Y.

35. See Alvin W. Gouldner's trenchant contemporary analysis of the affinity between functionalist sociology and the growth of the welfare state in chapter 9 of *The Coming Crisis of Western Sociology* (New York: Basic Books, 1970).

36. On this phenomenon, see Randall Collins, "Prediction in Macrosociology: The Case of the Soviet Collapse," *American Journal of Sociology* 100 (1995): 1552–93 (wherein the author recalls the frosty reception his prediction of the Soviet state's demise encountered at a Yale seminar in 1980); and Timur Kuran, "The Inevitability of Future Revolutionary Surprises," *American Journal of Sociology* 100 (1995): 1528–51.

37. David K. Cohen and Michael Garet, "Reforming Educational Policy with Applied Research," *Harvard Educational Review* 45 (1975): 17–43.

38. Stinchcombe, op. cit., 284.

39. *New York Times* (Sunday, June 25, 1995), 1. Huber (op. cit., 201) suggests that sociology's tendency to attract reform-minded and activist students is costly to the discipline because such students make poor impressions on businesspeople on college and university boards of trustees. This is likely to be true only in the absence of an activist, reform-minded state that legitimates and rewards the work of reform-minded scholars and students.

Part II

Introduction

Kai Erikson

Robert Merton has had at least two sets of students: those fortunate enough to have passed through his classrooms, and those—from the same sociological generations—who received their most decisive lessons about what sociology is and could be from his writings. I belong to the second group, and while I have no warrant to speak personally here, given that this book has drawn on the work of so many people, I will do so anyway because I know from conversations with colleagues that my experience has been very widely shared. *Social Theory and Social Structure* came out in 1949, the year I entered college, and although another two years would pass before I came across it in a classroom, it not only defined the field for me but was instrumental in drawing me to it. It seems to me now, looking back, that I learned to *see* sociologically and to *think* sociologically from those early exposures to Merton's mind, and I assume the same is true for many (and probably for most) of those who were attracted to the profession in that span of time. Younger colleagues and students may speak less now about Merton's influence on them, but if so, that is because they are moving across so familiar a conceptual landscape that they no longer need to specify how it was charted in the first place. If that does not qualify as an example of what Merton calls "obliteration by incorporation"[1]—the process by which a scientific finding becomes so widely known that its origins are forgotten and its author no longer cited—maybe it could be called "obliteration by absorption." "Obliteration" is an odd term to use when speaking of the most widely recognized and most widely cited sociologist of our times, but there is something to that idea all the same. (I was surprised to realize how seldom I have cited

219

Merton in my own work, even though, as these remarks make plain enough, my intellectual debt to him is immense.)

A number of scholars have made a special point of arguing that Merton has not offered anything like a comprehensive general theory of social life (Robert Bierstedt and Anthony Giddens, for instance). Others have argued with equal force (Peter Blau and Arthur Stinchcombe, for instance) that he has indeed done so, even if much of it is hidden deep in the folds of his work. Charles Crothers and Piotr Sztompka, who have written book-length studies of Merton's work, also take that latter view. And so, for what it is worth, do I. Bierstedt portrays Merton as "moving with the speed and grace of a hummingbird from one blossom to the next," and then notes somewhat archly: "If sociology were defined as that which sociologists do, one would have to conclude that in Merton's own case sociology is a rummage sale rather than a discipline."[2] I appreciate both of those similes, but I think it would be fairer to describe Merton's mind as shifting restlessly not from one blossom to the next but from one vantage point to another as he tries to obtain a rounder and more dimensional look at the social order—which is, after all, his central topic.

These matters have been discussed with considerable wisdom and at formidable length over the past two decades, along with a number of analyses of the body of work Merton is still expanding. There was a fascinating Festschrift edited by Lewis A. Coser in 1975 when Merton was turning sixty-five, and another arranged by the New York Academy of Sciences and edited by Thomas F. Gieryn when he turned seventy. Sztompka's and Crothers's volumes helped celebrate Merton's seventy-fifth birthday, and a collection edited by Jon Clark, Celia Modgil, and Sohan Modgil honored his eightieth. This volume, in turn, was in preparation at the time of his eighty-fifth birthday. So the subject continues to be well covered.[3]

Whether or not Merton can be said to have presented us with a systematic body of general theory, I would argue that he has presented us with something far more important in the long term—a coherent *vision* of how the social order works and how one should go about studying it. I would further argue that the vision he has presented us has worked its way so deep into the sociological grain that it has become a permanent part of our way of looking at things. Even those who want to protest some view that Merton has proposed seem to do so using languages and concepts and logics and forms of argument that derive from him.

When I first read "Social Structure and Anomie," to draw once more on personal experience, I filled whole notebooks with questions. It seemed to my undergraduate sense of things that most of the people who end up in prisons and mental hospitals—people about whom I knew nothing whatever—do not act the way Merton expected them to. But I have had an absorbing interest in matters deviant ever since, and more to the point, I doubt that a semester has gone by in a teaching career of thirty years without my showing to undergraduates that famous diagram of possible modes of adaptation with all its representational pluses and minuses—not because I find it so useful in conveying what I want them to know about crime and mental illness and other forms of socially defined deviation, but because it is so clean a sample of how to reason sociologically.

Merton notes in the autobiographical sketch included here that, for him, "teaching itself is a form of scholarship"—by which he means, I assume, that his ideas have been honed in his classrooms to the fine edge they always seem to have. We all have the right to think that our mentors are the people we have imagined them to be, and I am only exercising that right when I reverse the order of the above remark and suggest that, to Merton, "scholarship is a form of teaching." The Merton who resides in my imagination devises his carefully crafted writings as a form of professing. His life's work, then, has been not only to provide insights into the workings of society but also to offer instruction on how to visualize and to approach the human world sociologically. I obviously have no idea what he is thinking as he moves into his study each morning, but what he produces there has the look of paradigmatic essays as much as the look of scholarly reports. And the point of an essay is to inform, to educate, to tutor, to improve. I am still speaking of *my* Robert Merton, of course, but the real one said in an interview with Caroline Persell a few years ago: "When I think back on the papers I've published over the years, the ones that engaged me the most deeply derived from the lectures I developed for courses."[4]

The same might be said of Emile Durkheim. His writings often have the tone and the cadence of lectures. Even in print, he seems to be arguing, scolding, pacing excitedly in front of us, waving his arms for emphasis. His empirical researches and his historical accounts always look and feel like acts of teaching as well as acts of a more remote kind of scholarship; they are undertaken to make a point.

The tone and cadence of Merton's work are entirely different from Durkheim's, and his teaching style, from everything I have heard, could not be less like Durkheim's. But setting aside for the moment Merton's brilliant contributions to the history of science, his empirical work, too, appears to have been undertaken, at least in part, to make a point. Was he ever truly interested in deviant conduct as a topic of study? In bureaucracy? In anomie? The answer may very well be yes, of course, but it has always seemed to me that these papers belong to the same intellectual species as Durkheim's *Suicide*—studies chosen to elucidate a theme as well as to shed light on the concrete subject at hand. They are teachings as well as researches.

Bierstedt writes in a discussion of Merton's *On Theoretical Sociology* that "all of the essays in this book and indeed almost all of Merton's theoretical writing" are "metasociological," by which he has in mind "theory whose subject is sociology rather than society."[5] An interesting point. Merton certainly focuses on human society most of the time, so the comment cannot be read literally. But in his concern with instructing us, he attends as much to the disciplinary lens through which he is inviting us to look as he does to the social realities that are visible through that lens.

Merton's initial impact on sociology occurred in the 1940s and 1950s. What other voices and counsels were active in molding the discipline then? The sociological generation moving into senior ranks included Robert Lynd, Pitirim Sorokin, and Robert MacIver. Merton's own generation included Talcott Parsons, Everett Hughes, Paul Lazarsfeld, C. Wright Mills, David Riesman, and Samuel Stouffer. If one listens with a sensitive rhetorical ear to the sounds of modern sociology, it is impossible not to conclude that Merton has done more than all of them together—and the rest of us too, for that matter—to shape the language we speak. I mean this not only in the sense that the vocabulary we draw on is full of terms and expressions of his coinage, but also in the sense that he has done more than all of them together to map the conceptual terrain that the language was developed to describe. "Theories of the middle range" and "sociological ambivalence" and "opportunity structure" and "self-fulfilling prophecy" and "anticipatory socialization" and the combination of "status sets" and "role sets" are terrific images, but the reason they have worked their way so easily into sociological discourse is that they have done a brilliant job of capturing important parts of that terrain. To coin terms that aptly designate phenomena or concepts is to engage in a useful art. But to sharpen the very contours of reality in the act of doing so is scholarship of a rare and special kind.

Merton's vision of the social order has been challenged, of course. There are sociologists who resent what has seemed to them the somewhat imperious injunction that we should all turn our energies and talents to theories of the middle range, on the ground that general theory is a "premature" if not "grandiose" conceit for which "we are not ready."

And then there are sociologists who doubt that there really *is* much of a normative structure out there in social life, and who for that reason are suspicious of any vision of human society—Merton's being a very prominent example—that begins with an underlying assumption of orderliness. A number of scholars take the view that people in society improvise and accommodate and maneuver as they make their way across social space, and do so without a very strong sense of being governed by rules or of being compelled by custom or tradition or convention or anything else. According to that argument, those of us who think we see structure out there—an orderly tissue of roles and statuses, norms and values—are really imposing our own sense of pattern on the scenes we are observing. It is the tidiness of *our* vision rather than the tidiness of actual social life that is reflected in our research reports. We are looking straight into a mirror. "My argument," writes Richard Hilbert in a volume on Merton's work, "is that these constantly operating mechanisms are Merton's requirements, not necessarily requirements of the people observed or of their behavior."[6] That may be true enough at one level or another, of course, but how does one go about appealing a verdict like that? If I stare mightily at people in motion and conclude that there are regularities in the way they live their lives, I may be told that I am only revealing something about myself. But once I am on that level of discourse, the only available counter for me is to inquire in return: what can we learn about those who stare mightily at people in motion and conclude that there are no underlying structures out there? That an unusual number of them seem to live in California?

And then, most important, there are sociologists who regret that conflict plays so limited a role in Merton's vision of the social order. Randall Collins, in *Sociology Since Midcentury,* is sharp and to the point. Merton, he says, "takes phenomena that are basically matters of stratification and disinfects them by passing them through a bath of abstractions." Or again:

> If there is a central theme that underlies virtually all of Merton's work, I would say that it is the effort to diffuse stratification issues. In good American style, structural inequalities are simply settings for the drama of social mobility. Instances of conflict . . . are refocused onto the claim that they really are evidence for upholding or striving to obtain. Relationships of authority and subordination become instances of self-equilibrating systems.[7]

The social world envisioned in Merton's work is a patterned field of force in which order prevails. But it is also a world of tensions and strains, of contrary pulls and crosscurrents, of ambiguities and ambivalences, of contradictions and dysfunctions. If Merton does not in his own work focus all that often on raw displays of power or on conflicts between warring social classes or on scenes of outright domination, the social landscape he has envisioned is certainly hospitable to them. Sztompka, surveying that same terrain, sees Merton as "a conflict theorist par excellence." Few of us (Merton included, I suspect) would put the matter that flatly, but most would agree that Sztompka is basically correct. On that note I invite you to continue with Part II of this volume.

Notes

These introductory remarks have profited very greatly from readings by Cynthia Fuchs Epstein and Paul DiMaggio.

1. Robert K. Merton, *Social Theory and Social Structure*, 3rd. enlarged edition (New York: Free Press, 1968), 27–29.

2. Robert Bierstedt, *American Sociological Theory: A Critical History* (New York: Academic Press, 1981), 486, 444–45.

3. Lewis A. Coser, ed., *The Idea of Social Structure: Papers in Honor of Robert K. Merton* (New York: Harcourt Brace Jovanovich, 1975). Thomas F. Gieryn, ed., *Science and Social Structure: A Festschrift for Robert K. Merton* (New York: The New York Academy of Sciences, 1980). Piotr Sztompka, *Robert K. Merton: An Intellectual Profile* (New York: St. Martin's Press, 1986). Charles Crothers, *Robert K. Merton* (New York and London: Tavistock Publications, 1987). Jon Clark, Celia Modgil, and Sohan Modgil, eds., *Robert K. Merton: Consensus and Controversy* (London: Falmer Press, 1990). Carlo Mongardini and Simonetta Tabboni, eds., *Merton and Contemporary Sociology* (New Brunswick: Transachon Publishers, 1997).

4. Caroline H. Persell, "An Interview with Robert K. Merton," *Teaching Sociology* 11 (1984): 355–86, 361.

5. Bierstedt, op. cit., 460.

6. Richard A. Hilbert, "Merton's Theory of Role-Sets and Status-Sets," in Lewis A. Coser, ed., op. cit., 185.

7. Randall Collins, *Sociology Since Midcentury* (New York: Academic Press, 1978), 301, 303.

De-Gendering "Man of Science": The Genesis and Epicene Character of the Word *Scientist*

Robert K. Merton

Quel beau livre ne composerait-on pas en racontant la vie et les
aventures d'un mot?

> —Honoré de Balzac, *La Comédie humaine* (1835)[1]

I wish you would reflect seriously upon the moral aspect of
terminology.

> —C. S. Peirce to William James (1904)[2]

Faire l'histoire d'un mot, ce n'est jamais perdre sa peine. Bref ou long,
monotone ou varié, le voyage est toujours instructif.

> —Lucien Febvre (1930)[3]

Prologue

Encouraged by the epigraph drawn from the *Human Comedy* where Balzac has his hero exclaim "What a splendid book could be written about the life and adventures of a word" and alerted by Peirce to the moral dimension of terminology and reassured by Febvre that to probe the history of a word will not be labor lost, I continue my excursions into the sociological history of culturally strategic words by examining the genesis and de-gendered evolution of the English word *scientist*.[4] You will notice, however, that I do not explore at all the comparative history and distinctive implications of such not-quite counterpart terms as *Wissen-*

225

schaftler, savant (or later, *scientifique* and, more reluctantly, *scientiste*), and *scienziatio.*

You will also notice that the evolving usages of the word *scientist* turn out to engage a variety of theoretical problems in the history, philosophy, and sociology of science. Such problems as the historically changing concept of science; the perduring problem of the unity of the sciences; the problem of demarcation, that is, the question whether science differs fundamentally from other kinds of cognitive work; the problem of boundaries among the sciences or "the distributions and partitions and partitions of knowledge" about which Francis Bacon wrote in anticipatory style in his proto-sociology of science;[5] the cognitive consequences of the sometimes tacit, sometimes explicit, concept of the unity and hierarchy of the sciences; the diverse cultural imagery of science;[6] and, far from least, the historically changing access of women to the world of scientific inquiry. Of course, I shall not be speaking at length about these large subjects but as I proceed with this inquiry into the history of *scientist* you will hear echoes of all those problems.

Two further quotations, one of them quite familiar, the other not apt to be, will take us into the history of the genesis and de-gendering consequences of the word *scientist.* They are both from the hand of the incomparable Lewis Carroll, yet they seem rather at odds. But, of course, although his other self, the Reverend Charles Lutwidge Dodgson, was a certified mathematician and logician, the rather more memorable self of Lewis Carroll, the master of paradoxy, had his own version of an ultimate consistency. One can hardly accept his stammering self-caricature as Dodo in *Alice's Adventures in Wonderland.*

Here is the first quotation, the one in *Alice,* that has Humpty-Dumpty asserting quite unforgettably:

> When I use a word . . . it means just what I choose it to mean—neither more nor less.

And here is the other, not-at-all familiar, quotation from a letter Lewis Carroll wrote much later to a set of children who had asked about the meaning of the word *Snark:*

> . . . you know, words mean more than we mean to express when we use them. . . .[7]

There you have it. A paired sign of the demarcation between the Two Cultures as set forth in C. P. Snow's drastic portrait of scientists and humanists poised on opposite sides of a "gulf of mutual incomprehension."[8] For here is Humpty-Dumpty speaking for the would-be singular exactitude of scientific *de*notation, intent on abolishing overtones and undertones with all their interpreted ambiguities. And there is his reflective creator speaking, many years later, of the shades of meaning to be found in humanistic *con*notation, with its often more evident variety of meanings we need not wittingly mean.

As I proceed to examine the genesis and complex character of the word *scientist*, I shall side rather less often with Humpty-Dumpty than with the author of *The Hunting of the Snark*. From time to time, you will hear reverberations of the clash between the culture of the sciences and the culture of the humanities that attended the early biography of that word just as you will take note of historically induced meanings beyond those the new word was probably meant to express.

The Prime Origin of *Scientist*

First, all tribute due William Whewell, the Victorian historian-philosopher of science, dedicated coiner of scientific words, and longtime Master of Trinity College, Cambridge. For he is truly the *prime* begetter of the enduring coinage, *scientist*.[9] In 1834, he observes in an admiring, anonymous, good-humored, and quite long essay-review of a book by Mary Somerville—about which more, much more, later—that there was a widely felt deficiency

> in the want of any name by which we can designate the students of the knowledge of the material world collectively. We are informed that this difficulty was felt very oppressively by the members of the British Association for the Advancement of Science,[10] at their meetings at York, Oxford, and Cambridge. There was no general term by which these gentlemen[11] could describe themselves with reference to their pursuits. *Philosophers* was felt to be too wide and too lofty a term, and was very properly forbidden them by Mr. Coleridge, both in his capacity of philologer and metaphysician; *savans* was rather assuming, besides being French instead of English; some ingenious gentleman proposed that, by analogy with *artist*, they might form *scientist*, and added that there could be no scruple with this termination when we have such words as *sciolist, economist,* and *atheist*—but this was not generally palatable. . . .[12]

Here, then, ascribed to an un-named "ingenious gentleman"—who was none other than Whewell himself[13]—is the first appearance in print of the

English word _scientist_. This, we see, was in response to the recurrently expressed interest of the newly organized British "cultivators of science" in arriving at a term that will refer to themselves distinctively and collectively. Whewell's introductory passage contains a set of interesting assumptions and raises a set of correlative questions. First, it evidently assumes a unity of the sciences since the search for "a general term" called for a word that would indicate what they had in common rather than what distinguished them as, say, astronomers, chemists, or geologists. What, then, led to this perceived common identity that found organizational expression in formation of the "British Association for the Advancement of Science"? Be it noted, "science" rather than "the sciences." Second, it is said that the new "general term" was needed to designate "students of the _material_ world," thus implicitly excluding students of the society, economy, polity, or psyche (which made up the "moral sciences" of the time). This was surely not Whewell's own restriction as he made explicitly clear in his (1837) _History of the Inductive Sciences_ by noting that he did not exclude such subjects as "Ethnology and Glossology [Linguistics], Political Economy, Psychology . . . [from] the rank of Inductive Sciences."[14] And third, is the anticipated discomfort that linguistic purists might experience from that 'ingenious gentleman" making free with the Greek suffix -_ist_ by proposing to attach it, in questionable hybridizing style, to the Latin root _scient_-. I shall have more to say about each of these assumptions in due course.

A new "general term" may have been needed but Whewell's proposed _scientist_ elicited no further notice. Indeed, a half-century afterward, when the distinguished Victorian historian of mathematics, Isaac Todhunter—who, as it happens, had early on won a prize in moral science—took occasion to refer to Whewell's "spirited little paper" he tellingly did not pause to observe that it had introduced the still-suspect word _scientist_. In that essay, Whewell had gone on to report—whether literally or fictively is not known—that others at these earliest meetings of the new British Association had tried their hand at a direct English translation of the established German term, _Naturforscher_. But that didn't work out. It invited such "undignified compounds as "_nature-poker,_ or _nature-peeper,_" candidate words that were promptly and "indignantly rejected."

Having mastered the German language, Whewell would of course resist such unhappy literalisms. However, others at those first meetings of the British Association instituted for cultivators and friends of the _sciences of nature_ also focused on finding an English equivalent of _Naturforscher;_ the term that had been adopted by the explicitly emulated _Gesellschaft Deutscher Naturforscher und Aerzte_ founded a dozen years before. The need for such a generic term found emphatic expression in an account of the ninth, 1830, meetings of the *Gesellschaft* by the chemist James F. W. Johnston, a protégé of the influential Scottish physicist David Brewster who had been pressing for a like organization in Britain. Throughout that lengthy account, running to some 55 pages of print, Johnston wrestles with the problem of finding a single English word to serve as a suitable translation of *Naturforscher*. In the title of that account, he settles for the established phrase "cultivators of natural science," while the running heads at the top of each page condense this phrase into the term "naturalists." But in what seems to be a state of quiet desperation, he continues to fall back in the text on the long-established phrases, "men of science," and "scientific men." His patent terminological discomfort continues until, in final despair, he annotates his translation of *"Deutscher Naturforscher und Aertze"* thus:

> We have no words in our language corresponding to these two. The former means a cultivator of science in any of its branches, being much more comprehensive than our word Naturalist, as generally understood; while the latter includes all cultivators of the healing art,—surgeons as well as physicians.[15]

Nor were other German terms of much assistance. The compound *Naturwissenschaftler* had not yet come into being and the uncommon words *Wissenschaftler* and the antecedent *Wissenschafter* had too broad a scope of reference.[16]

What we see in process, then, is the collective search for a word that will signify the newly emerging *cognitive and social identities* that were becoming socially organized to advance the cause of all the then-institutionally recognized sciences. The emergence of the new science organizations is linked with a widening recognition of more-or-less common cognitive styles and objectives among those engaged in scientific inquiry.[17] In that slowly developing professionalization of science, active "cultivators of science" are being distinguished from "friends of science," although the term *profession of science* had not yet emerged to reflect that process. And in the rejection of the German core-term *Wissenschaft* as "too broad" in scope, we also see a not-so-tacit demarcation of science (in a distinctively English sense) from the other, loosely identified forms of scholarly and scientific knowledge.

It is in this historical context that Whewell undertook, through the agency of that unnamed "ingenious gentleman," to introduce a reflective neologism in the shape of the generic word *scientist*. But he did so only light-heartedly and tentatively rather than seriously and with conviction. For there is no evidence of his having deployed the new word again until he introduced it formally a half-dozen years later in his pathmaking *Philosophy of the Inductive Sciences*. His formulation there bears witness that the ingenious gentleman who had earlier proposed the new word was indeed none other than Whewell himself:

> We need very much a name to describe a cultivator of science in general. I should incline to call him a *Scientist*. Thus, we might say, that as an Artist is a Musician, Painter, or Poet, a Scientist is a Mathematician, Physicist, or Naturalist.[18]

Cultural Resistance to the New Word

In proposing the new word, Whewell had the moral courage to hazard the inevitable criticism his formal statement suggests he knew would be mounted by his classicist friends (and, for that matter, by a good many in the sciences as well). And indeed, they were quick to denounce the hybrid word *scientist*. Anticipating the purist attack, Whewell had prefaced his proposed new word by observing that "The terminations *ize* (rather than *ise*) are applied to words of all origins: thus we have to *pulverize*, to *colonize*, *Witticism*, *Heathenism, Journalism, Tobacconist*. Hence we may make such words where they are wanted." Despite this anticipatory defense, *scientist* was immediately stigmatized as a linguistic barbarity which appended the Greek suffix *ist* to the Latin root *scient* to form an agent-noun in quite unseemly fashion.

Excursus on Coinage of the Word *Sociology*

Coincidentally, while Whewell was minting *scientist* anonymously in 1833–34 and acknowledging the coinage in 1840, Auguste Comte was minting *sociologie*, this in 1839. Comte, too, had some misgivings about his coinage:

> I think I should risk introducing this new term [sociology]. . . . The necessity for this coinage will, I hope, excuse this last exercise of a legitimate right which I believe I have always used with proper caution and [he adds in proper obeisance to the cant of the time] without ceasing to experience a deep feeling of repugnance for the systematic use of neologisms.[19]

Expressions of etymological contempt for the barbarism *sociology* would be countlessly reiterated throughout the Victorian era and the brief Edwardian reign. An early stigmatizing version appears in an unsigned editorial (by an untraced author) in the influential *Fraser's Magazine* (of October 1851) which interpolates an altogether extraneous allusion to "the new science of sociology, as it is barbarously termed. . . . " And the seldom invoked word *sociologist* (coined by Mill rather than Comte) was plainly a barbarism twice over since it combined the Latin *socio* with the Greek root *logos* and the Greek suffix *-ist.*

No doubt Whewell would have been appalled by this pairing of his neologism with Comte's. For unlike his friend and philosophical adversary, John Stuart Mill, Whewell rejected Comte's positivism *tout à fait* as a contribution to both the philosophy and the history of science, let alone as the basis for a newly proclaimed science. He also condemned Comte's thesis that every branch of knowledge must go through theological and metaphysical stages before becoming truly scientific, that is to say, *positive.* Whewell took this as nothing more than a historical and epistemological figment, condensing his argument into a scornful anaphora.

> There is no science in which the pretended order of things can be pointed out. There is no science in which the discoveries of the laws of phenomena, when once begun, have been carried on independently of discussions of ideas. There is no science in which the expression of the laws of phenomena can at this time dispense with ideas which have acquired their place in science in virtue of metaphysical considerations. There is no science in which the most active disquisitions concerning ideas did not come *after;* not *before,* the first discovery of laws of phenomena.[20]

Whewell's unyielding contempt for Comte's doctrines until his dying day becomes evident from a passage in his last published work that virtually reiterates the mocking anaphora of "There is no science in which. . . . "[21] Tellingly enough, this last withering attack on Comte makes unhesitating and repeated use of his hybrid "sociology" but does not make use of Whewell's own, consequential, hybrid *scientist.* Instead it refers to the long-established term "man of science." We shall shortly encounter more evidence of Whewell's ambivalent attitude toward his own coinage.

The Continuing Purist Attack on the Barbarism, *Scientist*

The strong objection to the word *scientist* on purist etymological grounds remained largely intact in English high culture through the Edwardian regime, not least among clasically educated scientists themselves. Its every public usage contributed to the *cause célèbre.* The peerless physicist-peer Lord Kelvin did not take kindly to the word which, his biographer assures us, he used "once in his *Popular Lectures* vol. i, p. 405, where he refers with a touch of sarcasm to 'scientists speaking, as now, each in his own vernacular'!" Despite his announced dislike for the words " 'physicist' and 'scientist' . . . especially the latter," Kelvin did slip into the taboo usage a second time—this, at the Royal Society Banquet of 1894. At once, we are told, "a protest was raised against this interloper of doubtful etymology, and a newspaper correspondence arose. Huxley considered 'scientist' as degraded a word as 'electrocution' and it was condemned by the Duke of Argyll, Lord Rayleigh, and Sir John Lubbock."[22]

This long-lasting rejection of the offensive word evidently exhibited resistance not alone in the colloquial sense of opposition but also "in the technical psycho-social sense of motivated neglect or denial."[23] Long after Whewell had anonymously floated the trial balloon emblazoned with the new word and had then re-introduced it under his own name, *scientist* had not diffused into common usage among English men of science. Thus, it is symptomatic that, after reporting the denunciation of the etymological hybrid by the likes of Rayleigh and Kelvin himself, Kelvin's biographer, Silvanus Thompson, goes on to remark, almost in the very words used by the anonymous Whewell 80 years before: "A word seems needed, which is scarcely supplied by 'philosopher,' 'naturalist,' or sçavant.' "[24] Evidently it was still the case in England that the declared barbarism *scientist* was being judged as not fit to fit the bill.

All this provides a marker of the tension between the changing social structure of Victorian science and elements of Victorian high culture. On the side of social structure, science was becoming increasingly institutionalized and the "gentlemen of science" were in process of being professionalized. Social institutions and social mechanisms were required to provide for the legitimation of science as worthy of enlarged social support and to provide authoritative demarcation of authentic science from what were thought of as mere pretensions to science. Socially instituted "status-judges" were required to provide credentials for scientists as were credible scientific referees to pass judgment on claims to scientific discovery.[25] The evolving institutionalization and emerging professionalization of science—which Joseph Ben-David, Edward Shils, and Everett Mendelsohn documented decades ago[26]—generated both the British Association for the Advancement of Science and concerted pressure for reform of the Royal Society to center both on "cultivators of science" and on intensified relations with their constituencies. As Morrell and Thackray have observed:

The BAAS flourished and waxed fat. Opponents, critics, observers, and by-standers were not necessarily persuaded. Some wondered aloud about the remarkable phenomenon with which they were confronted. They not unnaturally asked what Science was, that it stood in such urgent need of Advancement. Their arguments are illuminating. They help to reveal the clash of ideas through which natural knowledge took on new meanings and came to serve fresh functions. The ideological categories into which natural knowledge was then cast remain familiar today: science as value-free and objective knowledge; science as the key to economic and technological progress; science as the firm fruit of proper method; science as an available, visible, and desirable cultural resource.[27]

These social, cognitive, and ideological changes were being reflected in the repeated insistence by Whewell, Brewster, Johnston, and many anonymous others that a generic term was needed to describe those engaged in doing science (of institutionally recognized kinds) to complement such discipline-specific descriptors as *botanist, geologist,* or *zoologist* (these being, of course, nicely Greek in both stem and suffix). On the side of high culture, however, the convenient barbarism *scientist* experienced passive resistance in the form of sheer avoidance and active resistance in the form of sardonic or indignant rejection.

Perhaps, as I am inclined to believe, it was this purist resistance to the word by Whewell's reference group—the group of respected colleagues whose values and judgments influence one's own judgments—that shaped his subsequent neglect of his own neologism. For it seems that only Faraday in Whewell's large circle of scientist friends took occasion to welcome the neologism, writing Whewell that "I perceive another new and good word, the *scientist*"[28] (although not to the point of actually employing it in print). In any case, Whewell himself joined the passive resistance, in effect if not in announced intent, by giving his apt new word the silent treatment. In the course of his quarter-century of active life in the domain of science after the declared coinage of 1840, he made public use of it precisely once and, so far as the evidence allows one to say, no private use at all.

A prime instance of Whewell's private neglect of his coinage appears in a letter to his good friend, the geologist Roderick Murchison. That letter has Whewell reluctantly accepting the idea of becoming president of the Brtitish Association (an outcome that Murchison was engineering). On three occasions in his long letter written in late 1840, Whewell refers quite traditionally to "men of science" but not once to "scientists."[29] His public silence becomes loud the year following in his presidential address to the "gentlemen" of the Association who, by his own early account, were seeking a "general term . . . to describe themselves with reference to their pursuits." There again, he speaks about the "man of science" but not about the "scientist."[30] Of course, Whewell may have regarded it as unbecoming to give even the appearance of imposing his very new word upon the assembled "cultivators of science"—as another common phrase had it—just a year after he had proposed it in his *Philosophy of the Inductive Sciences.* He may have felt that the proprieties called for a period of decent reticence. But then we note that, with one significant exception, his coinage remains absent from all his many later public addresses to the BAAS and to other scientific bodies just as it remains absent from his later voluminous historical and philosophical writings and his abundant correspondence.

That exception tellingly reveals Whewell's continuing ambivalence about his no-longer-quite-so-new word. The lone usage appears in a lecture to the Society of Arts, Manufactures, and Commerce Inaugurating the Great Exhibition of 1851, a lecture given at the "suggestion of H. R. H. Prince Albert, President of the Society." In that lengthy lecture (later issued in super-abundant 34 pages of print, as I fear my own protracted text will run), Whewell has occasion to refer three times to "men of science." Only at its virtual close does the word-master venture to speak once of "scientist," that single and singular utterance being swiftly followed by the diffident parenthesis ("if I may use the word").[31] One could scarcely ask for a more eloquent expression of an ambivalent affirmation-and-denial of a terminological brainchild. High culture had triumphed. The barbarism was hushed up.

Thereafter, Whewell abandoned that brainchild altogether to the chill winds of mocking resistance and public dismissal and, in his further abundant writings and lectures, reverted—I do not presume to say, regressed—to such long-established and less-concise terms as "cultivator of science," "scientific man," and, most often, "man of science" (about which rather a lot later). In sum, Whewell put his much-needed word to public or private use just three times all told: once, anonymously and lightly in his review-article on Mary Somerville's book in 1834; again, openly and seriously, in his *Philosophy of the Inductive Sciences* in 1840; and, finally and ambivalently, in his lecture at the Crystal Palace Exhibition of 1851.

Whewell's seemingly anomalous behavior of tacitly rejecting his own coinage may have been unwittingly reinforced by similar resistance to another of his words of like kind. Once again, caustic responses to his verbal invention testify to the varied purist grounds for the initial rejection of new terms that can be said, without lapsing into Whiggish historiography, to have been socially induced at the time and to have proved serviceable since. Not etymology but phonetics, not language roots and affixes but language sounds, came under attack when Whewell proposed the word *physicist* in the same paragraph of his book that introduced the word *scientist*: "As we cannot use *physician* for a cultivator of physics, I have called him a *Physicist*." As Sydney Ross and Pearce Williams have severally noted in a letter excavated from the archives at Trinity College (Cambridge), this one of the two new words led the sterling physicist Michael Faraday to follow his applause for "the new and good word, the *scientist*" with a complaint to his friend Whewell (who, upon request, had often invented scientific terms for Faraday's new concepts and discoveries):[32]

> Now can you give us [a new and good word] for the french physicien. Physicist is both to my mouth and ears so awkward that I think I shall never be able to use it. The equivalent of three separate sounds of *s* in one word is too much.[33]

Similar auditory discomfort led an anonymous author in the widely read *Blackwood's Magazine* to sound off in a fit of onomatopoeia on Whewell's " 'word *physicists*, where four sibilant consonants fizz like a squib' "[34]—this lampoon appearing, by the way, in the same magazine which, just four years before, had happily printed the word *classicists*, replete with its five sibilant consonants.[35] So much for hissing sibilances.

Plainly, William Whewell had ample cause to resonate to Ben Jonson's observation on the sociology of linguistic innovation:

> A man coynes not a new word without some perill, and less fruit; for if it happen to be received, the praise is but moderate; if refus'd, the scorne is assur'd.[36]

The scorn Whewell suffered from Victorian purists may have led him to virtual infanticide of his terminological brainchild, but we know that its evolving social and cognitive contexts nevertheless enabled it first to survive and then to flourish. The proximate social basis for the invention of the word *scientist* was provided by the growing institutionalization of science through the emergence of associations composed of those variously engaged in the doing and in the appreciation of what was defined as science. Those social formations in conjunction with the slowly evolving universities provided the immediate impulse for the repeated and emphatic cultural expression of the need for a generic term to identify and, by direct implication, to legitimatize the emerging professionals of science, individually and collectively.

Along with the social context was the constraining and evocative cultural context, partly cognitive, partly class-based, that provided the norms and practices of word-formation and evoked often deep-felt ambivalence about hybrid solutions. Hence, the sustained resistance to the convenient barbarism, *scientist*. The reiterated analogy between such a long-established word as *artist* was deployed to legitimatize the bastard word *scientist* though the then-and-there rules of word-formation prohibited such miscegenation between the Latin stem and the Greek suffix. And beyond the new associations of science workers (along with mere lovers of science) as proximate cause of the declared need for a newly appropriate collective term were the larger social and economic strata that in turn conferred legitimacy on the growing scope and scale of science and its practitioners. Of all these, I cannot undertake to speak in detail here.

In any case, those enabling contexts of the creation, early life, and adventures of the word *scientist* still tell us nothing about interesting properties of the word itself. Yet mindful as we are of Lewis Carroll's observation on the unintended meanings of the Snark, we are prepared to find that the new word has been taken to mean more than it was evidently meant to express when first invented. It will comfort you to learn that I shall briefly examine only one of those properties here—namely, its epicene character—and deal with it and its implications in smaller compass than is truly called for.

The Epicene Word *Scientist*

For this, I return to Ben Jonson who, in his *English Grammar* of 1640, proposed that along with the masculine, feminine, and neuter genders of nouns, the epicene be taken as a fourth gender applicable to an individual of either sex.[37] Unlike the inflected Latin and Greek, the proposed gender is of course grammatically alien to English, but I shall nevertheless follow Jonson's discarded terminological lead. For plainly, the agent-noun *scientist* is thoroughly epicene; that is to say, it is entirely and wonderfully gender-free. Thus, Whewell bequeathed a grand legacy to posterity. After all, an analogy with the then familiar terms as *postman* or *postmaster* might have led him directly to *scientman* or *scientmaster*. (Indeed, *scientman* in the extended sense of a "man of knowledge" had appeared as a nonce-word in the seventeenth century.)

That legacy has special import for our own age, with its belated and marked sensitivity to possibly invidious gender-laden and sex-laden oc-cupational terms. For, as we have ample cause to know, much semantic change his mirrored social and cultural change since H. W. Fowler issued his unique *Dictionary of Modern English Usage* some 70 years ago.[38] With little regard for the still matchless Fowler, history has been rendering obsolescent his magisterial declaration that "gender is a grammatical term only," this followed by a characteristic elucidation: "To talk of *persons* or *creatures of the masculine or feminine g[ender].*, meaning *of the male or female sex,* is either a jocularity (permissible or not according to context) or a blunder." But of course an enlarged public consciousness of prob-lems of equity between the sexes and a concurrent scholarship (along with the ideological ferment) have led to semantic changes. *Gender* is no longer an exclusively grammatical term. As Cynthia Fuchs Epstein observes: "Today scholars use the word *sex* to refer to attributes of men and women created by their biological characteristics and *gender,* to refer to the dis-tinctive qualities of men and women (or masculinity and femininity) that are culturally created. . . . "[39]

Still, this tribute to the talented word-coiner, William Whewell, must be tempered. For the happily epicene character of his new word was evi-dently an inadvertent, not a deliberate, accomplishment. Thus, in the de-fining passage of his book where he notes the need for a name "to de-scribe a cultivator of science in general," he goes on to say, quite understandably for that early moment of the Victorian era: "I should be inclined to call *him* a Scientist" (the audible italics emphasizing *him* are of course mine, not Whewell's). From that generally but not necessarily androcentric pronoun and from certain of Whewell's subsequent usages, we provisionally infer that he was proposing the single word *scientist* as an equivalent to the long-established and widely used term "man of sci-ence." As a historian of science past and present, Whewell knew of count-less men of science but precious few women of science. The sex-free word did not mirror the social reality of his time as he evidently experienced it. He therefore had scant occasion to reflect upon the special virtue of his new word which prophetically embraced both men and women of sci-ence.

And yet, and yet . . . Had the Victorian Whewell turned back to that immortal work of English literature *The Life and Opinions of Tristram Shandy, Gent.,*[40] which Laurence Sterne had bestowed upon an unsus-pecting world almost a century before, he would have found the idiomatic expression "man of science" neatly paralleled by the expression, still far from being idiomatic, "woman of science." And perhaps that would have given him pause for further reflection.

There is the more reason to think that this might have been the case as we examine the context in which Whewell first ventured the word *scientist*. As I noted at the outset, the fifteen pages of the anonymous review-essay in which he did so were devoted to the book *On the Connexion of the Physical Sciences*, written by his much admired friend and formidable woman of science, Mary Somerville.[41] She was an extraordinary expositor of science who had done some scientific work of her own; a good friend of many of the leading scientific men of her long-lived time in England, France, and Italy; an *honorary* (not a full-fledged) member of several Royal Societies; and even in those difficult times for the rare woman of science, a full member of other learned academies (including, far from least, the oldest American institution of that kind, the American Philosophical Society). Of her it could be said in an obituary published in London's *Morning Post* of December 2nd, 1872: "Whatever difficulty we might experience in the middle of the nineteenth century in choosing king of science, there could be no question whatever as to the queen of science."[42]

Rightly enough, for in each of the ten editions of Somerville's book, often revised "to keep pace with the progress of discovery," the dedication is in effect by one Queen to another, by an "Obedient and Humble" Queen of Science to Queen Adelaide of Great Britain and Ireland:

To the Queen

MADAM,

If I have succeeded in my endeavour to make the laws by which the material world is governed more familiar to my countrywomen, I shall have the gratification of thinking that the gracious permission to dedicate my book to your Majesty has not been misplaced.

I am,
With the greatest respect,
YOUR MAJESTY'S
Obedient and Humble Servant,
Mary Somerville

That dedication, most notably its reference to the primary audience of "country*women*," did not escape notice in the review-essay by her good friend William Whewell. Indeed, it launched that philosopher-historian of science on a veritable ocean of sex-laden and gender-laden reflections. However, as one would now retrodict, those admiring reflections proved at times to be perceptibly if unwittingly patronizing. Friendship and generous impulse are betrayed by socially defined realities as Whewell laboriously puns his way in this telltale fashion:

And if her "countrywomen" have already become tolerably familiar with the technical terms which the history of the progress of human speculations necessarily contains; if they have learned, as we trust a large portion of them have, to look with dry eyes upon oxygen and hydrogen, to hear with tranquil minds of perturbations and eccentricities, to think with toleration that the light of their eyes may be sometimes polarized, and the crimson of their cheeks capable of being resolved into complementary colours—if they have advanced so far with philosophy, they will certainly receive with gratitude Mrs. Somerville's able and *masterly* (if she will excuse the word) exposition of the present state of the leading branches of the physical sciences.

These studied and pun-itive allusions to "dry eyes" and "crimson cheeks" only begin to provide the strongly gendered context for emergence of the genderless word *scientist*. Speaking of both gender and sex, Whewell continues:

For our own part, however, we beg leave to enter a protest, in the name of that sex to which all critics (so far as we have ever heard) belong, against the appropriation of this volume to the sole use of the author's country*women*. We believe that there are few individuals of that gender which plumes itself upon the exclusive possession of exact science, who may not learn much from this little volume.[43]

And toward the close of that admiring essay, Whewell achieves a crescendo of sex-linked mental proclivities. From a distance of 150 years, one might say that he outdoes today's most dedicated exponents of intrinsically differing female and male mentalities, as may be gathered from this lengthy though reluctantly curtailed set of observations. Whewell goes on to say

that where we find a real and thorough acquaintance with these [scientific] branches of human knowledge, acquired with comparative ease, and possessed with unobtrusive simplicity, all our prejudices against such female acquirements vanish. Indeed, there can hardly fail, in such cases, to be something peculiar in the kind, as well as degree, of the intellectual character. Notwithstanding all the dreams of theorists, *there is a sex in minds*. [You will find that assertion reverberating should you turn to a recent scholarly book with an interrogatory title that asks: *The Mind Has No Sex?*][44] One of the characteristics of the female intellect [Whewell continues] is a clearness of perception, as far as it goes; with them, action is the result of feeling; thought, of seeing; their practical emotions do not wait for instruction from speculation; their reasoning is undisturbed by the prospect of its practical consequences. . . . Their course of action is not perturbed by the powers of philosophic thought, even when the latter are strongest. The heart goes on with its own concerns, asking no counsel of the head; and, in return, the working of the head (if it does work) is not impeded by its having to solve questions of casuistry for the heart. In men, on the other hand, practical instincts and theoretical views are perpetually disturbing and perplexing each other. Action must be comformable to rule; theory must be capable of application to action. The heart and the head are in perpetual negotiation, trying in vain to bring about a treaty of alliance, offensive and defensive. The end of all this is, as in many similar cases, inextricable confusion—an endless seesaw of demand and evasion. In the course of this business, the man is mystified; he is involved in a cloud of words, and cannot see beyond it. He does not know whether his opinions are founded on feeling or on reasoning, on words or on things. He learns to talk of matters of speculation without clear notions; to combine one phrase with another at a venture; to deal in generalities; to guess at relations and bearings; to try to steer himself by antitheses and assumed maxims. Women never do this: what they understand, they understand clearly; what they see at all, they see in sunshine. It may be, that in many or in most cases, this brightness belongs to a narrow Goshen; that the heart is stronger than the head; that the powers of thought are less developed than the instincts of action. It certainly is to be hoped that it is so. But, from the peculiar mental character to which we have referred, it follows, that when women are philosophers, they are likely to be lucid ones; that when they extend the range of their speculative views, there will be a peculiar illumination thrown over the prospect. If they attain to the merit of being profound, they will add to this the great excellence of also being clear.[45]

So much for a professedly benign and plainly ambivalent conception of the distinctively feminine intellect. For Whewell, as for some present-day theorists and speculators, there is a definite "sex in minds." Each sex has its distinctive value; each, its distinctive limitations. I do not venture to compare those doctrines of our own time which, if not substantively similar, also speak of deep-seated (natural) sex or (cultural) gender differences of intellect between women and men—on the whole, if not in every case. The comparison might have its moments.[46]

It will be noticed that in the course of his ruminations on female and male minds (which I have only touched upon here), Whewell paid no attention to a morphological and connotational feature of his new word *scientist*. Neither then nor later, does he pause to observe that in failing to distinguish between the sexes, his newly minted word *scientist* does not so much as hint at sex-linked kinds of intellect. This is further reason to suppose that its being a sex-free term was incidental rather than deliberate. That attribute was simply a morphological by-product. Once Whewell decided to fashion the new word *scientist* after the old words *artist* and *atheist*, the deed was done. In one felicitous stroke, the centuries-old term, *man of science*, widely used to refer to practitioners of science generically, was unwittingly transformed and emasculated. The epicene suffix *-ist* provided the handy tool for the terminological surgery. Ever since, the sex of an unknown individual anonymously described as a "scientist" could only be inferred in terms of empirical probabilities. This was not so with the earlier term, for even the most myopic of males would presumably have hesitated to describe a woman of science as a man of science.

Or so one would suppose. But not with assurance, for this is a matter of *social* identities—and ascribed social identities have a way of ignoring seemingly self-evident differences, as in the case of the "one-drop rule" which has the perceptually "white" person socially and legally defined as "black" by virtue of having "a drop of black blood."[47] So too it was that the first eleven editions of *American Men of Science* retained its restrictive title from 1906 to 1970, despite the early and growing numbers of women scientists appearing in that rather selective directory. It was not until 1971 that the 12th edition adopted the transitional title: *American Men and Women of Science, Formerly American Men of Science*. The new title is merely noted in the opening sentence of the Preface without explanation or further comment on this belated institutional recognition of social and cultural change. For, as the historian Margaret W. Rossiter has reported, as long ago as 1920 the "vigilant" Columbia University psychologist Christine Ladd-Franklin had suggested to Jacques Cattell, editor of the directory, that he change the title to register the changing social reality: " 'Do say Men and Women of Science, or Scientists [*n.b.*], or, like the English, Scientific Worthies.' "[48] The actual change of title came fifty years later, not quite a century-and-a-half after Whewell had provided the fortuitously epicene tag *scientist.*

That long-standing titular inclusion of women of science among men of science reminds us of the enduring ambiguity in the words "man" and "woman." At times, the word *man* is taken to refer to "a male adult of the human species"; at other times, *man* and such derivatives as *mankind* are understood to refer to the species *homo sapiens* irrespective of sex. Thus, long before the change in the title of *American Men of Science*, another directory had provided an eloquent instance of that ambiguity. The title page of the 12th edition of that directory read *MEN OF THE TIME: A Dictionary of Contemporaries, containing Biographical Notices of EMINENT CHARACTERS OF BOTH SEXES* (London: George Routledge and Sons, 1887). However, the tension generated by the juxtaposed allusions to "men . . . of both sexes" evidently proved too much even a century ago, for just four years later, the 13th edition carried the quite unambiguous title: *MEN AND WOMEN OF THE TIME: A Dictionary of Contemporaries.*

It is evidently not an idle guess that Whewell's new word *scientist* came to serve as a surrogate for the long-established term *man of science.* At any rate, the ever-instructive *Oxford English Dictionary* supplies varied evidence, some of it apparently inadvert, to support that hypothesis. To begin with, the title pages of its early volumes testify that this *"New English Dictionary on Historical Principles"* was "Edited by Dr J. A. H. Murray"—the now rightly recognized "pioneer in the field of historical lexicography"[49]—and go on to acknowledge that this was "with the assistance of scholars and men of science." Those designations—the epicene word *scholars* contrasting with what is now identified as the gendered *men of science*—continued to appear on the title page of every volume of that grandest of all English dictionaries for decades.

However, that acknowledgement of assistance from "scholars and men of science" no longer appeared on the title page of volume VIII which contained an entry for *scientist,* when it appeared in 1914. In that entry, the etymology and definition of the word read, with all the eloquence of stark simplicity, as follows:

Scientist (sci-entist) [L. *scient-*(in L., *scientia* SCIENCE, and in SCIEN-TIFIC) + -IST.] A man of science.

That lone four-word definition seems to say it all: A scientist is a *man* of science. The entry goes on to quote Whewell's defining sentences in his *Philosophy of the Inductive Sciences:* "We need very much a name to describe a cultivator of science. I should incline to call him a Scientist." Nevertheless, it will be noticed, the entry does not adopt Whewell's tacitly gender-less definition, "a cultivator of science." Was Whewell's pronoun "him" possibly taken to imply that a scientist was *necessarily* a man"?

Of course, as we have noted, the word *man* need not be androcentric, referring only to the male of the species. However, as the *OED* reminds us in its incomparably informative entry of thirteen columns on "man" as a substantive, the phrase *"a* man" has the delimited sense of "an adult male person, with special reference to sex" as distinct from the generic sense man can have in the absence of the qualifying article. And, as though to make it utterly clear that this is the case in its definition of *scientist* as "a man of science," the *OED* in effect proceeds to define its definition of *scientist,* thus:

> 6. **Man of science. a.** A man who possesses knowledge in any department of learning, or trained skill in any art or craft. *Obs.* **b.** In modern use, a man who has expert knowledge of some branch of science (usually, of physical or natural science) and devotes himself to its investigation.[50]

This reinforced definition of *scientist* as "a man of science" remained intact in the "corrected re-issue" of the *OED* published in 1933, a precise hundredth year after Whewell's first, anonymous, coinage. It also remained intact in the superb four-volume *Supplement* to the *OED* published half a century later (1982–86). Presumably reflecting the greatly changed social reality and climate of opinion, the second, 1989, edition in twenty volumes has abandoned the androcentric definition of Whewell's tacitly epicene *scientist* and defined it instead in thoroughly de-gendered terms:

> A person with expert knowledge of a science; a person using scientific methods.

In that respect, the *OED* evidently lagged far behind the 1864 revision of Noah Webster's *An American Dictionary of the English Language,* which had thoroughly (though we cannot with assurance say, advisedly) de-gendered the word *scientist* by defining it as "one learned in science; a savant; as, an enthusiastic scientist." And in 1890, when *An American Dictionary* was expanded and extended into Webster's *International Dictionary of the English Language,* the epicene character of its slightly changed definition was preserved thus:

> **Sci'entist, n.** One learned in science; a scientific investigator; one devoted to scientific study; a savant.[51]

And now that I near the close of these observations, full disclosure requires me to report that, in a manner of speaking, ontogeny does in this case recapitulate phylogeny. For once having searched out the long lag in definitional recognition of the epicene character of the word *scientist* in the grandest of English dictionaries, I could hardly remain unaware of the terminological lag represented by my own aperiodic but frequent use of the term "man of science" over the years. Canons of political correctitude aside, I am not likely to continue that practice.

Epilogue

William Whewell does us a final service in the preamble to his review-essay of Mary Somerville's book. He turns our attention from the one engaging property of the word *scientist* of which he took no notice—its morphologically epicene character—to other, rather more broadly theoretical, properties. Closely read, the preamble takes us to a series of concluding questions that have become part of the developing agenda of the philosophy, history, and sociology of science and the sciences.

Ever the philosopher and historian of science, Whewell observes:

> Mrs. Somerville's . . . professed object is to illustrate "The *Connexion* of the Physical Sciences." This is a noble object and to succeed in it would be to render a most important service to science. The tendency of the sciences has long been an increasing proclivity to separation and dismemberment. . . . The disintegration goes on, like that of a great empire falling to pieces; physical science itself is endlessly subdivided, and the subdivisions insulated. We adopt the maxim "one science only can one genius fit" [that, of course, is Whewell quoting Alexander Pope]. The mathematician turns away from the chemist; the chemist from the naturalist; the mathematician, left to himself, divides himself into a pure mathematician and a mixed mathematician, who soon part company; the chemist is perhaps a chemist of electrochemistry; if so, he leaves common chemical analysis to others; between the mathematician and the chemist is to be interpolated a *"physicien"* (we have no English name for him),[52] who studies heat, moisture, and the like. And thus, science, even mere physical science, loses all traces of unity.[53]

This passage indicates that if Mary Somerville did not herself invent the word *scientist,* the central theme of her book strongly underscored and reaffirmed the widely felt need for such a collective term. If not the cause she was at least the occasion for Whewell's putting his anonymous coinage into print.

As anticipated, we have seen that the generic noun *scientist* harbors a variety of historically evolving implications. On the surface, it connotes a belief in the unity of the sciences that transcends their ever-evolving partitions. It also reflects changes in applicaton of the concept of "science" and "the sciences." It directs our attention to the historically changing boundaries of science: *Who* can legitimately be described as a scientist? And where is the right to accord legitimacy lodged? Answers to these questions continue to differ among the competing and sometimes clashing groups laying claim to such legitimatizing authority. A growing awareness of the de-gendered aspect of the word reflects the social changes in the access of women and men to the opportunity structure of science. In its varied applications, the lone word *scientist* thus raises the question of the social and cognitive demarcation of science from non-science along with the correlative philosophical and sociological question of the grounds for distinguishing the sciences as one culture and the arts and humanities as another.

But you will be relieved to hear that I am postponing detailed examination of these and kindred questions for another time—perhaps for the celebration of the 125th anniversary of sociology at Yale. After all, as an honorary son of Eli, privileged to hold the still rare degree of Doctor of Social Science, I am bound to have a stake in the future of the first American university to provide for teaching and research in sociology.[54]

Notes

Copyright © 1993, 1995, by Robert K. Merton. I am indebted to I. Bernard Cohen, Morton N. Cohen, Gordon Ray, Stephen M. Stigler, and Harriet Zuckerman for their criticism and suggestions; to Rosa Haritos, Ona Bloom, and Ellen Tawil for their indomitable research assistance; and to Joshua Bender for technical aid. Once again, I gladly acknowledge aid of another kind from the John D. and Catherine T. MacArthur Foundation, the Russell Sage Foundation, and the Eugene Garfield Foundation.

1. *Etudes philosophiques et études analytiques: Louis Lambert* (Paris: Alexandre Houssiaux, [1835]), p. 111.

2. In Ralph Barton Perry, *The Thought and Character of William James* (Boston: Little Brown, & Co., 1936), II, p. 432.

3. In *Civilisation, Le mot et l'idée, 1ʳᵉ Semaine internationale de synthèse, 2ᵉ fasc.* Paris, 1930, 1–55, at page 1. ("It is never a waste of time to study the history of a word. Whether short or long, monotonous or varied, the voyage is always instructive.")

4. Other explorations include *On the Shoulders of Giants: A Shandean Postscript* ([1965, 1985] University of Chicago Press, 1993) on the history of the aphorism, "If I have seen further, it is by standing on the shoulders of giants"; a book written with Elinor Barber in 1958, *The Travels and Adventures of Serendipity: A Study in Historical Semantics and the Sociology of Science*, now being put in belated, Italian, print by Il Mulino; "On the Origin of the term *Pseudo-Gemeinschaft*," *Western Sociological Review*, 1975, 6, 83; "Our Sociological Vernacular," *Columbia* 1981, 42–44; an article written with David L. Sills and Stephen M. Stigler, "The Kelvin Dictum and Social Science: An Excursion into the History of an Idea," *Journal of the History of the Behavioral Sciences* 1984, 20, 319–331; "Opportunity Structure: The Emergence, Diffusion, and Differentiation of a Sociological Concept," in Freda Adler and William S. Laufer, eds., *The Legacy of*

Anomie Theory (New Brunswick, N.J.: Transaction Publishers, 1995), 3–78; "On the [W.I.] Thomas Theorem: A Sexist Eponym?" *Social Forces*, 1995, 74, 379–424.

5. On that proto-sociology of science, see Part I of the paper commemorating the 400th anniversary of Bacon's birth: R. K. Merton, "Singletons and Multiples in Scientific Discovery," *Proceedings of the American Philosophical Society*, 1961, 105, 470–486.

6. On socially conceived images of science, see Yehuda Elkana, "Science as a Cultural System," in V. Mathieu and Paolo Rossi, eds., *Scientific Culture in the Contemporary World* (Milan: Scientia, 1979), 269–290.

7. "To the Lowrie Children" in Morton N. Cohen, ed., *The Letters of Lewis Carroll*, (London: Macmillan, 1979), 2 vols., I, p. 548. Some years later, a resonating thought appears in *The Education of Henry Adams: An Autobiography* (Boston: Houghton Mifflin [1907] 1946), p. 451: "No one means all he says, and yet very few say all they mean, for words are slippery and thought is viscous."

8. C. P. Snow, *The Two Cultures and the Scientific Revolution* (Cambridge University Rede Lectures, 1959).

9. I say "prime begetter" rather than "only begetter" since the word *scientist* was evidently an independent multiple coinage. That possibility came to mind as I began the search for the historical, sociological, and philosophical contexts and properties of the word by turning first, naturally enough, to the ever-informative and evocative *Oxford English Dictionary* (1884–1928) and its *Supplement* (1972–86). The entry for *scientist* in the *OED* has its first two quotations from the same year, 1840, a coincidence which, given my enduring interest in "multiples" (independent appearance of the same discovery or invention), was enough to start my search into its history. My search was greatly aided when, well along in those explorations, I came upon the informative article by Sydney Ross, published a quarter-century before, which I found had in part anticipated, in other parts had gone beyond and, in still other parts, had not undertaken to define the problems and to seek the results of my own inquiry. See Sydney Ross, "Scientist: The Story of a Word," *Annals of Science*, June 1962 (published April 1964) 18, 65–85. I have elsewhere extended the evidence and the analysis of *scientist* as a multiple coinage (a subject that Ross treats on his pages 71–74) but will focus here on its unwitting origin as an epicene term (a subject which Ross, working in a much earlier day, left wholly untouched).

10. The major monograph on the history, sociology, and politics of the British Association as it emerged and evolved in the early Victorian era is by Jack Morrell and Arnold Thackray, *Gentlemen of Science: Early Years of the British Association for the Advancement of Science* (Oxford: Clarendon Press, 1981). On the basis of thousands of letters and other documents of the time, they show how the BAAS managed to convert "natural knowledge" into a "cultural resource," this largely through the efforts of an elite core of some two-dozen "gentlemen of science" who, as we shall see, did not, of course, include "gentlewomen of science." A collective volume edited by Roy MacLeod and Peter Collins, *The Parliament of Science: The British Association for the Advancement of Science* (Middle-

sex: Science Reviews, 1981) also provides context for understanding the social and cognitive realities that, as we shall also see, pressed for the variously symbolic neologism, *scientist*. Chapters 6 and 7 of Susan Faye Cannon, *Science in Culture: The Early Victorian Period* (New York: Dawson & Science History Publications, 1978) give a lively version of how the newly established BAAS, unlike the long-established Royal Society of that time, made for the "professionalization of Science" and provided an early arena for " 'men of Scientific eminence' " (p. 196) to "debate with one's peers before a large, admiring, quasi-informed audience of cultivators of science" (p. 222). But see the detailed monograph by Marie Boas Hall, *All Scientists Now: The Royal Society in the Nineteenth Century* (Cambridge: Cambridge University Press, 1984) with its theme that the history of the Society in that century was "in large part . . . the triumph of those who struggled to create a Royal Society all of whose Fellows should be eminent for their contributions to science" (p. 218).

11. Whewell's "these gentlemen" provides a further resonant basis for Morrell and Thackray's book-title, *Gentlemen of Science*, and will become another telling allusion for our impending examination of the then operative meaning rather than the literal epicene meaning of the word *scientist*. The integration of the social roles of "gentleman" and "man of science" emerging in nineteenth-century England contrasts with the frequent radical opposition in early seventeenth-century "polite society" between the roles of "gentleman" and "natural philosopher." On this, see Steven Shapin, " 'A Scholar and a Gentleman': The Problematic Identity of the Scientific Practitioner in Early Modern England," *History of Science*, 1991, 29, 279–325. However, the latter seventeenth century saw the emergence of new attitudes and judgments in "genteel society," as witness, among many other indicators, the sought-for membership of courtiers in the Royal Society established by Charles II; see R. K. Merton, *Science, Technology and Society in Seventeenth-Century England* (New York: Howard Fertig, Inc., [1938] 1970), Chapter 1.

12. [William Whewell], "Art. III. — On the Connexion of the Physical Sciences. By Mrs. Somerville." *The Quarterly Review*, 1834, 51:54–68, at 59–60.

13. The indispensable *Wellesley Index to Victorian Periodicals, 1824–1900*, edited by Walter E. Houghton (London: Routledge & Kegan Paul, 1966–79), 3 volumes, confirms yet again the fact that the anonymous author was indeed Whewell, as was long since indicated by Isaac Todhunter in his *William Whewell: An Account of His Writings, with Selections from His Literary and Scientific Correspondence* (London: Macmillan and Co., 1876), I, pp. 92–93.

14. See the perceptive analyses of Whewell's conception of science and his attendant terminology by Yehuda Elkana, "William Whewell, Historian," *Rivista di storia della scienza*, 1984, 1, 149–197 and by Richard R. Yeo, "William Whewell's Philosophy of Knowledge and Its Reception," in Menachem Fisch and Simon Schaffer, eds., *William Whewell: A Composite Portrait* (Oxford Press, 1991), pp. 175–199, esp. at pp. 176–187.

15. James F. W. Johnston, "Meeting of the Cultivators of Natural Science and Medicine at Hamburgh, in September 1830," *The Edinburgh Journal of Science*,

N.S. IV, April 1831: 189–244, at 218. The emulation of the German Association by the British Association extended to the detail of holding its annual meeting in different cities: Leipzig, Halle, and Würzburg in the one; York, Oxford and Cambridge in the other.

16. Early uses of both the outmoded *Wissenschafter* and the emerging *Wissenschaftler* are cited in the grand dictionary on historical principles initiated by the philologist brothers, Jakob and Wilhelm Grimm, *Deutsches Wörterbuch* (Leipzig: S. Hirzel, [1854–55] 1960, 14, 798b.

17. For a pioneering sociological study of the scientist role emerging in Germany, England, and France, see Joseph Ben-David, *The Scientist's Role in Society: A Comparative Study* (Englewood Cliffs, N.J.: Prentice-Hall, 1971) and, for extension of that analysis, his posthumously published volume edited by Gad Freudenthal, *Scientific Growth: Essays on the Social Organization and Ethos of Science* (Berkeley: University of California Press, 1991). For an early overview of the social organization of science in those countries, see Volume I, chapters 1–3 of John Theodore Merz, *A History of European Thought in the Nineteenth Century* (Edinburgh: William Blackwood, 1896–1914), 4 vols.

18. William Whewell, *The Philosophy of the Inductive Sciences, Founded Upon Their History* (London: 1840), 2 vols., I, Intro., p. cxiii; 2nd ed. 1847, II, p. 560.

19. Auguste Comte, *Cours de philosophie positive* (Paris: Bachelier, [1830–1842] 1839), 6 vols., IV, p. 252; translation by Yole G. Sills.

20. Whewell, op. cit., [n. 18] 2nd ed., II, p. 322.

21. William Whewell, *Of Induction, With Special Reference to Mr. J. Stuart Mills' System of Logic* (London, 1849), esp. at pp. 62 ff. On p. 183 in his "William Whewell, Historian," (op. cit., [n. 14]), Yehuda Elkana quotes the penultimate passage from Whewell's "Comte and Positivism," *Macmillan's Magazine* 1866, 13, 354.

22. Silvanus P. Thompson, *The Life of William Thomson: Baron Kelvin of Largs* (London: Macmillan, 1910), 2 vols. II, pp. 1119–1120n. Edwardian in tone and substance, this remains a valuable biography of Kelvin (which has proved to be a staple source for my studies in the historical sociology of science since the 1950s and has now been importantly supplemented by Carobs Smith and M. Norton Wise, *Energy and Empire: A Biographical Study of Lord Kelvin* [Cambridge University Press, 1989]). Sydney Ross has evidently located the source of Thompson's brief quoted summary of the resistance to the no-longer new word *scientist* that was persisting into the last decade of the century for he quotes the letters protesting the barbarism from J. T. Carrington, *Science-gossip*, N.S. 1894, 1, 242–243. These include not only the letters of Argyll, Rayleigh and Lubbock but of Huxley and Alfred Russel Wallace as well. *Cf.* Ross, op. cit., [n. 9], 75–78.

23. R. K. Merton, "Resistance to the Systematic Study of Multiple Discoveries in Science," *European Journal of Sociology*, 1963, IV, 237–282, at 239 which refers to an array of early studies of social, economic, and political sources of resistance to new developments in science, technology, and medicine. See, in particular, the

classic paper by Bernard Barber, "Resistance by Scientists to Scientific Discovery," *Science*, 1 September 1961, 134, 596–602.

24. Thompson, op. cit., [n. 22], II, p. 1120n.

25. On the emergence of the institutional structure of science with its arrangements for the exercise of socially "organized skepticism" in assessing claims to scientific work and the operation of the reward system of science, see R. K. Merton, "The Normative Structure of Science" (1942), "Priorities in Scientific Discovery" (1957), and Harriet Zuckerman and R. K. Merton, "Patterns of Evaluation in Science: Institutionalization, Structure and Functions of the Referee System" (1971) reprinted in Merton, *The Sociology of Science* (Chicago: University of Chicago Press, 1973), pp. 267–278; 286–324; 460–496.

26. Joseph Ben-David, "Scientific Productivity and Academic Organization in Nineteenth-Century Medicine" (1960) and "The Profession of Science and Its Powers" (1972) in *Scientific Growth*, op. cit., [n. 16], pp. 103–124, 187–209; Everett Mendelsohn, "The Emergence of Science as a Profession in Nineteenth-Century Europe," in Karl Hill, ed., *The Management of Scientists* (Boston: Beacon Press, 1964), pp. 3–48; Edward A. Shils, "The Profession of Science," *The Advancement of Science*, (June) 1968, 469–479. See also W J. Reader, *Professional Men: The Rise of the Professional Classes in Nineteenth-Century England* (New York: Basic Books, 1966).

27. Morrell and Thackray, op. cit., [n. 7], p. 224.

28. Faraday to Whewell, 20 May 1840 in L. Pearce Williams, *Michael Faraday* (New York: Basic Books, 1965), p. 261.

29. Whewell to Murchison, 2 October 1840 in Todhunter, op. cit., [n. 13], II, pp. 290–292.

30. "Address by the Rev. Professor Whewell, F.R.S., &c.," *Report of the Eleventh Meeting of the British Association for the Advancement of Science* (London: John Murray, 1841), xxvii–xxxv.

31. William Whewell, Inaugural Lecture, *The General Bearing of the Great Exhibition on the Progress of Art and Science* (London: David Bogue, Fleet Street, November 26, 1851), pp. 1–34. It is symbolically apt that when Prince Albert delivered *his* presidential address to the BAAS a few years later, he too referred several times to "men of science" but not at all to "scientists." I take incidental satisfaction in noting that having been tutored in his youth by Adolphe Quetelet—who my mentor George Sarton and my colleague Paul Lazarsfeld both regarded as a founder of sociology properly conceived—Prince Albert went on to urge members of the BAAS to accord "warmest approbation and good will" to the fields of "Political Economy" and "what is called 'Social Science'." His Address appears in *Victorian Science: A Self-Portrait from the Presidential Addresses to the British Association for the Advancement of Science*, edited by George Basalla, William Coleman, and Robert H. Kargon, eds., (Garden City: Doubleday, 1970), pp. 49–59.

32. Part of Faraday's terminological indebtedness to Whewell appears in the correspondence between them brought together in the second volume of Tod-

hunter, op. cit., [n. 13], e.g. pp. 363 ff. More is established in Robert E. Oesper and Max Speter, "The Faraday-Whewell Correspondence Concerning Electro-Chemical Terms," *Scientific Monthly,* 1937, XLV: 535–546. This paper, the authors note, publishes "for the first time [certain] extracts" from the 65 items composing the Correspondence in the archives of Trinity College, Cambridge. Oesper and Speter take evident scholarly pleasure in having captured the process of change in Faraday's terminology in transit from the oral to the printed version of his famous paper summarizing his work on electrochemistry, the paper having been read to the Royal Society early in 1834 and printed later that year. As they put it for the record which merits reinstatement here: "The electrochemical terminology for the most part was evolved during the period between the reading and the publication of the paper, a fact that hitherto has either been unknown or disregarded, with the result that Whewell has never been given adequate credit for the predominant part he played in the coinage of these new terms" (538–539). An expanded list of Whewell's neologisms, supplementing the items appearing in the OED, is assembled in P. J. Wexler, "The Great Nomenclator: Whewell's Contributions to Scientific Terminology," *Notes and Queries,* January 1961, 8:27–29, 33, a paper that draws upon Oesper and Speter. Both papers are superseded by Sydney Ross, "Faraday Consults the Scholars: The Origins of the Terms of Electro-chemistry," *Notes and Records of the Royal Society of London,* November 1961, 16:187–220 which is in turn "heavily" and gratefully drawn upon by Pearce Williams in his superb biography, *Michael Faraday,* op. cit., [note 28], pp. 257–272.

33. Quoted by Ross, ibid., 216; Ross, op. cit., [n. 9], 72; Williams, ibid., p. 261. The two scholars differ slightly in their reading of this passage. Ross has the phrase read "three separate sounds of *i* in one word" while Williams has it as "three separate sounds of *s.*" The variation may result from what Ross describes as "the difficulty posed by Faraday's handwriting" (while Williams says much the same about Whewell's handwriting). I have adopted the Williams reading not so much for first having come upon this passage in his book as for the resulting emphasis on sibilance which was soon to be publicly voiced by others. No great difference; either way leads to much the same sort of complaint. As we have seen, that other physicist of the very first rank, Kelvin, was still objecting to *physicist* a half-century later.

34. The *OED* quotes this remark in its entry for *physicist,* thus leading me to the unsigned article in which it appears: "Physical Science in England," *Blackwood's Magazine,* October 1843, 54:514–524 (at 524) as it may have led Ross there as well (1962, op. cit., [n. 9], 73). The *OED* thus exhibits once again the value of a dictionary founded "on historical principles" in leading students to sources. Neither the *OED,* of course, nor Ross had occasion to cite the title of the article or to note that this complaint about sibilance appears in the course of a strong criticism of Whewell as "a word-maker [who] seems peculiarly deficient in ear." Thanks to Walter Houghton's *Wellesley Index,* one now knows that the anonymous critic was a William R. Grove, described in the *Dictionary of National Biography* as a "man of science and a jurist,"—not, be it noted, as a scientist and a jurist.

35. Unsigned, "On the English Language," *Blackwood's Magazine,* April 1839, 45:455–462, at 460. The anonymous author turns out to be that nineteenth century master of seventeenth century prose style, Thomas De Quincey. The *OED* adopts this as its first example of "classicist" in use but of course the word had appeared before, notably in the drawing of contrasts between classicism and romanticism.

36. Ben Johnson [*sic*], *Timber: Or Discoveries: Made Upon Men and Matter: As They have flow'd out of his daily Readings, or had their refluxe to this peculiar Notion of the Time.* (London, M.DC.XLI). Reprinted in *Ben Jonson,* C. H. Herford, Percy and Evelyn Simpson, eds. (Oxford: Clarendon Press, 1947), vol. 8, p. 622.

37. *The English Grammar* made by Ben. Johnson [*sic*], MDCXL, as reprinted in Ben Jonson, ibid., vol. 8, pp. 507–508.

38. (Oxford: Clarendon Press, 1926), p. 211.

39. Cynthia Fuchs Epstein, *Deceptive Distinctions: Sex, Gender, and the Social Order* (New Haven: Yale University Press, 1988), pp. 5–6, citing Ann Oakley, *Sex, Gender and Society* (London: Temple Smith, 1972).

40. Laurence Sterne, *The Life and Opinions of Tristram Shandy, Gent.* (London, [1759–67], 1819); in this edition of 1819, "man of science" turns up on page 16 of the first composite volume; "woman of science," on page 72 of the second volume.

41. Mary Somerville, *On the Connexion of the Physical Sciences* (London: John Murray, 1834). I rather like the thought that in 1975 when—to cite for a rare equity, a *reverse*-alphabetical ordering of the compilers—Harriet Zuckerman, Arnold Thackray, Robert K. Merton, and Yehuda Elkana put together a collection of 60 out-of-print volumes for republication by the Arno Press under the title *History, Philosophy, and Sociology of Science: Classics, Staples, and Precursors,* we included Mary Somerville's book. Our catalogue entry described it in part this way: "First published in 1834, with each of its ten editions revised 'to keep pace with the progress of discovery,' this dedicated *vulgarisation* was described a generation later by Clerk Maxwell as shadowing forth a 'unity of the method of science' with 'facility and occasional felicity of expression.' Its indomitable author continued her writing into her nineties, learning much of her science from her circle of friends and, often, invisible collaborators. These included some of the foremost practitioners of the time: Faraday, Lyell, Sir John Herschel, and even the rebel Charles Babbage."

42. I quote from the opening lines of the biographical article by Elizabeth C. Patterson, "Mary Somerville," in *The British Journal of the History of Science,* 1969, 4, 331–339. Thanks to Stephen M. Stigler I learned that the article has been expanded into an excellent monograph: Elizabeth Chambers Patterson, *Mary Somerville and the Cultivation of Science, 1815–1840* (The Hague: Martinus Nijhoff, 1983) where it is noted on page 138 that it was in his anonymous "review that Whewell's suggestion [of *scientist*]—widely adopted—was first made public and a new term added to English usage." Understandably, that brief aside takes

no notice of the decades of vicissitudes encountered by the new term before it was widely adopted nor does it pause to take note of the term's fortuitously epicene character.

43. Whewell, op. cit., [n. 12], pp. 55–56.

44. Londa Schiebinger, *The Mind Has No Sex?* (Cambridge: Harvard University Press, 1989). The epigraph quotes François Poullain de la Barre as claiming in 1673 that *"L'ésprit n'a point de sexe"* and is followed by Whewell's counterpoint claim of a century-and-a-half later.

45. Whewell, op. cit., [n. 12] 65–66 (italics added).

46. For diverse sources and orientations, see Evelyn Fox Keller, *Reflections on Gender and Science* (New Haven: Yale University Press, 1985) and "The Wo/Man Scientist: Issues of Sex and Gender in the Pursuit of Science" in Harriet Zuckerman, Jonathan R. Cole and John T. Bruer, eds., *The Outer Circle: Women in the Scientific Community* (New York: W. W. Norton, 1991), pp. 227–236; Sandra Harding, *The Science Question in Feminism* (Ithaca: Cornell University Press, 1986); Nancy Tuana, ed., *Feminism & Science* (Bloomington: Indiana University Press, 1989).

47. F. James Davis, *Who Is Black? One Nation's Definition* (University Park: Penn State Press, 1992).

48. Margaret W. Rossiter, *Women Scientists in America: Struggles and Strategies to 1940* (Baltimore: The Johns Hopkins University Press, 1982), p. 112. The titular phrase "women scientists" of course tacitly registers the epicene character of the word *scientist.*

49. It is Robert W. Burchfield, editor of the superb *Supplement* to the heroic *OED* who describes Dr. Murray so in his Preface to the concluding volume IV (Oxford: Clarendon Press, 1986), p. ix while meticulously noting that "The *OED* was not in fact the first historical dictionary. Jacob Grimm and Wilhelm Grimm started their *Deutsches Wörterbuch* at an earlier date and their first volume was published in 1854." See also the biography by Dr. Murray's granddaughter: Catharine Murray, *Caught in the Web of Words: James A. H. Murray and the Oxford English Dictionary* (Oxford, 1977).

50. The entry on "man of science" appears on page 222 of Volume IX of the 1933 re-issue of the *OED.* The criterion for the word *man* to be understood in the generic sense of "a human being (irrespective of sex or age)" or in the specific sense of "an adult male person, with special reference to sex" is drawn from the entry on *Man* as a substantive (which appears on pages 99–103 of Volume VI of the same edition).

51. Unabridged and tellingly described as an *American* dictionary, the 1864 Webster's ascribes the word *scientist* to an unidentified "Gould," without date or title of specific source. And when in 1890 it was transformed into an avowedly "International" rather than provincially "American" Dictionary, *Webster's* still ascribed the word, not to the 1840 work of the British William Whewell but to the readily identifiable American astronomer, "B. A. Gould" who had claimed in his presidential address to the American Association for the Advancement of Sci-

ence in 1869 that he had "ventured to propose . . . the word *scientist*" twenty years before. *Scientist* probably was an independent multiple coinage as can be seen from cumulating investigations of the matter by Sydney Ross, "Scientist: The Story of a Word" 1962 [see n. 9] and an expanded edition of that paper in Ross, *Nineteenth Century Attitudes: Men of Science* (Dordrecht/Boston/London: Kluwer Academic Publishers, 1991), pp. 1–39; and from Robert K. Merton "Le molteplici origini e il carattere epiceno del termine inglese Scientist," *Scientia: Rivista internationale di sintesi scientifica,* 1988, 82:279–293 and "Ueber die vielfältigen Wurzeln und den geschlechtslosen Charakter des englischen Wortes 'scientist' " in Peter H. Hofschneider and Karl Ulrich Mayer, eds., *Generationsdynamik und Innovation in der Grundlagenforschung-Symposium,* Juni 1989 (Munich: Max-Planck-Gesellschaft Berichte und Mitteilungen, 1990), 3:259–294.

52. As we have ample cause to know, here is a foreshadowing moment of Whewell's invention, a half-dozen years later, of that "English name for *physicien": physicist.*

53. [Whewell], *"On the Connexion of the Physical Sciences.* By Mrs. Somerville," op. cit., [n. 12], 58–59.

54. Successive editions of this paper have been presented to the American Philosophical Society, the Harvard University Department of the History of Science, the Rockefeller University, the New York Academy of Sciences, and the University of Oslo. These pre-print lectures have been aided by the ensuing discussions. Although the unexamined mores of publishing do not ordinarily allow for successive editions of printed papers as they do for books, "oral publication" in the form of lectures and seminars does. (The term oral publication may seem an oxymoron until we recall that for centuries before Gutenberg "to publish" meant simply "to make public"—that is, to make something known to members of a collectivity.) Note 51 of this paper cites the two earlier editions that have also appeared in print.

On Robert Merton, Mary Somerville, and the Moral Authority of Science

Gerald Holton

I am happy to participate in this celebration of the long and distinguished tradition of sociology at Yale University. Meeting at a time of national and international upheavals unparalleled in recent memory, we know that there is now no politically more urgent or intellectually more demanding area of study than the social sciences. Within that area of scholarship, the sociology of science is one of its very lively frontiers, and our main contributor is of course the founder of that field. So there is much to say, and as his commentator, I find myself struggling, within the frame of the allowed space, to do justice to his learned and elegant discourse.

On the surface, Robert Merton's challenge to us is to comment on the social study of science as reflected in William Whewell's and Benjamin Gould's coinage of their noneuphonious word "scientist."

Let me confess that on first reading his manuscript I fell into Merton's well-placed trap for those who would be seduced merely by the word itself. I began to ponder that a scientist today is painfully aware of the ambiguities in the meaning of the words "scientist," or even "science" in actual usage—and of the fact that these ambiguities are indicators of the place of science in society today. To much of the population, basic science is indistinguishable from applied or from engineering, or research from development. Jerome Wiesner told me that when he became President John Kennedy's Science Adviser, he thought that yet another new word in place of science might be needed to indicate the total span of his mandate, from research to technology, from mathematics to public health. So he announced a prize competition among his staff for coining the necessary new term, to be used in renaming the Office of the Science Adviser. The competition was won by a chap who persuasively argued that the word science itself, as commonly understood, was already suitably diluted, that it was generally held to embrace the whole spectrum anyway, and that therefore no new name was needed at all. And so it stayed the Office of the Science Adviser.

Possibly for similar reasons, however, a scientist now almost never calls himself or herself a scientist in public, except while giving testimony at a congressional hearing, or the like. Yet the media love to pin the label on you anyway on every occasion. An on-line search for the term shows the word scientist is now appearing about two thousand times each month in the *New York Times* alone. If credit were given each time to the co-coiners, Whewell and Gould would instantly become the world's most frequently cited authors.

As a physicist and a historian of science, I have had occasion to wonder what *those* descriptive words really signify to others. Sometime ago I was handing in an application for a credit line at a bank. The desk officer, a young woman of athletic appearance, read my application form, then scanned me up and down with obvious disbelief, and finally said, "And you are a professor of physique?" On another occasion, I was asked with some embarrassment what it is that a professor of physic really does. As to the term history of science, it now describes quite inadequately a portion of a large and fast-growing field that encompasses history, philosophy and sociology of science, and technology and medicine. The members of this general professional field now really need a new term for their self-description, for much the same sociological reasons as obtained for scientists in the nineteenth century in Merton's example.

But here I must catch myself before I really get caught in the trap laid for the philologue or logophile. For the chief point of Merton's paper is in another direction entirely. As I see it, his essay can be read, at a deeper level, as a series of cleverly placed clues, a rebus that suggests by word and symbols its own solution. That is to say, his examples can be understood as pointers to a series of research projects in the sociology of science. He broadly hints at their existence throughout the text, but lest one missed it, he reemphasizes it near the end of the essay, in the third sentence of the epilogue: "Closely read, the preamble takes us to a series of concluding questions that have become part of the developing agenda of the philosophy, history, and sociology of science and the sciences."

Let us follow the design in the rebus, one by one. The first clue is the early introduction of an essay-review on Mary Somerville's book, written by the "*prime* begetter of the enduring coinage, *scientist*," namely William

Whewell. We thus are gently directed to look into the volume containing that essay: *The Quarterly Review*, for March and June 1834. We notice, perhaps initially without making anything of it, that Whewell's essay on Somerville appears there in unexpected company, such as the review of a book by the Reverend J. B. Clarke of Trinity College, being an account of the worthy life of one of his worthy ancestors, and a review of the Reverend Alexander Crombie's dense speculations on natural theology and the immortality of the soul.

As we ponder why Whewell would have chosen a journal that could provide such neighbors for his essay, the idea suggests itself that it was not an accident. Whewell must have known that at the birth of the new word, such divines might stand at either side of the cradle. It is a signal worth following up. After all, Whewell was not merely a scientist distinguished in physics and astronomy, and just then, in 1834, at work on his great three-volume history of inductive sciences. He also was an ordained deacon and then a priest in the Church of England, long before being made Master of Trinity. Indeed, soon he was to become professor of moral philosophy at Cambridge. For such a man, quite characteristic of that part of the century, science and theology were not separate, but rather could be conceived as existing in wonderful symbiosis—mutually validating each other. As Whewell's biographer, Robert Butts, put it, the essence of Whewell's view on scientific progress was the attainment of more and more general theories, the increasing discovery of a generality and an underlying unity worthy of the creator himself. For the final aim of science was that we "would know the way it is because that is the way God made it."

We'll come back to this point later. Looking now further at Whewell's seemingly lighthearted review, we note, as Merton says, that the main object was not the coining of the epicene word scientist, but the agitating question, here and elsewhere in Whewell's writings, how to oppose the unfortunate tendency of science to subdivide and subspecialize. The word "scientist" seems intended by Whewell to give symbolic reality to the underlying unity of all sciences to which our diverse, incomplete sciences should progress. And precisely in those years, the 1830s, the possibility of increasingly achieving unity seemed very clear. After all, this was the time when Thomas Young had recently announced the close analogy of the wave nature of light and sound. Alessandro Volta had demonstrated the direct kinship of animal electricity and electric currents from his newly invented batteries. Humphry Davy had found the bridge between electricity and chemistry. Hans Christian Oersted and Michael Faraday had discovered the unification of electricity and magnetism into electromagnetism. Intellectual synthesis was beckoning everywhere; that could be the best weapon for counteracting the splintering effects of professional specialization and the other diseases within the scientific establishment in the 1830s, on which Charles Babbage had so recently issued his thundering denunciation.

In this light, Whewell and like-minded friends could only welcome with pleasure Somerville's veritable ode to the underlying connections within the physical sciences; for as Whewell indicated in his review, nothing would be worse for science than to forget its "traces of unity."

But Whewell was evidently enchanted by her work also for another, quite different reason. Behind his donnish and now rather absurd-seeming attempts at levity, this is nevertheless the Whewell who was regarded as perhaps the most effective educational reformer of his day. Through Somerville's book, he could point to her as a worthy role model for scientists, for amateurs of science, and for laymen and laywomen who might be attracted to science.

We begin to see that Whewell's essay lays bare some of the issues of interest in the sociology of science, not only for the nineteenth century, but also for our day: the place of science in the educational system, the place of women in science, the difference in the career paths of men and women, the theories of scientific progress, the growth of social institutions, the phase in that growth when the old rhetoric of science has to give way to new rhetoric, and so on.

Having now indirectly signaled these multifaceted tasks for the sociologist of science, Merton drops another clue for us to follow up, in order to enlarge the scale of our labors. That clue is introduced by his bringing into the picture Gould's review of 1849 of John Herschel's book, *Outline of Astronomy* (a book, as it happens, written by one of Somerville's friends and admirers). In the pamphlet version of that review, Gould also happened to fashion the word *scientist*. The great astronomer Herschel was interesting to Gould chiefly as a popularizer, almost as successful on the whole as Whewell's Somerville. But there is more to this, as we discover quickly. Following Merton's implicit directions, we take the volume with Gould's review of Herschel off the shelf. The journal has the full title, *The Christian Examiner and Religious Miscellany,* and the Widener Library copy, properly enough, still has the bookplate of its year of acquisition, 1850, showing a group of heroic figures above the seal with the inscription: Sigillum Academiae Harvardianae, below which is added most appropriately the college's old motto: Christo et Ecclesiae.

So alerted, we now focus on the fact that Gould's lengthy article finds itself among rather similar neighbors as Whewell's review had. To either side of the review of Herschel's astronomy are reviews of books on Christian hymns, on the problem of evil, on the "philosophy of religion," on a history of the American Baptist missions abroad, and even on a book entitled "Scripture Vindicated against some Perversions of Rationalism, with a Sketch of the Lake of Galilee."

What does all that have to do with Herschel's writings on Neptune or the comets, which Gould examines with great care and occasionally criticizes with unseeming lack of charity? The answer is given at the very end of the review, where Gould quotes Herschel himself, to the effect that by following the proper scientific method, the effort of the devotee of science "is the first movement of approach toward that state of mental purity which alone can fit us for a full and steady perception of moral beauty. . . ."

With this hint—if it were really needed—we add to our implied research project the issue of science and religion in pre-Darwinian England. Our list of work to be done is growing.

But by now we can no longer contain our curiosity about Somerville's own writings, and so we lay aside for the moment Whewell and Gould, and turn to her book. It is entitled simply *On the Connexion* [significantly singular] *of the Physical Sciences,* and it was published in 1834 when she was 54 years of age. The title and the dedication to Queen Adelaide make clear that Somerville has three main aims. The first, to take her at her own word, is the upgrading of the education of her follow countrywomen. Her own experience had taught her how difficult it was for a bright woman to enter on and pursue a study of the sciences. She had to teach herself at first from books and in secret, hiding to escape the charge of so-called "unwomanly behavior." As for so many others before her and since, a turning point in her intellectual life seems to have been the self-study of Euclid's geometry and of algebra. That was followed by a course in Latin; by studying physics directly from Isaac Newton's *Principia;* and by going on to a rigorous sequence of readings in advanced mathematics, astronomy, Greek, botany, and geology. Her highly acclaimed translation, with her commentary, of Pierre-Simon Laplace's *Traite de mécanique céleste* was in fact used as a textbook at Whewell's Cambridge. The last of her books on a scientific subject appeared when she was 89, and she retained her mental vigor to the end, working on a paper on quarternions shortly before her death in 1872 at the age of 92. Yet, while she had an enormous circle of friends and admirers among scientists, one must note that a reviewer, two years after her death, could confidently announce in the journal *Nature* that her genius was so unique "that her case . . . [may] be adduced in proof of the rule that women are not by nature adapted for studies which involve the higher processes of induction and analysis."

If improvement of the access of women to science was Somerville's first priority in her book—which would also fit with her work on behalf of emancipation—another seemingly quite different aim was not far behind. It was the exhibition of a set of unifying connections among "the laws by which the material world is governed." Her brief preface following the dedication shows that she is not interested in discussing a ragbag of disconnected laws of nature. On the contrary, she explicitly notes that the whole point of the "progress of modern science" in her time is to show that there is "a tendency to simplify the laws of nature, and to unite detached branches by general principles." She has indeed absorbed the chief lesson arising from the work of scientists such as Young, Davy, and Faraday, all of whom were incidentally in her close circle of friends. She reveals herself in her book also as a seeker after unity, one who, in the terminology of that great pluralist Isaiah Berlin, is possessed by the Ionian fallacy, defined as the search, from Aristotle to our day, for the ultimate constituent of the world.

But as we read in the almost encyclopedic test of over four hundred fifty pages in her book, it becomes clear that there is yet another, third aim also at work in her endeavor, showing itself most strikingly perhaps in her introduction and in the last pages. That aim, to put it simply, is to discover and exhibit the moral warrant of science. This question was on many minds then as now. Somerville had lived through the height of what Friedrich Schlegel had termed "the romantic ideal," and through the romantic reaction against Newtonian science. And yet here she was launching her paean to science with an explanation of the Newtonian dynamics of the planetary system.

She begins calmly, reassuring her reader that even without higher mathematics and advanced physics, it is possible to grasp the unifying "mutual dependence of the different parts of the system," as well as how these "most extraordinary conclusions have been arrived at." This in turn will enable one to contemplate the "works of creation" in a manner that "elevates the mind to the admiration of whatever is great and noble." And that, finally, will bring us nearer to "that supreme and eternal mind which contains all truth and wisdom." Perhaps we begin now to see why the word scientist appeared first among pages frequented by divines.

At the end of her book, Somerville holds out the ancient and ever dizzying prospect that tracing the immediate connection among the parts of science, "which is daily extending its empire, and will ultimately embrace almost every subject in nature in its formulae," is essentially a religious act. For, as she says, "these formulae [are] emblematic of Omniscience." She ends with the stirring prospect of the ultimate unification of mankind, nature, and the deity: "This mighty instrument of human power [the formulae of science] itself originates in the primitive constitution of the human mind, and rests upon a few fundamental axioms, which have eternally existed in Him who implanted them in the breast of man when He created him after His own image."

The moral authority of science, in Somerville's formulation, derives from the inherently transcendent function of scientific thought. That was of course an ancient preoccupation, from Psalm 19 ("The heavens declare the glory. . . .") through the Platonists and on to Johannes Kepler's outburst that God specifically created man with a mind that "carries in it the concepts built on the category of quantity," in order that man may directly communicate with the deity: As Kepler put it in 1599, in almost the same way as Somerville: "Those laws [which govern the material world] lie within the power of understanding of the human mind; God wanted us to perceive them when he created us in His image in order that we may take part in His own thoughts. . . . Our knowledge [of numbers and quantities] is of the same kind as God's, at least insofar as we can understand something of it in this mortal life." Newton thoguht so too, although in writing on physics he did not often let his stern, public mask slip. But at the very end of his *Opticks,* he predicted: "If natural philosophy in all its parts . . . shall at length be perfected, the bounds of moral philosophy will be also enlarged." Newton's contemporaries in the Royal Society said as much, and at greater length. Indeed, Somerville's rather characteristic view of science in nineteenth-century England owed much to the tradition of the relation between science and religious thought in seventeenth-century England.

Having said that, we realize with a start that we have arrived here at the very problem from which the sociology of science itself originated as a field of study in Merton's own seminal volume, now over half a century ago, on the social and religious origins of the scientific revolution in seventeenth-century England.

With this, my commentary has come back full circle to the beginning. Somerville, Gould, Whewell, the word scientist, the book of 1834, and even the review journals: each of them a nodal point in an intimate network of connections. Together they define a promising research site for the still rather neglected field of pre-Darwinian English science; separately, each symbolizes an entrance point for the sociological imagination at work.

If there were space, we could use Somerville's example to urge us on to the obvious next questions: If she now came back in new guise to join us today, what would she find to be the same or different? Would she not ask whether her hopes for the upgrading of her countrywomen have really succeeded? How does the unification program for the sciences stand today? In what, if anything, is the moral authority of science grounded now? These, as it happens, are some of the main questions around which my own research is centered, questions with clear policy implications that fascinate many historians and sociologists of science in this last decade of our century. I join in expressing the hope that from the scholars at this great university there will radiate continued illumination on these problems for many decades to come.

Strange Relation

Denis Donoghue

In the preface to the second edition of *Lyrical Ballads* William Wordsworth has a few sentences about the relation between science and literature. If the time should ever come, he says, when "what is now called
Science . . . " shall be ready to put on "a form of flesh and blood," the
poet "will lend his divine spirit to aid the transfiguration." He seems to
mean that if a scientific discovery becomes common property, part of
ordinary lore, the poet will take as much interest in it as in writing poems
about revisiting the Wye, looking at London from Westminster Bridge,
or considering the fate of old Cumberland beggars. Poets will try to convert the new knowledge into experience, carrying it to the heart. Over the
years, as we know, a few such discoveries have become common lore and
are part of daily reference. Such phrases as "the survival of the fittest,"
"inferiority complex," "self-fulfilling prophecy," and "Oedipus complex" are spoken even by people who have never read a word of Charles
Darwin, Alfred Adler, Robert Merton, or Sigmund Freud. Wordsworth
seems to say that when science makes these discoveries and offers them
as knowledge, the poet is ready to transfigure this knowledge by bringing
it into the common stock of affections and interests; presumably by imagining lives of which this knowledge is the incipient form. Poets don't—or
shouldn't—regard scientific knowledge as alien, but as incomplete: the
completion of it is experience.

I have quoted Wordsworth mainly to show that poets did not invariably
construe the relation between science and literature as one of mutual distrust. Also to note certain consequences from the fact that in 1800 the
English language, as Merton and Sydney Ross have noted, did not contain

the word "scientist," which would have corresponded to such words as artist and humanist. Wordsworth's phrase "what is now called Science" seems to refer to a historical moment in which the physical and natural sciences stepped forward as assured forms of knowledge and claimed to distinguish themselves from other forms that were merely skills or crafts. Medicine, for instance. Not that the distinction between a professional and an amateur practitioner could be firmly held. In 1800 sciences were not yet institutions. There were gentlemen with some learning and much curiosity. There were gentlemen with great learning and endless curiosity; but the lines were not sharply drawn. In effect, Wordsworth is calling upon the hard sciences—as we now think of them—to commit themselves to a distinctive human and social purpose, not merely the production of knowledge but ultimately the enhancement of affection.

I assume that the context of Wordworth's phrase was the recognition of a scientific project that in English would eventually be called the Enlightenment. Immanuel Kant's essay "What Is Enlightenment?" was published in November 1784, but the OED hasn't found any instance of the word "Enlightenment" in the Kantian sense earlier than 1865. This seems late for the acknowledgment, in England, of an ideology of science. By that phrase I mean the conjoined claims entailed by reference to the values of Enlightenment, inductive method of inquiry, and the confident expectation of progress; what Gerald Holton describes in *Thematic Origins of Scientific Thought* as "the generally accepted thema of the unlimited possibility of *doing* science, the belief that nature is in principle fully knowable."[1] If this belief is in the context of Wordworth's preface, the poet may have been saying to the young men of the Enlightenment, the men whom he can't yet call scientists: "the claim you make to rescue us from superstition and the empire of error may be valid, but please don't assume that your discoveries will in their scientific form satisfy the people who receive them: they won't, by themselves, appease the desires still widely gratified by superstition." He may even have been saying: "whatever you discover will remain mere knowledge, the stuff of books, until it has been brought into the stream of common feeling."

Some such admonition is implicit in the humanist part of the great Victorian dispute about the role science should play in education: a dispute so well known that it may sufficiently be recalled if I merely list such names as Matthew Arnold, T. H. Huxley, Henry Sidgwick, Cardinal Newman, and C. S. Peirce. But I may remark that in the documents of that dispute there is, on the scientific side, a note of condescension: we hear it in Huxley's implication that the *Zeitgeist* has already made its decision in favor of science. The humanities are to be patronized and protected, much as Victorian fathers undertook to protect their women. The note is heard again in the first replies to *Culture and Anarchy;* as if Arnold's appeal to values beyond positive culture merited chiefly ridicule. We hear the same note of teasing condescension even in Whewell's review of Somerville's *On the Connexion of the Physical Sciences.* I agree with Merton that Whewell is good-humored, but if Whewell were reviewing a book of the same title by a man of science, perhaps an Anglican divine given to writing such books, he would not even advert to a question of gendered intelligence.

Humanists, in turn, attacked science because they feared it. They saw that it must inevitably play the major role in industrial development—essential in any country that proposed to develop in terms of Empire—railways, roads, ships, factories, mechanization, imports, and exports. Humanists were afraid of the social changes science would bring. This is Charles Dickens's theme in *Dombey and Son* and *Hard Times;* though his sense of the matter was complex and not at all reactionary. It is a theme of English literature from Thomas Hardy to E. M. Forster. Some humanists feared that the extension of scientific method would break the national connection to the past and undermine the values that depended on that connection. In the event, long after scientists found a name for themselves, science made its way into the curriculum—mainly, I think, because most people came to admire scientists as exemplars of a moral type, serious, conscientious, truthful. In effect, the dispute was yet another version of the seventeenth-century quarrel between the Ancients and the Moderns, between tradition and modernity, between the intellectual value ascribed to the classics of Greece and Rome and the inductive procedures of modern science. Even those who accepted that the future was to be increasingly in the hands of scientists felt misgiving to the degree sometimes of dread. Mary Shelley expressed this fear by inventing Frankenstein. Newman thought to take the harm out of the ideology of science by invoking the merit of the pursuit of knowledge for its own sake, not for its useful application; he proposed to internalize knowledge, speeding up Wordsworth's program. But in the end the scientists won the argument because they presented themselves not only as exemplars of a better domestic and national economy but as men who were willing and able to give reasons for their actions and to take responsibility for them. Humanists came off badly from the comparison: they seemed vague, "praisers of gone times because they had none of their own"—a rebuke I recall from R. P. Blackmur's essay on Irving Babbitt. In practice, men of power saw their own interests fulfilled in the national interest, a consequence of the relation between scientific knowledge and the human ability to live in the world.

The success of scientific method and its development in technology had profound consequences, most of them beneficial but one or two of them regrettable. In his lecture in September 1919 called "Science as a Vocation," Max Weber makes the point that modern science is "a 'vocation' conducted through *specialist* disciplines to serve the cause of reflection on the self and knowledge of relationships between facts, not a gift of grace from seers and prophets dispensing sacred values and revelations."[2] The claim is valid, though Weber is glib in disposing of the superstitions and prophecies he refers to. In his emphasis on the specialist character of scientific disciplines he didn't foresee that the disciplines would become, one after another, inaccessible even to reasonably well-read people; that their lore would become common property only in much diminished if not disheveled form, like the survival of the fittest, inferiority complex, self-fulfilling prophecy, and Oedipus complex. Or if he foresaw this development, he decided that it wouldn't matter, since the important application of scientific knowledge would remain in the hands of experts.

The opacity of scientific knowledge to lay readers played a considerable part in the situation that Georg Simmel described in *The Philosophy of Money* (1900). The situation is one in which many people feel that their lives are divided into two unequal if not opposed parts. There is the official or public part, largely involving one's career, making a living, earning money: it is the place of routine, or of that careerist striving that is still routine. This part of one's life is predicated upon a scientific and mostly positive sense of reality, and it is subject to the disposition of specialists and experts. The second part is unofficial, it is one's private life, the site of the conviction of freedom, leisure, the place where—according to a perhaps facile assumption—one is most truly oneself. Simmel's explanation of this division is that "the modern division of labour permits the number of dependencies to increase just as it causes personalities to disappear behind their functions." Speaking of "the preponderance of objective over subjective culture," he argues that "every day and from all sides the wealth of objective culture increases, but the individual mind can enrich the forms and contents of its own development only by distancing itself still further from that culture and developing its own at a much slower pace."[3] It follows that people come to regard their public lives—indeed public life itself—as inauthentic, a state of entrapment, and they regard their private lives as the sole region of their authenticity. If they can afford the luxury, they live for the weekend. Weber, too, in the lecture from which I have quoted, has this passage:

The fate of our age, with characteristic rationalization and intellectualization and above all the disenchantment of the world, is that the ultimate, most sublime values have withdrawn from public life, either into the transcendental realm of mystical life or into the brotherhood of immediate personal relationships between individuals. It is no accident that our greatest art is intimate rather than monumental, nor is it fortuitous that today only in the smallest groups, between individuals, something pulsates *in pianissimo* which corresponds to the prophetic *pneuma* which formerly swept through great communities like fire and welded them together.[4]

One of the clearest expressions of this withdrawal of value from public life and the concentration of energy upon one's private life is the conclusion to Walter Pater's *Studies in the History of the Renaissance* (1873) in which he presents the supreme value as one's conversion of time into experience by force of consciousness:

> Failure is to form habits: for habit is relative to a stereotyped world; meantime it is only the roughness of the eye that makes any two persons, things, situations, seem alike. While all melts under our feet, we may well catch at any exquisite passion, or any contribution to knowledge that seems, by a lifted horizon, to set the spirit free for a moment, or any stirring of the senses, strange dyes, strange flowers, and curious odours, or work of the artist's hands, or the face of one's friend. Not to discriminate every moment some passionate attitude in those about us, and in the brilliance of their gifts some tragic dividing of forces on their ways is, on this short day of frost and sun, to sleep before evening.[5]

Pater speaks of setting the spirit free for a moment. He doesn't think it can be set free for a longer interval. Presumably one's energy is not enough to sustain the effort. Inevitably we sink again into habit; till we take another deep breath and exert our consciousness on some chosen provocation. In this act we resume our true life. To achieve this momentary sense of freedom, one must (Pater, Weber, and Simmel seem to agree) withdraw from the public world and discount the values we practiced there.

I assume that the Enlightenment hoped to find—or to render—any such division of one's life unnecessary. Men of the Enlightenment appear to have hoped that the consistent application of reason and method to the evidences of nature would make sense of our entire lives. They would deem it miserable to find the use of reason rebuffed at any point. Perhaps they didn't sufficiently allow for the habit in each of us of requiring the world to resemble ourselves. When James Frazer wrote *The Golden Bough,* having studied the legends, myths, and practices the book tries to account for, he brought to bear upon them the habits of mind of a Victorian positivist. He wrote of the myths as if they should not only make sense but make his sense, or find themselves relegated to the already vast stock of superstition. Ludwig Wittgenstein's comments on Frazer rebuke him for his provincialism, for his lack of imagination, his inability to see that one community's sense is another's nonsense. René Girard has developed this rebuke further in *La Violence et le sacre* (1972).

It appears to be as true of science as of art and literature: there is never a beginning. The beginning is not the beginning. Nobody starts from zero. Even a zero would not constitute an absolute beginning. Gerald Holton's work on the thematics of scientific discovery allows us to think of a *thema* as a working prejudice from which the scientist begins: it is what the particular scientist starts from, and may have no more formal justification, at that stage, than a hunch or a notion. Like Holton, Merton allows for the starting point of research, in a particular case, as a hunch or indeed a religious faith. In one of his papers, "The Puritan Spur to Science," he joins Wittgenstein and Holton in warning against provincialism:

> The commitment of the Protestant leaders to have reason and experience "test" all religious beliefs, except the basic assumption, which, just as in science, is simply accepted as a matter of faith, is in part grounded upon the previously mentioned conviction of the inherent consistency, congruence, and mutually confirmatory nature of all knowledge, sensory and supersensory. It would seem, then, that there is, to some extent, a community of assumptions in ascetic Protestantism and science: in both there is the unquestioned basic assumption upon which the entire system is built by the utilization of reason and experience. Within each context there is rationality, though the bases are nonrational.[6]

To that paragraph Merton added a footnote. "A modern logician," he reported, "has aptly remarked that the social scientists must locate the irrational (rather, nonlogical) sources of both rational and irrational thought." The logician was Rudolf Carnap, his book *Factors Determining Human Behavior* (1937).

I take it that the correction of "irrational" to read "nonlogical" is a small instance of Merton's large virtue, of his being edifyingly unprovincial; of his noting that irrational and nonlogical are not synonymns. Unless corrected in turn, I shall assume that irrational means contrary to reason in any of its certified forms, and that nonlogical refers to something in discourse that, rational or not, does not observe the particular form of reasoning which is called logic. Rationality is a larger term than logicality. A Cubist painting may or may not be rational, but it is almost certainly nonlogical.

Merton's correction or clarification exhibits—without making an exhibition of it—the scruple attendant upon the finest activity of social science. It touches, too, upon a further matter of moment, the determination of the boundaries—if there are any—of such terms as knowledge, reason, and science. I refer again to Holton's phrase, "the belief that nature is in principle fully knowable." Michel Foucault has argued, in his study of madness in the eighteenth century, that each society determines for itself where to draw a line between reason and the irrational. Foucault was concerned not only with the definition of madness but with the official treatment of people deemed mad. I presume that there are experts in any community who say where the lines are to be drawn between reason, madness, faith, prejudice, and fiction.

Drawing lines is not one of my favorite activities. I invariably find that wherever I draw one, some value I cherish falls outside it. So I have been gratified to infer that disputes between scientists and humanists have largely died away, perhaps because neither side has persisted in making exclusive claims for itself. We no longer find humanists saying that scientists are predators; that, as John Crowe Ransom charged, they wound "the world's body" by the quality of the attention they bring to it. Nor do we find scientists rejecting the fictive capacity in art and literature. They have assimilated the fact that they, too, exert this capacity. It is pleasant to feel that such quarrels are finished, and that we can now quarrel about local issues, such as the discrepancy between the grants available to scientists and those, smaller indeed, available to humanists.

But my sense that there is peace at large may be premature. A while ago I was reading Michel de Certeau's *The Writing of History* and well into the chapter called "The Fiction of History: The Writing of *Moses and Monotheism*" I came upon a disturbing passage. De Certeau has been arguing that "historical discourses are *themselves* deceived by failing to admit the fundamental debt that they owe, over distance, in respect to what, now *silenced,* was known in the traditions (and which remains within them)." Then he says:

> The gap on which history is constructed may never be denied without a fall into doctrine and "genealogical legend"; yet this gap, an exodus of the "son" and the means of his victory in the place of the father, can also never impede the return (under a different name) of the repressed—of the "uncanny familiarity" *in the very place* of a scientific rationality and production. There are many indications of this. Thus, to select one of the most glaring signs, we

see that in remaining a narrative, historiography retains this "element of grandeur" that once characterized religion. In effect, narrative means impossible totalization. It takes charge of the relation of "science" with its repressed. A "reason" (a form of coherence, the delimitation of a field of study) is endlessly conjoined to the "rubbish" that it creates by being established as such.[7]

De Certeau gives the word "rubbish" protective quotation marks to indicate that it is rubbish in someone else's eyes, not in his. There is every evidence that he feels well disposed to it, all the more for its lowly, excluded character.

When I ask myself what this rubbish is, I think of a passage in Wallace Stevens's poem "Notes toward a Supreme Fiction" in which the poet uses the word "gibberish" and another passage in the same poem in which he uses the word "nonsense." In one he says that "Life's nonsense pierces us with strange relation." In the frame of mind in which one adverts to that relation, one feels well disposed toward rubbish, nonsense, and gibberish. These words refer to matters—feelings, fears, desires—excluded from official designations of usefulness, discourse, and reason. They point toward forms of perception that for the time being evade or transcend the category of knowledge. I quote this passage from Stevens's poem:

The poem goes from the poet's gibberish to
The gibberish of the vulgate and back again.
Does it move to and fro or is it of both

At once? Is it a luminous flittering
Or the concentration of a cloudy day?
Is there a poem that never reaches words

And one that chaffers the time away?
Is the poem both peculiar and general?
There's a meditation there, in which there seems

To be an evasion, a thing not apprehended or
Not apprehended well. Does the poet
Evade us, as in a senseless element?

Evade, this hot, dependent orator,
The spokesman at our bluntest barriers,
Exponent by a form of speech, the speaker

Of a speech only a little of the tongue?
It is the gibberish of the vulgate that he seeks.
He tries by a peculiar speech to speak

The peculiar potency of the general,
To compound the imagination's Latin with
The lingua franca et jocundissima.[8]

This passage of Stevens's poem gives in pianissimo his theory of poetry, or his apology for poetry. The poet's gibberish is what he discovers among the words when he doesn't feel constrained by the conventions having to do with diction, syntax, and communication; or when he feels that these conventions prevent him from saying what he wants to say. The speech is "only a little of the tongue" because it is exiled from its origin, like a recent immigrant in a new, official country. If the speech becomes more of the tongue, it degrades itself, submits to being naturalized. The gibberish of the vulgate is also exempt from the proprieties of diction and syntax, and it communicates by procedures highly informal. I should note that Stevens has printed "vulgate" with lowercase v, else we would feel bound to think it referred to the Latin translation of the Bible (the *editio vulgate*) made by St. Jerome and completed at the beginning of the fifth century. The Vulgate has many specimens of the gibberish of the lowercase vulgate, besides the kind that Stevens designates as the poet's gibberish, peculiar indeed.

There is much to be said about these matters, though not now. But I am inclined to apply Stevens's words to science and literature. It strikes me that we may associate the poet's gibberish with the scientist's gibberish, even in their difference. The poet's gibberish is likely to be peculiar, sublime, or abysmal; it has no prior authority, and in modern literature—think of *The Waste Land*—it has only such authority as it acquires while going along, achieving itself in the words. It convinces, when it does, by its presence, its presence of mind among the peculiarly disposed words. In our time the scientist's gibberish is likely to be mathematical and therefore speechless, to most people nearly as obscure as the poet's gibberish. Whether this matters or not, I can't say, but I recall Hannah Arendt saying, in *The Human Condition,* with the atomic bomb and its devastations in view, that "the reason why it may be wise to distrust the political judgment of scientists *qua* scientists is not primarily their lack of 'character'—that they did not refuse to develop atomic weapons—or their naiveté—that they did not understand that once these weapons were developed they would be the last to be consulted about their use—but precisely the fact that they move in a world where speech has lost its power."[9] There is cause of meditation there, especially on the theme of trust and its bearing upon a shared discourse. As for the gibberish of the vulgate: is it not a matter of peculiar interest to social scientists? What else is Freud on the interpretation of dreams but a social scientist, almost a poet, trying to make sense of the gibberish of the vulgate? What do social scientists do, if not try to draw toward the condition of discourse all the feelings in the world that otherwise roam wild? What is psychoanalysis but the effort to talk into discourse what is otherwise speechless and intolerable for that reason? If the poet tries by a peculiar speech to compound the imagination's Latin with the lingua franca et jocundissima, so too do the social scientists.

But I touch here upon a difficult issue. When social scientists do research in the ways of the vulgate and come upon its gibberish, what are they trying to do? Are they trying to turn that gibberish, with normative intent, into proper sentences? In Freud's case it is an old question: was he a man of the Enlightenment or a Romantic poet? Was it Franz Kafka or Rainer Maria Rilke who noted: "if I get rid of my devils, I fear for the loss of my angels." One of the merits of the visual arts and of music is that they can show particular states of feeling without the obligation of saying anything about them. Is the damage, the intrusion, the normative zeal, inevitable in the scientific form of paying attention? Or does it arise only in discourse when sentences are formed?

For the past year or two I have been returning to two books that seem crucial to me, Jürgen Habermas's *The Philosophical Discourse of Modernity* and Emmanuel Levinas's *Totality and Infinity*. More particularly, I have been mulling over the argument common to both books, that the entire tradition of Western philosophy has been a philosophy of consciousness turned upon being. Habermas thinks the tradition exhausted, but he seems to believe that the cure for the flaws of Enlightenment is more Enlightenment. He proposes that philosophers should devote their energies to the facilitation of "communicative action." Levinas urges philosophers to devote those energies to issues of ethics and justice. "Ethics precedes ontology." I hope that social scientists are willing to take part in this endeavor and, specifically, to recognize what Levinas calls "the primordial face-to-face of language." But when I find myself telling people what they should be doing, I know it is time to stop.

Notes

1. Gerald Holton, *Thematic Origins of Scientific Thought*, rev. ed. (Cambridge: Harvard University Press, 1988), 18.
2. Peter Lassman and Irving Velody with Herminio Martins, eds., *Max Weber's "Science as a Vocation"* (London: Unwin Hyman, 1989), 27.

3. Georg Simmel, *The Philosophy of Money*, trans. Tom Sottomore and David Frisby (London: Routledge & Kegan Paul, 1978), 296.

4. Weber, supra, 30.

5. Walter Pater, *Studies in the History of the Renaissance* (London: Macmillan, 1873), 210–11.

6. Robert K. Merton, *The Sociology of Science*, Norman W. Storer, ed. (Chicago: University of Chicago Press, 1973), 252.

7. Michel de Certeau, *The Writing of History*, trans. Tom Conley (New York: Columbia University Press, 1988), 346.

8. Wallace Stevens, *Collected Poems* (New York: Knopf, 1965), 396–97.

9. Hannah Arendt, *The Human Condition* (Chicago: The University of Chicago Press, 1958), 4.

A Life of Learning

Robert K. Merton

1994 Charles Homer Haskins Lecture,
American Council of Learned Societies

I doubt that any of my learned predecessors experienced as much harmless pleasure as mine when *they* were asked to give the Haskins Lecture. After all, none of them was a sociologist, happy to learn that his work was thought humanistic enough to warrant this great honor. And surely, none of them had their lecture mark the seventy-fifth anniversary of ACLS and also take place in their hometown.[1]

Other coincidences of time and place deepen my pleasure in this meeting. For one, this new Benjamin Franklin Hall of the American Philosophical Society happens to be within walking distance of the house in which I was born almost 84 years ago. For quite another, the daunting invitation to give the Haskins Lecture reached me just as I was preparing a new edition of my prodigal brainchild, *On the Shoulders of Giants*. And naturally, *OTSOG*, as I have come to call it in a breath-saving acronym, draws often upon Haskins's magisterial work, *The Renaissance of the Twelfth Century*.

But enough. Now that I have subjected you to this brief recital of coincidences, some of you no doubt ache to remind me that the humanist Plutarch anticipated this sort of thing when he observed: "Fortune is ever changing her course and time is infinite, so it is no great wonder that many coincidences should occur. . . ." And no doubt others of you would

---

1. Since my long-term memory is distinctly limited, this essay draws freely upon reminiscent passages in previous publications.

prefer to draw upon the mathematical statisticians, Persi Diaconis and Frederick Mosteller, who conclude that "we are swimming in an ocean of coincidences. Our explanation is that *nature* and we ourselves are creating these, sometimes causally, and also partly through perception and partly through objective accidental relationships." As will soon become plain, I am inclined to agree with both the humanist and the scientists.

After much ego-centered meditation about the Haskins Lecture, I have come to two conclusions: one, that my life of learning has been largely shaped by a long series of chance encounters and consequential choices, and not by anything like a carefully designed plan. The other that, in my case at least, "the Child is [truly] father of the Man," a conclusion that invokes Wordsworth and Laurence Sterne rather more than Sigmund and Anna Freud. Those conclusions will lead me to focus this evening, far more than I had at first intended, on my early years. And since few, if any, of you gracing this ACLS celebration will have known the vanished world of my distant youth and since my word portraits of that world are bound to be imperfect, I shall resort from time to time to the use of more lifelike visuals, pictures from a family album.

I

My very first chance encounter occurred, of course, with my birth. For who or what dictated that I, and not another, should be born to my loving mother and father? Not the genetic me but the entire me as I have come to be. As it happens, my first appearance also involved a coincidence of time and place, for I was a Yankee-Doodle-baby, born on Independence Day eight blocks from Independence Square. This I report on the firm testimony of my mother, who was presumably close at hand. As she vividly described it more than once, the event took place in the family house well before midnight of July 4th—while local patriots were still noisily celebrating the holiday. It did *not* take place on July 5th, as mistakenly recorded on the birth certificate after a forgetful lapse of a month by the family doctor who helped bring me into the world; said doctor plainly being a latter-day version of Tristram Shandy's accoucheur, Dr. Slop. My parents did not discover the error until they needed evidence that I was old enough to enter public school; by that time, the bureaucratic damage had been done. Ever since, I've had two birthdays a year: July 4th for the family and July 5th on public documents (until, in a much-delayed show of independence, I recently began to set the record straight).

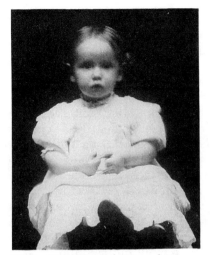 

Figures II.1 (left) and II.2 (right)

(Incidentally, the same sort of thing also happened to Saul Bellow. His birth certificate has him born on July 10th although he generally lists it as *June* 10th, since his mother insisted that it *was* June. And yet, his impending biographer James Atlas tells us, Bellow entered that misconceived July birth-date on his application for a Guggenheim fellowship just as I did, in turn, on my own Guggenheim application. A continuing reign of bureaucratic error.)

At any rate, here at least is visual evidence of my having appeared at all (Figure II.1). Followed by apparent evidence of my being oriented to the glories of the book years before I began my formal schooling (Figure II.2). I suppose that my mother was making a statement by placing her only son in that Little Lord Fauntleroy garb.

The document wrongly attesting the time of my birth sensitized me early on to an elementary rule of historical method: when reconstructing the past, draw gratefully on archival documents but beware of taking them at face value. So it was that decades later, when I became apprenticed at Harvard to the pioneering historian of science, George Sarton, I found myself resonating to his cautionary remark that even "the dates printed on the covers of periodicals are often inaccurate." Just as I resonated later to the infectious seventeenth-century John Aubrey who, while doing strenuous field work in English cemeteries to discover when little lives were *actually* rounded with a sleep, concluded that even epitaphs etched on tombstones might deceive; as, for example, the epitaph which asked passers-by to "Pray for the soul of Constantine Darrel Esq. who died Anno Domini 1400 and his wife, who died Anno Domini 1495." But no more about rules of historical evidence and back, for another Shandean moment, to my birth.

That event received *no* public notice. Not, I believe, because it was obscured by another historic event that same day: the battle for the heavyweight championship of the world between the "black giant" Jack Johnson and the "white giant" Jim Jeffries (if I may adopt Jack London's description of that pugilistic pair). Nor do I think that the *Philadelphia Inquirer* failed to record my arrival simply because it was busy reporting that "not since October of 1907 has the financial district been thrown into such a state of demoralization . . . by the panicky markets in stocks." Nor again, do I believe for even a moment that word of my birth went unnoticed simply because "mid-summer clearance sales" had the ladies hurrying to Philadelphia's Lit Brothers for their pick of "$6 dresses marked down to $3.50" while the men were off to Blum Brothers, just two blocks away at Market and Tenth, where they could find "white serge suits with black stripes" for a mere $10—both of these being obvious good buys in a consumer society even for that distant time.

Not at all. I suspect that my birth went unregarded for quite another reason. It was probably because, as a *New Yorker* profile by Morton Hunt put it some 35 years ago, I was born "almost at the bottom of the social structure" in the slums of South Philadelphia to working-class Jewish immigrants from Eastern Europe. But since a proper slum involves wretched over-crowding in dismal housing, perhaps our family situation did not truly qualify as slum-like. After all, upon being delivered by our own Dr. Slop, I found myself at ease in the ample six-room quarters above my father's newly acquired milk-butter-and-egg shop located at 828 South Third Street. When the uninsured shop was destroyed by fire a few years later and the family's fortunes declined, my father became a carpenter's assistant in the Philadelphia Navy Yard and we moved into a smaller, red-brick, row house. There too, I had no cause to feel deprived—or, as the sociologists now say, I did not experience "relative deprivation." Our house had an occasionally used parlor and a diversely used dining room—where, for example, I developed a slender interest in technology by building a crystal radio set, followed by a peanut-tube set and ultimately by a grand heterodyne set. The coal-burning stove in the kitchen provided heat for the entire house. The gas-lighting served admirably for years and, having nothing better, we made do with the privy in the backyard. In short, we were living the lives of those who would come to be known as "the deserving poor," fueled with the unquestioned premise that things would somehow get better, surely so for the children.

Figure II.3   *Figure II.4*   *(Jerzy Kosinski)*

(As you see from Figure II.3, I still have a picture of my mother and her darling son, then aged 10 or thereabouts, standing tall in that tiny backyard, his innocent child's head encircled by what appears to be . . . a saintly nimbus. Coincidences continue to abound. Some 40 years later, Jerzy Kosinski, author of that haunting autobiographical novel of the Holocaust, *The Painted Bird,* and sometime student of sociology at Columbia who also happened to be a prize-winning photographer, takes a snapshot of his sometime teacher, with this result (Figure II.4). As you see, my older, rather less innocent head is again nearly encircled by what surely can no longer be a *saintly* nimbus.)

Those early appearances notwithstanding, I was not greatly deprived during the rest of my 14 years in that urban village. Thanks to its great array of institutional riches close at hand, I soon began to discover the larger world. From the start, I had a private library of some 10,000 volumes, located just a few blocks from our house (Figure II.5), a library thoughtfully bestowed upon me by that ultimately beneficent robber baron, Andrew Carnegie. The neighborhood was secure enough for me to make my way alone to that library of mine from the tender age of five or six. From then on, I spent countless hours there, having been adopted by the dedicated librarians—all women, of course—who indulged and guided my interest in literature, science, and history, especially in biographies and autobiographies.

It was not at school but there in the Carnegie library that I was introduced to *Tristram Shandy* which, read and re-read over the years, often to cope with bouts of melancholy, eventually found expression in my Shandean Postscript, *On the Shoulders of Giants*. It was there also that I came upon James Gibbons Huneker, the Philadelphia-born-and-reared music, drama, and literary critic who introduced my teen-age self to new aspects of European culture. To the French symbolists, Baudelaire, Verlaine, Mallarmé, and Rimbaud, for example, and to Ibsen and George Bernard Shaw who, more than any other critic of his time, Huneker brought into the American consciousness. To say nothing of that "Beethoven of French prose," Gustave Flaubert. I still treasure the half-dozen Huneker volumes I later acquired at Leary's grand four-story bookstore, located, as I seem to remember, next to Gimbel's at Ninth and Market.

Evidently, the child was engaged in becoming father of the man as my presumably slum-bound self managed to travel widely in time and space. It may also have been in the Carnegie library that I first read David Brewster's engrossing and Victorian *Life of Newton* although I have no documents to support that conjectural memory. In any case, those early years turned out to be prelude to the years I lived in seventeenth-century England where, thanks to Harvard's Widener Library and archives, I hobnobbed with the likes of Newton, Boyle, and Christopher Wren. Just as that early addiction to biographies may have been prelude to a quantitative analysis in my doctoral dissertation of some 6,000 entries in the *Dictionary of National Biography*, a mode of analysis which, I learned only much later from a paper by the Princeton historian Lawrence Stone, contributed to the research art of "historical prosopography": "the investigation of the common background characteristics of a group of actors in history by means of a collective study of their lives."

Those sojourns in libraries exemplify the Bernard-Bailyn-and-Lawrence-Cremin thesis that much consequential education takes place outside the walls of classrooms. In defense of the South Philadelphia High School of that time, however, I must report that it did provide some of us with four years of Latin, two of French, and several years of physics, chemistry and mathematics. Not quite Groton, or Exeter, or the Bronx High School of Science, or, for that matter, Philadelphia's *Gymnasium*-like Central High School, but I might easily have done worse.

Other institutional assets were there just for the asking. A few blocks from the library was the local settlement house with its Graphic Sketch Club (Figure II.5), ever engaged in search of artistic talent among the culturally deprived but emphatically finding no trace of such talent in me. Still, it was there that Sundays brought us chamber music, at times by members of the celebrated Philadelphia Orchestra.

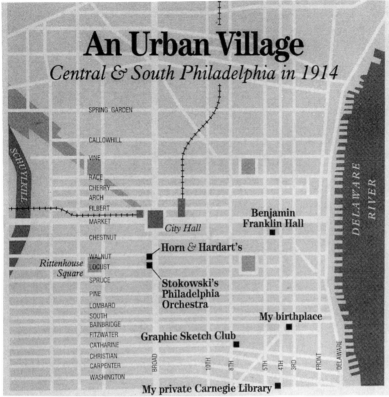

An Urban Village
Central & South Philadelphia in 1914

Figure II.5 *(Bill Marsh)*

The Orchestra itself was also ours since we were within easy walking distance of its Academy of Music (Figure II.5). First as children and then as adolescents, we had only to wait in line for hours on end to be admitted to the Saturday night concerts. The princely sum of first 25, then 50 cents would entitle us to a seat in the last six rows of the amphitheatre; that allowed us to hear and almost get to see the charismatic Leopold Stokowski taking his orchestra of world-fame through his masterly and controversial renditions of Bach—this, of course, without the customary baton. Those far-up seats also permitted us to hear him scolding the Philistine audience for noisily objecting to the new complex music of a Schoenberg, Varèse, or Alban Berg. And, after the concert, we could repair to the lavish Horn & Hardart Automat where we would sit near those of Stoki's men we had come to know and eavesdrop on their talk about the concert or, on occasion, about the baseball triumphs of Connie Mack's A's. But that too was not enough to turn me into howsoever mediocre a musician, though I do detect traces of that early musicological experience in the footnotes of *OSTOG.* Our horizons were further extended in the mid-1920s by the new, rather overwhelming Central Library and monumental Museum of Art.

At this point, my fellow sociologists will have noticed how that seemingly deprived South Philadelphia slum was providing a youngster with every sort of capital—social capital, cultural capital, human capital, and, above all, what we may call public capital—that is, with every sort of capital except the personally financial. To this day, I am impressed by the wealth of public resources made available to us ostensible poor. *Ostensible* poor, of course, since we held important property-rights in the form of ready access to valued resources otherwise possessed only by the very rich. The opportunity structure of our urban village was manifestly and rapidly expanding. But it is also the case that, in the absence of capability, all manner of opportunities being presented to me—for example, in music and the graphic arts—were without visible result. As I would argue long afterwards, in elucidating the sociological concept of opportunity structure, opportunity is probabilistic, not deterministic; it opens possibilities but does not assure their being realized. Just another biographical reminder of the continuing interplay between social structure and individual agency.

My own youthful life was also expanding through an encounter of the first magnitude with Charles Hopkins—or "Hop," as he was known to his friends—the man who became my sister's husband and, in effect, my surrogate father. And a truly chance encounter it was. Soon after my father lost his job at the Navy Yard and we moved once again, we were startled by white mice racing through our newfound row house and intrigued by rabbits in our back yard. Our next-door neighbor, Hop, came by to ask if we had happened to see his pet mice or rabbits. They turned out to be part of his stock-in-trade as an avocational magician. (Only later did I discover that his accomplished craft and artful inventions had won him a secure reputation among prime professional magicians of the time.) That encounter began Hop's courtship of my sister Emma and my idolization of Hop as he began to induct me into the art of prestidigitation. The apprenticeship continued so that I became fairly adept by the time I was 14. Enough so, for this arcane practice to help support me through my studies when I entered Temple College three years later. I still have copies of the card which Hop, as a Ben Franklinesque printer, designed for me (Figure II.6).

Robert K. Merton

Enchanting Mysteries

414 Wilder Street
Philadelphia

Figure II.6

As you see, against a background of top hat and wand etched in soft blue, it declares in flowing script that Robert K. Merton was ready to produce "Enchanting Mysteries," presumably for a modest fee; as it turned out, chiefly at children's parties, at Sunday schools and, for part of one summer, in a small and quite unsuccessful traveling circus.[2]

When I began that short-lived practice as a magician, Houdini became a "role model" (if I may resort to that once well-defined sociological term now become blurred if not vacuous by frequent and indiscriminate use; a term, incidentally, which *A Supplement to the Oxford English Dictionary* maintains was first used in 1957 by my Columbia research group then at work on *The Student Physician*). But I swiftly end this tiny digression into sociological semantics to return to another consequential moment in my youth, when I seized upon Houdini as my subject for a biographical sketch required in a high school course. During research for the paper, I soon learned that names in the performing arts were routinely Americanized; that is to say, they were transmuted into largely Anglo-American forms. For this, of course, was the era of hegemonic Americanization, generations before the emergence of anything resembling today's multiculturalism. The process of symbolic renaming was then in full force as we know, for example, from Leonard Rosenberg becoming Tony Randall, Issur Danielovitch Demsky becoming Kirk Douglas, and Irving Grossberg becoming first the musician and then the artist, Larry Rivers. And so, just as Ehrich Weiss, the son of Rabbi Mayer Samuel Weiss had become

---

2. I need hardly remind this company that Vladimir Nabokov and Edmund Wilson, those closest of friends and most devoted of antagonists, also took pleasure in the esoteric art of magic, as do Persi Diaconis and Frederick Mosteller, that pair of mathematical statisticians I have quoted on the complex subject of coincidence.

Harry Houdini, naming himself after the celebrated French magician, Robert Houdin, the 14-year-old Meyer R. Schkolnick fleetingly became Robert K. Merlin, after the far more celebrated magician of Arthurian legend. Merlin, in turn, soon became Merton when my mentor Hop gently observed that Merlin was a bit hackneyed. By the time I arrived at Temple College, my close friends were more often than not calling me Bob Merton and I did not discourage them. I rather liked the sound of it, no doubt because it seemed "more American" back then in the 1920s. With the warm consent of my devoted Americanizing mother—she attended night school far more religiously than the synagogue—and the bland agreement of my rather uninterested father, this was followed by the legal transformation of my name some 65 years ago.[3]

II

It was at Temple, a secular college established in 1884 by the Baptist minister Russell H. Conwell for "the poor boys and girls of Philadelphia," that another chance encounter changed the direction of my life. Brought there by a scholarship, I had ventured into a class in sociology given by a young instructor, George E. Simpson, and there I found my subject. Then still at work on a doctoral dissertation on *The Negro in the Philadelphia Press*, Simpson recruited me as his research assistant and soon had me doing some of the routine work: classifying, counting, measuring, and

---

3. Of course, Hop and I had no idea back then that the name *Merton* had been adopted by the Moses family of British and German industrialists. That I learned only in the 1970s in noticing that a biographical sketch of me in the *Encyclopedia Judaica* followed an entry for another, rather wealthier and vastly more philanthropic, Merton family. (They had founded *Metallgesellschaft*, one of the largest metallurgical firms in Germany.) Once again, coincidence reigns. For it was the philanthropic Wilhelm Merton who founded the Academy that eventually became the University of Frankfurt where the group advocating critical theory located its Institute for Social Research, later known as "the Frankfurt School" of social philosophy, sociology, politics and economics. When Hitler came into power, members of the Frankfurt School found their way to New York and a peripheral affiliation with Columbia University and it was there that Leo Löwenthal and occasional others of the School eventually became members of the Bureau of Applied Social Research founded by my longtime collaborator, Paul Lazarsfeld. It was not until those entries in the *Encyclopedia Judaica*, however, that Löwenthal and I took note of the wholly-secularized ethnic if not national coincidence of the German and the American Mertons.

statistically summarizing all the references to Negroes over a span of decades in Philadelphia newspapers. The purpose was, of course, to gauge changes in the public imagery of Negroes (not, I recall, of "Blacks," a term which, in those days, was regarded by us white liberals as a demeaning epithet). Only years later would George Simpson and I learn that we had engaged in the research procedure which Harold Lasswell came to designate as "content analysis"—no more aware that *that* was what we were doing than Molière's Monsieur Jourdain had been aware, before the moment of epiphany, that he had actually been speaking prose all his life. It was that research experience which sealed my decision to enter upon the still fairly new and, for many, exotic and dubious field of sociology.

It was also through George Simpson that I entered into new social and cognitive networks, especially with Negroes. Through him, I came to know Ralph Bunche and Franklin Frazier from the time they were instructors at Howard University, along with the Arthur Fausets and others in the reclusive Negro Philadelphia élite of physicians, lawyers, writers, artists and musicians. While at Temple, I also came to know the Philadelphia-born, Harvard-trained philosopher, Alain Locke, who had been the first black Rhodes scholar. I had invited him to address our nascent Sociology Club at Temple and several years later he invited me to join him for a summer in Paris but, to my great regret, time-and-circumstance kept me from what would have been my first direct experience of Europe. That wide array of Negro friends provided early contexts for my later assisting Kenneth Clark to put together the much-debated Social Science Brief on desegregation in the public schools for *Brown v. Board of Education* just as they provided contexts for my later studies of racism, Negro-white intermarriage, and the social perspectives of Insiders and Outsiders.

Taking his assistant in hand, George Simpson also saw to it that I would see and hear key figures at an annual meeting of the American Sociological Society. There I met Pitirim Alexandrovich Sorokin, the founding chairman of the Department of Sociology then being tardily established at Harvard. That too proved to be a consequential encounter. For I would surely not have dared apply for graduate study at Harvard had Sorokin not encouraged me to do so. After all, my college advisers had warned me that Temple was still not fully accredited. To which I replied, rather ineptly, that it was the scholar Sorokin, not the institution Harvard, that mattered most to me. For, as a rather arrogant undergraduate, I had brought myself to believe—not entirely without foundation—that I knew just about everything American sociology had to offer in the late 1920s, although I had to confess to having only peripheral knowledge of the older and, to me, more evocative European traditions of sociological thought. Sorokin had recently published his *Contemporary Sociological Theories*, a wide-ranging, contentious overview of, in the main, European sociology, and plainly he was the teacher I was looking for. Moreover, it was evident that Sorokin was not your ordinary academic sociologist. Imprisoned three times by czarists and then three times by the Bolsheviks, he had been secretary to Alexandr Kerensky, the Socialist Revolutionary Prime Minister of Russia, and had had a death sentence commuted into exile by the normally unsparing Lenin. That too was bound to matter to me since, like many another Temple College student during the Great Depression, I was a dedicated socialist. In the event, I did nervously apply to Harvard, did receive a scholarship there, and soon found myself embarked on a new phase in a life of learning.

III

Harvard proved to be a serendipitous environment, full of evocative surprises. The first definitely consequential surprise was Sorokin's inviting me to be his research assistant, this in my first year of graduate study, and then his teaching assistant as well. That meant, of course, that I became his man-of-all-work—and, as I was soon to learn, his occasional stand-in as well. Summoning me to his office one day, he announced that he had stupidly agreed to do a paper on recent French sociology for a learned society and asked if I would be good enough to take it on in his stead. Clearly, this was less a question than an unforgiving expectation. Abandoning all pretense at attending classes, I devoted days and nights to the vast *oeuvre* issuing forth from Émile Durkheim himself and from such eminences in the Durkheim school as Lévy-Bruhl, Mauss, Halbwachs, and Bouglé. This turned out to be the first of several such unpredictable and fruitful occasions provided by the expanding opportunity structure at Harvard. This one was doubly consequential, for it catapulted me at once, in my second year of graduate study, into the role of a published scholar and led to my being invited to do the first essay-review of Durkheim's newly translated *Division of Labor in Society*. The intensive work on those two papers resulted in my becoming a transatlantic Durkheimian and laid the groundwork for what would become my own mode of structural and functional analysis.

As I've said, Sorokin, not the University, was the lodestone that drew me to Harvard. But, in the event, it was not the renowned Sorokin who most influenced my sociological thinking there; instead, it was a young instructor with no public identity whatever as a sociologist. Talcott Parsons had then published only two articles, both based on his dissertation; moreover, these had appeared in the *Journal of Political Economy*, a journal, it is fair to suppose, not much read by undergraduates in sociology bent on deciding where to do their graduate work. However, those few of us who did come into Talcott Parsons's very first course in theory (despite its long, seemingly humdrum title, "Sociological Theories of Hobhouse, Durkheim, Simmel, Toennies, and Max Weber") soon experienced him as a new sociological voice. The corpus of social thought which Sorokin summarized, Parsons anatomized and synthesized. As we students could not know and as I later learned Parsons himself did not anticipate, those lectures would provide the core of his masterwork, *The Structure of Social Action*. That monumental book did not appear in print until five years later, only after having been worked and reworked in lectures and seminars.

I truly cannot say whether that experience of observing Talcott Parsons virtually write his book in the course of his teaching led me to adopt, quite self-consciously, a similar and lifelong practice of engaging in what can be described as "oral publication"—the working out of ideas in lectures, seminars, and workshops—before finally converting their developed substance into public print. For some of us, teaching is itself a mode of scholarship. Continually revised lectures amount to new if unprinted editions. At least, that has been my experience. On exceptionally good days, the effort to re-think a subject or problem in advance of a lecture or seminar session is capped by new tentative ideas emerging in the lecture or seminar itself. On bad days, I feel that such continuities in lectures over the years risk my becoming a repetitive bore. At any rate, I notice that a dozen years raced by between the time I first lectured on "manifest and latent functions" at Harvard and the time those ideas took printed form in a "paradigm for functional analysis." Just as a dozen years intervened between my 1936 paper focused on the unintended consequences of intentional action and the paper introducing the kindred concept of "the self-fulfilling prophecy."

Although much impressed by Parsons as a master-builder of sociological theory, I found myself departing from his mode of theorizing (as well as his mode of exposition). I still recall the grace with which he responded in a public forum to my mild-mannered but determined criticism of his kind of general theory. I had argued that his formulations were remote from providing a problematics and a direction for theory-oriented empirical inquiry into the observable worlds of culture and society and I went on to state the case for "theories of the middle range" as mediating between gross empiricism and grand speculative doctrines. In typically civil fashion, Parsons paid his respects to my filial impiety and agreed that we both had cause to disagree.

However, it was not the sociologists Sorokin or Parsons but the Harvard economic historian E. F. Gay who, with no such intent, triggered my enduring sociological interest in science and technology. Gay had studied at Berlin with the economic historian Gustav Schmoller, notorious, among other things, for his sociological bent and famous for his insistence on archival research. I decided to take Gay's course rather than an alternative in sociology and that led to still another truly consequential encounter. An assignment in the course had me doing an analytical essay on A. P. Usher's recent *History of Mechanical Invention*. Gay liked the essay and suggested that I audit Harvard's sole course in the history of science given jointly by the biochemist and self-taught Paretan sociologist, L. J. Henderson, and by George Sarton, the world doyen among historians of science. I did so but it was only after I began work on a dissertation that I dared seek guidance from Sarton. For he was reputed to be a remote and awesome presence, so dedicated to his scholarship as to be wholly inaccessible. Thus do plausible but ill-founded beliefs develop into social realities through the mechanism of the self-fulfilling prophecy. Since this forbidding scholar was unapproachable, there was no point in trying to approach him. And his subsequently having very few students only went to show how inaccessible he actually was. But when in the fall of 1933 I knocked on the door of Sarton's office in Widener Library, he did not merely invite me in; he positively ushered me in. That first audition had me sketching plans for a dissertation centered on sociological aspects of the growth of science in seventeenth-century England—a problem not exactly central to sociology back then. I cannot say that Sarton greeted those plans with enthusiasm; in his knowing judgment, so large a canvas as seventeenth-century English science might be a bit much for a novice. But he did not veto the idea. Then began my intensive, sometimes unruly, apprenticeship, followed by an epistolary friendship that continued until his death some 25 years later.

From the start, George Sarton did much to set me on a new path of learning. He proceeded methodically—he was methodical in most things—to transform me from a graduate student (Figure II.7), struggling with early work on a dissertation, into a tyro scholar addressing an international community of learned scholars in print. This he did first by opening the pages of his journal *Isis* to me. During the next few years, he accepted several articles of mine along with some two dozen reviews and scores of entries for the annotated critical bibliographies appearing in *Isis*. Sarton then went on to bestow a "threshold gift": the special kind of gift

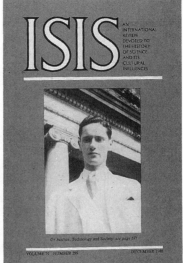

Figure II.7*   Figure II.8

which, in the words of the anthropological poet-ethicist Lewis Hyde, acts as an "agent of individual transformation." Sarton offered to publish my dissertation in *OSIRIS*, the series of monographs typically written by distinguished scholars in the history and philosophy of science, but not, surely, a series designed to include monographs by newly minted Ph.D.s at work in what was becoming the sociology of science. Half-a-century later, his daughter, the poet and novelist May Sarton, took occasion to

*Only now does this ancient snapshot call back to mind how it was that Filene's bargain basement of world fame allowed an impecunious graduate student to indulge himself by sporting a heavy, white-linen and originally expensive suit long before it became Tom Wolfe's signature. That Harvard student's standard of living can be gauged from a segmented summary of his weekly expenses in the academic year 1931-32 and from a sampled daily record maintained by his roommate, budgeter, and chef, Richard Deininger, during the next academic year (Figure II.7A).

Figure II.7A

say that were her father still with us, he would have felt renewed pleasure in that decision to publish *Science, Technology and Science in Seventeenth-Century England* as he observed its fiftieth year being commemorated in fine Sartonian style by a symposium in *Isis,* replete with a picture of his onetime student on the cover (Figure II.8).

Completion of the dissertation had other consequences. Sorokin and Parsons lifted my spirits by seeing to it that I was appointed an instructor and tutor in the department. Given the dismal state of the job market, that was something of an event. But only temporarily so. This was, after all, the midst of the Great Depression—and even Harvard was hurting. Its still fairly new president, James B. Conant, signaled his intention to do away with the rank of assistant professor altogether and to limit promotions to the replacement of retiring or otherwise departing professors. That meant, of course, that a permanent post at Harvard would largely depend on the age distribution of faculty in each department. To be sure, Conant, self-described as "an amateur historian of seventeenth-century science in England," had gone out of his way to let me know "how much I enjoyed your work"—the language is his. However, the presiding elder in our fledgling department, Sorokin, was still in his forties; reason enough for me to leave the to-me indulgent yet alien Harvard before my instructorship had run its course. And so when Tulane University beckoned with a professorship in that bleak economic time, the decision was over-determined and the die was cast. Besides, for a provincial whose life had been confined to Philadelphia and Cambridge, the fanciful culture of New Orleans provided a distinct attraction. After a relaxing—and intellectually rewarding—two years at Tulane, I moved to Columbia and entered upon another, wholly unpredictable, phase of learning: what turned out to be 35 years of an improbable collaboration with the mathematician-psychologist turned sociologist, Paul F. Lazarsfeld.

IV

I say "improbable collaboration" because Paul Lazarsfeld and I may have been the original odd couple in the domain of social science. He, the mathematically minded methodologist, inventor of powerful techniques of social inquiry such as the panel method and latent structure analysis; I, the confirmed social theorist albeit with something of an empirical bent, insisting on the importance of sociological paradigms (in a pre-Kuhnian sense of "paradigm"); Paul, a founder of systematic empirical research on mass communications, voting behavior, opinion leadership, and individual action; I, engrossed in developing the paradigms of functional analysis and deviant behavior while trying to bring a nascent sociology of science into fuller being by exploring science as a social institution with a distinctive, historically evolving ethos, normative structure and reward system; Paul, from his early days in Vienna, the inveterate creator of research institutes unable to imagine himself working outside of a research organization; I, the inveterate loner working chiefly in libraries and in my study at home; he, the matter-of-fact but methodologically demanding positivist; I, something of a doubting Thomas who, in my very first published paper, had dared satirize the "enlightened Boojum of Positivism." But, when I joined Paul in his prime institutional creation, the Columbia University Bureau of Applied Social Research, presumably for just one research project, we soon discovered elective affinities and common ground. That temporary affiliation with the bureau lasted some 30 years. Throughout that time, our shared lives of learning would center on a continuing program of theory-guided and methodologically disciplined empirical social research on a wide variety of substantive problems.

I have failed miserably in every attempt at even a meagre digest of the influence Paul Lazarsfeld and I may have had on each other. Documentary evidence does testify, however, that I finally did persuade this resolute mathematician-psychologist that there really was a discipline of sociology. For eventually Paul published a little book with the engaging title *Qu'est-ce que la sociologie?* which, in his private idiom, translated into the question: "What on earth *is* sociology all about?" Or, as his self-mocking inscription in my copy of the book put it: "All the questions you always wanted to have answered but never dared to ask."

Correlatively, Paul's abiding concern with research methods rubbed off on me and once resulted in a codification of what I called the focused interview. Designed to elicit responses of groups to texts of various kinds—say, a journal article, radio program or educational film—the focused interview took hold in academic sociology and then, after dubious sea changes, boomed its way into what we all know as the focus group. In their enthusiasm for the now ubiquitous focus group, marketeers and political advisers of every stripe, not excluding habitués of the White House and of Congress, often mislead themselves and others by failing to recognize or to acknowledge that such group interviews can at best only yield guesses about the current state of the public mind. Not being representative samples, focus groups cannot, of course, provide reliable knowledge about the extent and social distribution of public preferences, practices, and sentiments.

In retrospect, I am persuaded that the most consequential result of Paul's and my working together went far beyond our collaborations in print. It was of a quite different sort, one nicely summed up about a century ago by the French mining engineer and self-taught sociologist, Frédéric Le Play: The most important thing to come out of the mine, he wrote, is the miner. In much the same spirit, it can be said that the most important thing to come out of Columbia sociology back then was the student. Owing in no small part to the war's end and to the GI Bill, successive cohorts of brilliant students brightened our department and research bureau in the 1940s and '50s and did much to bring about the intellectual excitement that then brought us a continuing flow of new talent. Paul Lazarsfeld and I had no doubt that a good many of those students would go on to leave an indelible imprint on sociological scholarship. As has proved to be the case. Indeed, I now find myself periodically diverted from work-in-slow-progress by writing papers designed specifically for those honorific volumes known as *Festschriften*. Not, as might be supposed, *Festschriften* in honor of teachers or aged peers but in honor of onetime students. Hardly the usual pattern. Most recently, I have found myself gladly paying tribute to James S. Coleman, as I had gladly paid tribute before to Lewis Coser, Franco Ferrarotti, Peter Blau, Rose Coser, and Seymour Martin Lipset along with Alvin Gouldner and Louis Schneider though abjectly missing out on the two-volume *Festschrift* for Juan Linz. Contemplating the extraordinary run of gifted students over that period of decades, I see more *Festschriften* in the offing. In anticipatory celebration, I have begun work on a paper entitled "The Emergence and Evolution of the *Festschrift:* A Sociological Study in the Reward-System of Science and Learning." Prefaced by individualized tributes, it may serve as a template for contributions to future *Festschriften* honoring onetime students whose scholarship has happily advanced beyond that of their onetime teachers.

V

In this retrospect on a life of learning, I have dwelt upon the private life rather than upon the public learning. After all, the fruits of that learning are accessible in the public domain to those who care to sample them; the private life is not. But now that my time and your patience are rapidly drawing to a close, a few scattered remarks that bear variously upon the theme of the child as father of the man and upon oddities in my style of work over the years.

I first give way to the intrusive thought that age has its strange reckonings. I find it hard to believe that I was born a mere 45 years after the Civil War and exceedingly hard to believe that I have lived through more than a third of our nation's history. All the more difficult to believe since, as a young romantic, I was convinced that the good die young and that, like Byron, Keats, and Shelley, I'd not live much beyond the age of 30. A latter-day reminder that if age is renewed opportunity, it is also continuing obligation.

With regard to my work, I only touch upon three quite discrete matters: an almost lifelong addiction to editing, a preferred expositional style, and lastly, certain thematic orientations in social theory.

If Schopenhauer had it right in declaring that to put away one's own original ideas in order to take up the work of another is a sin against the Holy Ghost of scholarship, then indeed *peccavi, peccavi.* I have truly and chronically sinned. For almost as soon as sociology became my vocation, editing became my avocation. This began as early as my student days. Following upon a moderately effective editing of Sorokin's Russified English prose, I agreed to try my hand at editing Parsons's classic *Structure of Social Action.* Although kindly appreciated in the Preface, that editorial effort plainly had an indifferent effect. But this failure was evidently not enough to stay my editor's pen. For, based on some sample lists, a back-of-the-envelope estimate has me editing some 250 books and 2,000 articles over the course of the past 60 years. Behavior hardly in accord with the Schopenhauer canon.

My preferred style of exposition also emerged from the start. As in the 1936 paper on the "Unanticipated Consequences of Purposive Social Action," the 1938 paper on "Social Structure and Anomie," and the 1948 paper on "The Self-Fulfilling Prophecy," I have generally set out my sociological ideas in the form of highly condensed paradigmatic essays, typically running to few more than a dozen-or-so pages. By adopting the relatively discursive form of the essay, I have no doubt irked some sociologist-peers by departing from the tidy format long since prescribed for the scientific paper. Designed to instruct fellow scientists about a potential new contribution to a field of knowledge, the stylized scientific paper presents an immaculate appearance that tells little or nothing of the intuitive leaps, false starts, loose ends, opportunistic adaptations, and happy accidents that actually cluttered up the inquiry. After all, the scientific paper is not designed as a clinical or biographical account of the reported research. In contrast, the essay provides scope for asides and correlatives of a kind that interest historians and sociologists of science and is, in any case, better suited to my ungovernable preference for linking humanistic and scientific aspects of social knowledge.

However, those sociological essays of mine are not wholly discursive. They are disciplined by being "paradigmatic" in, as I've said, a pre-Kuhnian sense of the term "paradigm." That is to say, the analytical paradigm identifies the basic assumptions, problems, concepts, and hypotheses incorporated in the sociological idea in order to generate researchable questions and to provide for continuities of theoretical and empirical inquiry. Thus, the "paradigm of anomie-and-opportunity structure" laid out in a set of essays has been put to use by successive generations of scholars over the past half-century, first in the sociological and criminological study of deviant behavior and then in continuing researches in a variety of other disciplines, just as the "paradigm of the self-fulfilling prophecy," which was first applied to the sociological problem of ethnic and racial discrimination, has since led to traditions of theoretical and empirical inquiry in social psychology, political science, anthropology, economics, and public administration.

Reflecting briefly on thematic orientations emerging in my theoretical work, I take note of a prime aversion, a prime preference, and a prime indulgence.

My prime theoretical aversion is to any extreme sociological, economic, or psychological reductionism that claims to account uniquely and exhaustively for patterns of social behavior and social structure. By way of rationale for this aversion, I confine myself to the William James parable about the reductionist fallacy: "A Beethoven string-quartet is truly . . . a scraping of horses' tails on cats' bowels, and may be exhaustively described in such terms; but the application of this description in no way precludes the simultaneous applicability of an entirely different description."

As I have intimated, my prime theoretical preference is for sociological theories of the middle range which, I hasten to say in accord with Arthur Stinchcombe, can be shown to derive in principle from a more general theory if they are worth their salt in providing an improved understanding of social behavior, social structure, and social change.

And my prime theoretical indulgence finds its fullest expression in my one avowedly humanist and self-winding book, *On the Shoulders of Giants,* which adopts a non-linear, divagating Shandean mode for examining the enduring tension between tradition and originality in the transmission and growth of knowledge along with a variety of related themes.

And now, as befits a short essay on an improbable life of learning, a final brief thought about autobiography, that mode of self-reflection in historical contexts which has held my interest since those distant days in the Carnegie library. But not, of course, with reference to myself. Until recent decades. For it happens that ever since the publication in 1961 of *The New Yorker* profile, with its condensed South Philadelphia story, kindly disposed friends, colleagues, and publishers have been urging me to write an autobiography or, at least, a longish memoir. Would that I could. But, as all of us know, God is in the details. Without thick, textured detail, an autobiography is bound to be weary, flat, stale, and unprofitable. But the sinful fact is that I simply haven't access to the needed detail. Cursed my life long by a scant and episodic memory, I dare not rely on vagrant memories without visible means of documentary support. But, alas, I've not kept a diary or a journal, with documentation thus confined to notebooks and voluminous but still inadequate files of letters. And so, when asked to venture upon an autobiography, I have only to recall the caustic review of a memoir by the prolific novelist and playwright, Heinrich Böll. The reviewer notes Böll's many tiresome passages lamenting his inability to remember and concludes that the author "seems almost to boast of his mnemonic failures." For me, that review amounts to a preview. It provides timely warning that any memoir of mine would surely display an even more humiliating amnesia. But perhaps, just perhaps, this slight remembrance of things past will serve in its stead.

About the Contributors

Daniel Bell is scholar in residence at the American Academy of Arts and Sciences, and Henry Ford II professor of social science, emeritus Harvard University.

Paul DiMaggio is professor of sociology, Princeton University.

Denis Donoghue is Henry James professor of English, New York University.

Jean Bethke Elshtain is Laura Spelman Rockefeller professor of social and political ethics, University of Chicago.

Kai Erikson is William R. Kenan, Jr. professor of sociology and American studies, Yale University.

Gerald Holton is Mallinckrodt professor of physics and professor of the history of science, Harvard University.

Michael Katz is Sheldon and Lucy Hackney professor of History, University of Pennsylvania.

Ira Katznelson is Ruggles professor of political science and history, Columbia University.

Robert K. Merton is university professor emeritus, Columbia University.

Daniel Patrick Moynihan is senior senator from New York.

Neil J. Smelser is director of the Center for Advanced Study in the Behavioral Sciences.

Charles Tilly is Joseph L. Buttenwieser professor of social science, Columbia University.

Margaret Weir is professor of sociology and political science at the University of California, Berkeley.

William Julius Wilson is Malcolm Weiner professor of social policy, Harvard University.

Alan Wolfe is university professor of sociology, Boston University.

Viviana A. Zelizer is professor of sociology, Princeton University.